Statelessness in the Caribbean

PENNSYLVANIA STUDIES IN HUMAN RIGHTS

Bert B. Lockwood, Series Editor

A complete list of books in the series is available
from the publisher.

Statelessness in the Caribbean

The Paradox of Belonging
in a Postnational World

Kristy A. Belton

PENN

UNIVERSITY OF PENNSYLVANIA PRESS

PHILADELPHIA

Copyright © 2017 University of Pennsylvania Press

Published by
University of Pennsylvania Press
Philadelphia, Pennsylvania 19104-4112
www.upenn.edu/pennpress

Printed in the United States of America
on acid-free paper

10 9 8 7 6 5 4 3 2 1

A Cataloging-in-Publication record is available
ISBN 978-0-8122-4944-6

To those who fight injustice in all its forms

CONTENTS

ABBREVIATIONS

CARL   Canadian Association of Refugee Lawyers
CEJIL   Center for Justice and International Law
CESDEM   Centro de Estudios Sociales y Demográficos
COB   College of The Bahamas
CRC   Convention on the Rights of the Child
DRIP   Declaration on the Rights of Indigenous Peoples
DESA   Department of Economic and Social Affairs
DoI   Department of Immigration
DR   Dominican Republic
ECOWAS   Economic Community of West African States
FNM   Free National Movement
GULSHRI   Georgetown University Law School's Human
              Rights Institute
GAP   Global Action Plan to End Statelessness: 2014–2024
GDJ   Global Distributive Justice
GNI   Gross National Income
HRC   Human Rights Committee
HRW   Human Rights Watch
ISI   Institute on Statelessness and Inclusion
IRB   Institutional Review Board
IDPs   internally displaced persons
IACtHR   Inter-American Court of Human Rights
ICCPR   International Covenant on Civil and Political Rights
IOM   International Organization for Migration
JCE   Junta Central Electoral
MENAMIRD   Mesa Nacional para Migrantes y Refugiados
MFA   Ministry of Foreign Affairs
MUDHA   Movement for Dominican Women of Haitian Descent

NSU	Nationality Support Unit
NOS	National Office of Statistics
NGO	Nongovernmental organization
OBMICA	Observatorio Migrantes del Caribe
OSJI	Open Society Justice Initiative
OAU	Organization of African Unity
OAS	Organization of American States
PLP	Progressive Liberal Party
SIDS	Small Island Developing States
MOSCTHA	Sociocultural Movement for Haitian Workers
SSD	Statelessness Status Determination
SCJ	Supreme Court of Justice
UDHR	Universal Declaration of Human Rights
UN	United Nations
UNCTAD	United Nations Conference on Trade and Development
UNICEF	United Nations Children's Fund
UNDP	United Nations Development Programme
UNHCR	United Nations High Commissioner for Refugees
UN HRC	United Nations Human Rights Council
OHCHR	UN Office of the High Commissioner for Human Rights
UNSG	United Nations Secretary General
USCIS	United States Citizenship and Immigration Service

PREFACE

This book is about belonging in a world carved into states. It asks us to examine our taken for granted assumption that we all seamlessly fall into place as citizens of one state or another and that we are able to retain the citizenship we acquired at birth throughout our life. Millions of people around the world have no citizenship. They do not formally belong anywhere.

Take a moment and imagine what it must be like not to exist in the eyes of a state's bureaucratic machinery, not to be protected by national laws, not to have access to—or the ability to exercise—the rights and freedoms that are bound up with a particular state's citizenship. What must it be like to be physically present, to have tried to make a life in a place, yet to be rejected by the place you consider home? What must it be like to see others, born in the same place that you were, growing up in the same place that you did, be self-determining agents and take advantage of opportunities that come their way because they happen to have citizenship—a status that they hold through no merit or action on their part?

In essence, what is it like to be a noncitizen insider? To be displaced from belonging, even as your roots lie within the same land as the "citizens"?

*   *   *

I make no pretense to neutrality in this book: I believe that everyone has the right to belong to the community of her or his birth. I believe that the current international system of states that generates and perpetuates statelessness is unjust and I believe that the need to resolve statelessness is one of the greatest tasks and duties that we have in the twenty-first century. Before trying to convince the reader of these positions, however, it is important in a book about belonging and place identity to situate myself in this research project and note my particular subjectivities at the outset. As Ruth Arber reminds us, "We construct ourselves through the other and yet leave that which is ourselves silent" (2010, 57). "We must [therefore] properly define the place from which we speak, the person we are, and the way we might affect, or be affected by, the interpretations inscribed within ethnographic texts" (46).

My "place identity" is shaped by the fact that I consider myself a person who is always coming from elsewhere. I am the "Other" nearly everywhere I have lived (and I have lived in many places). I hold two citizenships, but neither is from the country that I was born in. I was born in a colony that had no citizenship of its own to grant, but I was able to acquire the citizenship of my father's country. If I had not been able to do so, I could have been stateless. I was born to a Bahamian mother and Bahamian women do not, as I explain in this book, have the same right to pass on their nationality to their children as their male counterparts do. Akin to the Bahamian-born persons of Haitian descent that I interviewed for this study then, I am a Bahamian via "registration."

Although I identify as Bahamian, I am acutely aware that possessing Bahamian citizenship formalizes my membership, but does not actually make me belong in the eyes of many Bahamians. My skin color, place of birth, and heritage single me out as not really belonging, as coming from somewhere else. I thus have a personal interest in how state membership practices—and society's acceptance of the "Other"—affect one's ability to belong and the ways that we can go about ameliorating exclusionary membership practices, especially among those who hold no citizenship from anywhere.

PART I

Reconsidering Forced
Displacement

CHAPTER 1

Displaced in Place

Something much more fundamental than freedom and
justice . . . is at stake when belonging to the community
into which one is born is no longer a matter of course
and not belonging no longer a matter of choice.
—Hannah Arendt, *The Origins of Totalitarianism*

The sun is shining warmly as the ocean breeze gently moves among the pine
trees. We have been sitting here a while, our only company a lone crab scav-
enging for food at the water's edge. "She had just graduated out of high
school," says Luzena Dumercy, looking out to sea. "She graduated that Fri-
day and that Sunday she left on the boat."[1] The young woman to whom Dumercy refers never came back. She was one of at least eleven people who
drowned in Bahamian waters on June 11, 2012, attempting to make it somewhere else.[2] "You have to understand why we get to that point to begin with,"
continues Dumercy. "They don't want us here. They don't make us feel like
we belong. . . . Why would you stay somewhere you're not wanted?"

Although we are discussing why some people of Haitian descent undertake the perilous sea voyage to leave their Bahamian home, Dumercy's story
is a local echo of a global phenomenon—the widespread movement of people
from one place to another in the contemporary era. According to the United
Nations (UN), over two hundred million people are on the move globally
(UN DESA 2016, 1 and 5). Of these, more than nineteen million are refugees
(1 and 9). Whether people are fleeing conflict or persecution, seeking better
economic opportunities, or attempting to reunite with family members, the
recent images of bodies washing up on Mediterranean shores, of people scaling seemingly impenetrable fences in places like Ceuta and Melilla, and of

individuals running across weakly managed borders, add flesh, if not individual stories, to these statistics. What distinguishes the people in Dumercy's
account from many other migrants, however, is that they are driven to leave
their home not because of conflict, crisis, or persecution, or because they
are trying to escape from an autocratic, failing, or failed state. Instead,
they are trying, in Dumercy's words, "to flee" because they feel as if they do
not belong. "They want to leave this place because it's toxic sometimes," Dumercy explains. "You shouldn't be stateless in the place [where] you were
born and where you feel like you're not included or not wanted."

This book examines the situation of those who are excluded from formal
belonging by practices of citizenship deprivation and denial in the countries
of their birth. Unlike the majority of forced migrants and other people on
the move, these individuals are not recognized as nationals[3] by any state
under the operation of its law (UN 1954). They are stateless. Statelessness
affects more than ten million people worldwide (UNHCR 2015e).[4] Without
any formal bond of citizenship, stateless people are susceptible to an array of
human rights violations, social exclusion, and pervasive insecurity, among
other concerns.

While their plight can be just as troubling as that suffered by refugees,
internally displaced persons (IDPs) and other forced migrants, stateless people
are rarely forced to flee their homes, whether within a state as IDPs or across
state borders as refugees.[5] They are consequently not considered forcibly
displaced persons. The UN High Commissioner for Refugees (UNHCR), the
body mandated with the protection of refugees and stateless people globally, for instance, remarks that a "staggering crisis" faces the world as nearly
sixty million people are forcibly displaced (Murray 2015, n. pag.); but it does
not include the stateless within this figure because "being stateless doesn't
necessarily correlate to being displaced" (UNHCR 2014f). In this book, I
challenge this position.

Whereas Hannah Arendt, one of the twentieth century's great political
theorists, lamented that the stateless were referred to as "'displaced persons' . . . for the express purpose of liquidating statelessness once and for all
by ignoring its existence" (Arendt [1948] 2004, 355), I contend that we must
reconceptualize statelessness as a form of forced displacement precisely to
understand and address this extreme form of noncitizenship. By reconceptualizing statelessness as a form of forced displacement in situ—that is, one
does not have to be physically pushed across borders or made to flee one's
home within a state due to conflict, crisis, or persecution to be forcibly

displaced—I demonstrate how states can engage in practices that forcibly displace the unwanted among them, often through seemingly neutral membership policies and laws or ostensibly banal bureaucratic procedures.

Using a comparative case study of The Bahamas and the Dominican Republic (DR), I show how the stateless are either forced into liminality—a realm of formal nonbelonging everywhere—or made to take on the nationality of a country with which they do not identify (Haiti) when the state of their birth can no longer tolerate their ambiguous status. In both instances, I illustrate how the stateless are simultaneously rooted and displaced. They are rooted in that they are born and continue to reside within the country of their birth (although the latter excludes them); yet they are displaced in that they face similar constraints on their ability to be self-determining agents and to enjoy human rights, freedoms, and protections akin to other forced migrants. In fact, their lack of movement is one of the primary differences between them and the "rightless" of whom Hannah Arendt wrote last century.[6]

Citizenship, the State, and Human Rights

Writing in the immediate aftermath of World War II, Arendt described how millions of people were essentially rendered nonhuman through denationalization procedures and forced migratory movement. These people, who had once belonged to the community of nations as citizens of some state, were now stateless, "the scum of the earth" (Arendt [1948] 2004, 341). They "lived outside the pale of the law" (353) and were homeless, unprotected beings that no state was willing to adopt. Human rights, which were supposed to apply to all persons regardless of national origin or other status, had ceased to exist for them because "it turned out that the moment human beings lacked their own government and had to fall back upon their minimum rights, no authority was left to protect them and no institution was willing to guarantee them" (370).

The stateless epitomized the hollowness of human rights discourse for Arendt. When a man "is nothing but a man," she argued, he loses "the very qualities which make it possible for other people to treat him as a fellow-man" (Arendt [1948] 2004, 381). Arendt, herself a stateless person for many years, consequently argued that the great "calamity" to befall the stateless "is not that they are deprived of life, liberty, and the pursuit of happiness, or of equality before the law and freedom of opinion . . . but that they no longer belong to any community whatsoever" (375). She therefore proposed that human rights be "redefined as a right to the human condition itself, which depends upon *belonging to some human community*" (631; italics added).

Since Arendt's time, the "right to have rights" has been interpreted in many different ways.[7] The first and most common usage is that of the right to formal citizenship in a state or the right to a nationality.[8] In other cases the nonformal aspect of political belonging, such as "the right of political inclusion" (Michelman 1996, 205) or "the right to politics" (Schaap 2011, 33), is considered. Others define it as the right to personhood, whether this is "the right . . . to be a *legal person*, entitled to certain inalienable rights, regardless of the status of their political membership" (Benhabib 2004b, 3) or "the right to human personhood—recognition as a moral equal" (Somers 2008, 25). Yet despite the various understandings of the "right to have rights," no right to belong, at least as Arendt understood it, exists.

The Universal Declaration of Human Rights (UDHR) perhaps comes closest to a right to belong when it asserts that each person has a right to a nationality (UN 1948, Article 15),[9] that is, to belong formally as a member to a state. But the UDHR nowhere describes how this right is to be enacted. Even its hard law offspring[10] are silent when discussing how to translate the right to a nationality "into a specific, actionable duty on the part of any particular state" (Goldston 2006, 339). As Paul Weis writes, "There are no rules of international law which impose a duty on States to confer their nationality on certain individuals at birth" (1956, 242). The right to a nationality is therefore "a right without a remedy."[11]

The American Convention on Human Rights, the human rights treaty organ of the Organization of American States (OAS), also asserts that each person has the right to a nationality, and goes further than the UDHR and its affiliated human rights treaties by declaring that it is a nonderogable right (OAS 1969, Articles 20 and 27). The OAS is also remarkably Arendtian in that it contends that the right to a nationality is not only inviolable, but is "one of the most important rights of man, after the right to life itself, because all the prerogatives, guarantees and benefits man derives from his membership in a political and social community—the State—stem from or are supported by this right" (OAS 1977, n. pag.). The human right to a nationality, therefore, is both an intrinsic and an instrumental human right. It is an essential component of recognized, formal belonging in a world carved into states; yet, as I show in this book, its fulfillment is also necessary for people to access any number of other human rights (from education, work, and healthcare to social security, a juridical personality, and freedom of movement).[12] Moreover, citizenship is of such import in the international sphere that no international norm or recognition of the right to be voluntarily stateless exists. One must be a citizen of somewhere[13] and there is an international norm against statelessness (Adjami and Harrington 2008, 103; Donner 1994, 196; Spiro 2004, 99; van Waas 2008, 39).

While most states seem to accept the international norm that people must not be deprived arbitrarily of their citizenship, fewer are willing to accept that states must provide membership to the stateless populations on their territory,[14] or that they cannot deny or revoke citizenship from individuals on "reasonable" grounds, even if it renders people stateless. It is for these reasons, and others, that more than ten million people are stateless globally.

Whereas Arendt firmly believed that formal belonging, or citizenship in the state, is necessary to access rights, freedoms, and protections,[15] recent scholarship challenges this position. Beginning with Yasemin Soysal's *Limits of Citizenship* (1994), it has become increasingly common for scholars to describe citizenship as a status that is losing importance in a globalizing world of increased migratory movements and human rights provisions. Soysal's work concretized the concept of postnationalism, wherein "the logic of personhood supersedes the logic of national citizenship" as the "organizing principle of membership in contemporary polities" (Soysal 1994, 164). Through her study of guest workers in several European countries, Soysal argued that citizens and noncitizens were basically treated the same way when it came to rights provisions in state policies. She found that the basis for this similarity in treatment was host-state respect for the human rights regime, which acknowledges the rights of all *persons* regardless of race, national, or social origin. Soysal therefore posited that

contemporary membership formations have superseded the dichotomy that opposes the national citizen and the alien, by including populations that were previously defined as outside the national polity. Rights that used to belong solely to nationals are now extended to foreign populations, thereby undermining the very basis of national citizenship. (137)

Works from diverse scholarly genres have since taken a postnational orientation and sought to illustrate the changing nature of the citizen-state relationship. Some authors have followed in Soysal's footsteps by investigating the impact of the human rights regime on state treatment of noncitizens. David Jacobson, for example, contends that the new international order is based upon human rights and has effectively devalued citizenship in the state as it erodes "the distinction between 'citizen' and 'alien' " (1996, 8–9, 39). Linda Bosniak similarly argues that "the status of aliens in liberal democratic societies is, in many respects, hardly distinguishable from that of citizens" (2006, 34) due to noncitizens' ability to press human rights claims and enjoy the rights of citizenship without possessing formal citizenship status. Seyla Benhabib also concludes in her respective works on noncitizen rights that "one does not have to be part of a territorially defined people to enjoy human rights" (Benhabib 2001, 36).[16]

Thus, whereas Arendt deemed personhood insufficient for rights enjoyment, the premise of many scholars writing in the postnational vein is that personhood is enough to access human rights. Bosniak, for instance, directly challenges Arendt's position by asserting that "Citizenship . . . is *not* actually 'the right to have rights,' despite the conventional wisdom. In many situations, only personhood is required" (2006, 117). Jean Cohen likewise declares that "many rights that used to be construed exclusively as the rights of citizens are now deemed the rights of persons that must be respected everywhere" (1999, 258). Yishai Blank similarly observes how states are granting "an impressive and ever-growing catalogue of social and economic rights, as well as various political rights" to noncitizens (2007, 438). He further contends that states are "moving in the direction of granting de facto citizenship, that is, the substantive content of citizenship (often devoid of the political rights)" to those who hold no citizenship from anywhere—the stateless (438).

Beside examining the human rights regime's impact on the citizen-state relationship, other scholars have taken another *Limits of Citizenship* approach, focusing on "the emergence of membership that is multiple in the sense of spanning local, regional, and global identities, and which accommodates intersecting complexes of rights, duties, and loyalties" (Soysal 1994, 166). Thus while Arendt focused on formal membership in the state, these scholars study the diverse citizenship types or ways of belonging that exist in the contemporary era: from cultural (Kymlicka 1995), transnational (Bauböck 2007), deterritorialized (Ferme 2004; Teune 2009), denationalized (Sassen 2006), documentary (Sadiq 2009), flexible (Ong 1999; Nyamnjoh 2007), (Kostakopoulou 2008), postnational (Soysal 1994; Benhabib and Resnik 2009), post-sovereign (Murphy and Harty 2003), and global (Cabrera 2010) to irregular (Nyers 2011; Ni Mhurchú 2015), quasi (Gilbertson 2006), the "citizenship of aliens" (Bosniak 2006) and "citizenship light" (Caglar 2004). In so doing, they illustrate—contra Arendt—that formal, legal citizenship is no longer so important to act in a polity.

These works tend to directly or indirectly portray formal citizenship in the state as a "waning," "partially obsolete," "anachronistic," "possibly changed institution" or one that is undergoing "crisis" (Benhabib, Shapiro, and Petranovic 2007, 14; Hailbronner 2003, 75; Cohen 1999, 247; Sassen 2006, 280; Benhabib 2004b, 143; McNevin 2011, 143).[17] They question whether "the idea of territorial state citizenship—as distinct from personhood— remain[s] important?" and whether "human rights [are] replacing citizenship as the most important rights-bearing ideas and legal norms?" (Jackson 2009, 443).

Using the statelessness as forced displacement in situ framework, however, I find that the postnational portrayal of a world of blurred boundaries, flexible memberships, and denationalized rights is not global in scope.[18] The boundaries of belonging are hardening against the racial, ethnic, or religious Other and citizenship remains a crucial status to hold to access rights, freedoms, and protections. Moreover, the postnational worldview that democracies are providers of rights based upon personhood, as opposed to citizenship, also needs to be qualified.

Challenging the Postnational Worldview

The majority of postnational-oriented scholarship is limited in two primary ways: first, by its focus on developed world democracies and their provision of rights and protections to noncitizens[19] and, second, by its examination of noncitizens who are not stateless when making claims about the decoupling of human rights from citizenship. With regard to the first limitation, very few works have examined the relationship between citizenship status and access to rights, freedoms, and protections in developing world democracies.[20] This is somewhat surprising given that Soysal clearly states that her postnational arguments "are not exclusive to Europe. As the transnational norms and discourse of human rights permeate the boundaries of nation-states, the postnational model is activated and approximated world-wide" (1994, 156).

More recently, Bosniak asserts that "the status of aliens in liberal democratic societies is, in many respects, hardly distinguishable from that of citizens" (2006, 34) as "a great many of the rights commonly associated with equal citizenship and economic citizenship are not confined to status citizens at all but are available to territorially present persons" in "most other liberal democratic states" (117).[21] Such a position is in line with the accepted truism that democracies promote and protect human rights.[22] As Russell Bova notes,

> democracy is presumed to foster basic human liberties and freedoms to a degree that is unmatched by authoritarian regimes. . . . It is, in fact, this connection between democracy, on the one hand, and human rights and liberties, on the other, that constitutes the most powerful argument in favor of democratic government. (2001, 63)

This selection bias toward developed world democracies within the postnational literature results in an overly optimistic assessment of the degree to which citizenship is no longer important to access rights, freedoms, and protections in the contemporary era. It also obfuscates the myriad ways in which democratic regimes can engage in forced displacement within their own borders under nonconflict and noncrisis conditions against the racial, ethnic, or religious Other. I therefore examine the relationship between citizenship, human rights, and the state within developing world democracies to see if postnational claims about the severance of human rights from citizenship are generalizable to the developing world.

As regards the second limitation, I contend that we must examine whether citizenship has lost its significance as the conveyor of rights, freedoms, and protections by choosing as subjects those who are noncitizens everywhere— the stateless. Despite the increased attention that has been given to noncitizens in recent migratory, citizenship, and human rights research, as well as in political theory, scant consideration has been given to the stateless who represent the epitome of what it means to be a noncitizen. The stateless are distinct from refugees, the undocumented, guest workers and their descendants, and other types of noncitizens who may be noncitizens in their country of residence or employment, but who are not necessarily stateless as they have a "country of origin" and are still recognized as citizens under the operation of some state's law.

Also, unlike the former groups, who in most instances are migrants of one type or another, stateless people are "noncitizen insiders" (Belton 2011). They are insiders because they have not migrated from elsewhere. They are "rooted" as they remain, for the most part, in the states where they were born.[23] They are noncitizens, however, because the state where they were born either rejects them as members or does not fully provide the means by which they can be prevented from falling into statelessness. In both instances, they are forced into liminality and unable to enjoy many of the rights that immigrant noncitizens enjoy because they are not always considered legal or "lawful" residents of the states within which they reside. Moreover, unlike those deemed "unlawful" immigrants, the stateless cannot easily be deported because they do not always have a country of their "own" to which to be returned.[24] Indefinite detention is thus often a real possibility (Perks and de Chickera 2009, 49).

It bears mentioning that the stateless are also distinct from refugees. Refugees are sometimes considered de facto stateless because they do not enjoy the protection of their state of citizenship or few (if any) of the rights and freedoms associated with that state's citizenship. They are defined as persons who have a well-founded fear of persecution in their countries of citizenship because of certain political beliefs that they hold or ascriptive criteria (UN 1951). They consequently flee across an international border in order to seek safety from such persecution.[25] Refugees are still typically recognized as nationals under the operation of a given state's laws, however, and they are not penalized for their "irregular" presence in the same way that stateless people can be. The Convention relating to the Status of Refugees, for example, asks states parties to

> not impose penalties, on account of their illegal entry or presence, on refugees who, coming directly from a territory where their life or freedom was threatened in the sense of Article 1, enter or are present in their territory without authorization, provided they present themselves without delay to the authorities and show good cause for their illegal entry or presence. (UN 1951, Article 31)

No similar stipulation exists in the statelessness conventions. Stateless people can thus be penalized for their "unlawful" presence by the very states that made them unlawful in the first place via their practices of citizenship deprivation and denial.

Despite this protection gap, and notwithstanding the myriad human rights violations they face, stateless people have yet to be afforded the same type of developed, international protection framework that exists for refugees. As UNHCR senior protection officer Janice Marshal admits, "It is not that we are responsible for every stateless person worldwide, the way we more or less are for refugees because of the statute of the UNHCR" (Voice of America 2009 n. pag.).[26] Thus, by focusing upon those who are noncitizens everywhere—the stateless—we can test whether postnational claims about the decoupling of human rights from citizenship are applicable to all noncitizens.

Reconceptualizing Statelessness

While offering a more nuanced understanding of the relationship between citizenship, human rights, and democracies in this book, I also offer a reconceptualization of statelessness itself, adding to the emerging field of statelessness studies. It is only in the past few years that academic research on statelessness has begun to develop. This scholarship has generally been either legal or technical in nature, focusing on differences in nationality laws, lack of birth registration, crises of state succession, and gaps in protection;[27] or advocacy-based, describing the living conditions of stateless people, recording human rights violations against them, and making policy suggestions.[28] While a few comparative and single-case studies exist,[29] no work to date has offered a comparative analysis of statelessness in the developing world democracies of the Caribbean.

Moreover, "although there have been considerable strides in the machinery of human rights, political theory with respect to statelessness has hardly moved on since Arendt's day" (Sawyer and Blitz 2011, 306). Most recent theoretical work on statelessness has taken two forms: the application of an Arendtian framework to explain how some nonstateless noncitizens—such as the *sans papiers* and others who live on the fringes of legality within their host states—are in a stateless situation;[30] or the analysis of statelessness from a global ethics or justice perspective.[31] No work to date has argued that statelessness is a form of forced displacement.

Victoria Redclift's *Statelessness and Citizenship: Camps and the Creation of Political Space* (2013) is informed by a forced displacement lens through its analysis of the camp-based displacement of the formerly stateless Biharis of Bangladesh. Redclift's focus, however, is on exposing the messiness of contemporary membership practices and on how individuals are able to negotiate, and maneuver between, the boundaries of citizenship inclusion and exclusion. I come at displacement from a different vantage point. Instead of illustrating how acts of citizenship are performed outside statist understandings of belonging from spaces of displacement,[32] I argue in this book that we need to reconceptualize statelessness as a form of forced displacement in situ.[33] One need not be encamped or physically pushed across borders to suffer the effects of displacement from home.

Thus, whereas David Hanauer describes how migrants and their host-state born children "are defined in essentialist terms as representatives of their heritage countries" and "are symbolically returned to their native lands" in the process (2011, 203), the case studies I present in this work reveal that the displacement suffered by the descendants of migrants who are at risk of statelessness is much more than symbolic. As I describe in Chapters 3 and 4, the Bahamian- and Dominican-born offspring of Haitian migrants are forcefully "returned" to a "native land" they have never seen (Haiti) via practices of citizenship denial or deprivation in the countries of their birth.

Moreover, although other noncitizens, such as refugees, travelers, and different types of migrants, have been the subjects of "an explosion of work which considers the role of place in the production of outsiders" or people "who are said to be 'out-of-place' " (Cresswell 2004, 103), stateless people have not been included in this scholarship. Reconceptualizing statelessness as forced displacement highlights how practices of citizenship deprivation and denial render the stateless "out of place," disrupting their ability to carry out key life projects, be self-determining agents, and access rights and protections. Furthermore, it illustrates how being forced "out of place," whether by being rendered liminal subjects or by being made to take on another state's nationality, affects the stateless' sense of place identity and belonging in very concrete ways.

Place identity answers the question—Who am I?—by countering— Where am I? or Where do I belong? From a social psychological perspective, place identities are thought to arise because places, as bounded locales imbued with personal, social, and cultural meanings, provide a significant framework in which identity is constructed, maintained, and transformed. Like people, things, and activities, places are an integral part of the social world of everyday life; as such, they become important mechanisms through which identity is defined and situated. (Cuba and Hummon 1993, 112)

When people lack a national home, it affects their "expectations for the future" (Weil 1955 quoted in Relph 1976, 38) and psychologically displaces them, even though they remain physically rooted. They consequently lack "a secure point from which to look out on the world, a firm grasp of [their] position in the order of things" (38). The realm of statelessness then is more than one where the law ceases to operate or where rights are difficult to achieve. It is one, as Arendt recognized, in which one's place in the world becomes ambiguous, or even outright negated.

Reconceptualizing statelessness as a form of forced displacement in situ is important for several reasons. First, statelessness is a human rights issue that most people do not know exists. As UNHCR admitted, it is "one of the most neglected areas of the global human rights agenda" (UNHCR 2011b, 2). While the plight of refugees, IDPs, and other forced migrants has garnered the attention of the international, humanitarian, policy-making, and scholarly communities over the decades, statelessness has not. It is only in the past three years that the first Global Forum on Statelessness[34] was held and that UNHCR launched its global #IBelong Campaign to End Statelessness, even though statelessness has existed since before the organization's inception and is one of its primary mandates. It is also only in the past few years that scholarly interest in the subject has begun to develop and that regional intergovernmental organizations, such as the OAS and the European Union (EU),[35] have begun to address the issue.

The lack of attention given to statelessness is problematic because stateless people, as I describe in Chapters 2 and 5, are susceptible to a range of human rights violations as noncitizens everywhere. As UN Secretary General (UNSG) António Guterres declares, "The daily suffering of millions of stateless people is an affront to humanity" (cited in van Waas 2013, n. pag.). Yet because their situation typically lacks the humanitarian or emergency nature of other types of forced displacement—they may live in democracies and face little to no persecution; they may have never had to leave their home due to conflict or crisis; they may outwardly appear like any citizen you meet—their particular plight has often gone unrecognized or been made secondary to other human rights concerns. But, as I explain later in the text, statelessness is an insidious form of displacement, with invidious effects. Reconceptualizing statelessness as forced displacement in situ thus demands that we consider statelessness as important to address as other types of forced displacement.

Second, embedding statelessness within the forced displacement framework forces us to interrogate our assumptions about the relationship between displacement and movement. In an insightful article, Stephen Lubkemann argues for the need to critically examine the assumed relationship between displacement and mobility that permeates forced migration and refugee studies. Examining the case of the 1977–1992 Mozambican civil war, Lubkemann describes how those who were unable to flee the conflict suffered "a form of displacement in place" (2008, 457) as the war prevented them from using various forms of "mobility-based" coping strategies (464). Because of this, Lubkemann argues that displacement should be redefined as "immobilization" generated by the involuntary "disruption of key life projects" (468, 471n8). Reconceptualizing statelessness as a form of forced displacement that takes place in situ broadens our understanding of the diverse forms that forced displacement can take and illustrates that one does not have to be forced to flee one's home to suffer its effects. One can be physically rooted, yet displaced.

Third, the forced displacement in situ framework illuminates the myriad, yet subtle, ways in which democracies in nonconflict and noncrisis situations engage in forced displacement. Thus, whereas the focus within forced migration, conflict, and human rights studies has typically been upon those who are made to move (whether internally or externally) as a result of ethnic conflict, insurgency, persecution, foreign invasion, and other types of crises (Wood 1994, 612; Troeller 2003, 50),[36] the comparative case analysis presented here reveals that democracies can—and do—engage in the forced displacement of peoples through legal, bureaucratic, and political means that have consequences just as portentous as the more commonly studied drivers of forced migration, such as environmental catastrophe, civil war, or persecution.

Methods

In order to address the aforementioned gaps in the human rights, forced migration, and (non)citizenship literatures, and to challenge the postnational claim that human rights have decoupled from citizenship, I conduct a comparative case study of statelessness in the Caribbean democracies of The Bahamas and the Dominican Republic. I contend that the Caribbean stands as a valid testing ground for evaluating postnational claims about the decoupling of human rights from citizenship because "no other region" in the developing world "has had, for so long, so many liberal democratic polities" (Domínguez 1993, 2).

Freedom House, which scores states according to their practices in the areas of civil liberties and political rights, classifies all the countries in the Caribbean—with the exception of Cuba and Haiti—as "free" (2015, n. pag.). Caribbean states thus score well in the categories of political participation, freedom of speech and of the press, social and economic freedoms, and the rule of law, among other criteria. Specifically, The Bahamas earns the highest freedom scores possible (1 out of 7) in both civil liberties and political rights, while the Dominican Republic scores slightly lower, with a score of 3 and 2 (out of 7) in each category, respectively.

Beside the comparative "liberal/democratic" nature of the region, UNHCR is concerned about statelessness in the Caribbean, making the area a significant case study of this phenomenon from both a policy and an academic vantage. Statelessness is an issue in the region for several reasons. First, several countries do not grant citizenship automatically to children born of noncitizens on their soil if a parent is not a citizen, a permanent resident or legally present. Individuals are thus at risk of statelessness if they are unable to acquire the nationality of their parents and if the state of their birth has no provision in place to grant citizenship to stateless children. For example, and as I explain in Chapters 3 and 4, both The Bahamas and the Dominican Republic have stipulations in their laws that make it difficult to obtain citizenship at birth if one is born to noncitizen or "illegally" resident parents.

Second, few Caribbean states have ratified the two UN statelessness conventions and incorporated preventative measures against statelessness into their national legislation. For instance, only four Caribbean states (Antigua and Barbuda, Barbados, St. Vincent and the Grenadines, Trinidad and Tobago)[37] have ratified the Convention relating to the Status of Stateless Persons (UN 1954), which delineates the rights and duties of a stateless person in a state party to the treaty; and only Jamaica has ratified the Convention on the Reduction of Statelessness, which aims to prevent and reduce statelessness globally (UN 1961; UN 2016 Treaty Collection).[38] Moreover, the majority of these states lack statelessness status determination (SSD) procedures, making it difficult to determine who is and who is not stateless in a systematic and transparent manner and to thereby furnish the stateless with a legal, protective status.

The problem of statelessness is of such significance in the Caribbean that UNHCR's office for the Americas stated that one of its four strategic priorities for 2012 was to: "Prevent statelessness in the Caribbean by advocating for accession to international instruments, mapping the population concerned or at risk, providing technical and legal support and helping them with their registration and documentation" (UNHCR 2012e, 96). For 2013, this theme continued as "there will be a strong focus on the prevention and reduction of statelessness and other nationality issues, mainly through birth registration and documentation" (quoted in Belton 2015, 129). And, in 2015, following on the cusp of the successful Cartagena +30 process, the organization declared that one of its strategic priorities is to resolve statelessness in the region (2015c, n. pag.). Furthermore, UNHCR is expressly focused on "ensur[ing] access to a nationality for undocumented people of Haitian descent" (2012e, 97). This policy development is important because, as I explain in Chapters 3 and 4, in both The Bahamas and the Dominican Republic, the two main destination sites for Haitian migrants (IOM 2013, 23), individuals of Haitian descent struggle to obtain, or retain, citizenship.

I chose The Bahamas and the Dominican Republic as case studies not only because they are democracies with a large presence of Haitian migrants and their children—and therefore an increased likelihood of containing populations who are at risk of statelessness—but also because of the notable differences that exist between them. From a demographic perspective, The Bahamas has a much smaller population at just over 350,000 persons (Government of The Bahamas 2012, 1), while the Dominican Republic has a population of around 9.4 million (Government of the Dominican Republic 2010a). The estimated tens of thousands of Haitians and their descendants in The Bahamas therefore make up a larger percentage of the Bahamian population than the estimated 380,000 in the Dominican Republic.[39] Additionally, black Bahamians make up the majority of the population in The Bahamas (Government of The Bahamas 2012, 10) and thus share the same racial classification as most Haitian migrants. The DR, on the other hand, consists of a largely mixed population. These racial differences could play a role in mitigating or exacerbating any tensions toward Haitian migrants and their offspring, as well as affect how each community approaches the inclusion of noncitizen insiders.

Culturally, The Bahamas is a mixture of Baptist, Anglican and Catholic adherents, with the majority identifying as Baptist (Government of the Bahamas 2012, 11), while the DR is largely Catholic.[40] The former was a British colony whose residents' primary language is English, while the latter was a Spanish colony whose residents' principal language is Spanish. From a legal and political perspective, The Bahamas and the DR are also distinct.

The Bahamas is a common law country, while the DR observes continental legal praxis ("civil law"). Although both states are classified as democracies, The Bahamas operates under the Westminster-style parliamentary system and the DR is a republic headed by a presidency. Significant differences thus exist between the two cases, yet both states engage in exclusionary membership practices that primarily affect individuals of Haitian descent. By choosing to undertake fieldwork in two countries that exhibit significant demographic, cultural, and institutional differences—and that similarly generate forced displacement on their territories—I strengthen the external validity of my findings (Leedy and Ormrod 2005, 99–100).

I undertook fieldwork in The Bahamas and the Dominican Republic between 2009 and 2013 to examine how each state's laws operated in practice with regard to the fulfillment of a human right to a nationality and to investigate how lack of formal membership in a state affects a person's sense of place identity and ability to be a self-determining agent. The 2009 fieldwork in The Bahamas was exploratory in nature as questions of citizenship denial and potential statelessness had not yet been investigated, whether by academics, policymakers, lawyers, or other experts. I was thus trying to establish whether statelessness existed, why it existed if it did (through which procedures or processes), where it existed (specific islands), and what ethnic groups were affected. I therefore conducted the 2009 interviews under the condition of anonymity for the study participants because I wanted them to speak as freely, and provide as much information as they could, on questions surrounding citizenship, discrimination, and national identity, given these subjects' sensitive nature in the country.

I conducted sixteen anonymous interviews in 2009.[41] Fourteen of these took place in the capital, Nassau, while the remaining two were conducted via telephone. Participants included former and current government officials, academics, community leaders, lawyers, a civil servant, a journalist, an amateur film documentarian, and a graduate student who had worked in the local Haitian communities. None of those interviewed were stateless or at risk of statelessness, but two were Haitian and held prominent positions in the Haitian community. Due to lack of data on statelessness in The Bahamas, I purposely selected the majority of the participants because they held (or had held) leadership positions in the foreign affairs or immigration sectors of government or the nascent human rights community, or were experts on Bahamian migration or nationality law and data collection.

I returned to The Bahamas in the fall of 2012 to carry out a second wave of interviews. I interviewed thirteen individuals in Nassau and seven in Marsh Harbour, Abaco. Participants included lawyers, activists, elected and appointed officials, educators, businesspersons, healthcare professionals, a police and a defense force officer, as well as the Haitian ambassador and Bahamian-born students of Haitian descent from the College of The Bahamas (COB).[42] An official from the Ministry of Foreign Affairs provided the Ministry's perspective via email. Of the twenty-one persons interviewed in 2012, eight had either faced the risk of statelessness or were stateless at some point.[43] As in the 2009 study, I performed purposeful sampling, but limited such sampling to government officials and lawyers. I obtained interviews with the other participants via snowball sampling or because I came into contact with them at a public forum on statelessness[44] at COB and requested interviews from them.

Those who participated in the 2012 portion of the study reflected a broad set of opinions: from those affected by statelessness and those affected by the presence of Bahamian-born individuals of Haitian descent in their communities, to those who held leadership positions in diverse professions that come into contact with individuals of Haitian descent (such as the armed forces, the police, the Ministry of Foreign Affairs, health professionals, lawyers, and teachers). In total, I interviewed thirty-seven individuals for the Bahamian case study. Of these, twenty-three were Bahamian of non-Haitian descent, seven were registered or naturalized Bahamians,[45] six were foreign residents (American or Haitian), and the remaining person was born in The Bahamas of Haitian descent who had not yet applied to register as a Bahamian. The majority of the interviewees were black (twenty-seven) and male (twenty-four).

In addition to the thirty-seven interviews from The Bahamas, I traveled to the Dominican Republic in the summer of 2012 and the spring of 2013. I interviewed ten individuals in the capital, Santo Domingo, and five in the batey[46] of El Caño in the province of Monte Plata. Four of the five participants from the batey were stateless, while one had previously been in that situation but now had her documents to prove Dominican citizenship. The interviewees from Santo Domingo consisted of two UN officials, nongovernmental organization (NGO) activists, lawyers, a diplomat from the Haitian Embassy, academics, as well as the local representative of the Open Society Justice Initiative (OSJI). Of the fifteen interviewees, six were Dominican (one had previously been stateless), five were foreign residents, and four were presently stateless or unable to prove Dominican nationality. The majority of the interviewees were black[47] (ten) and female (ten).

Participants for this part of the fieldwork once again reflect diverse viewpoints on the effects, and existence, of statelessness in the country. As in the Bahamian 2009 portion of the study, I selected the majority of the interviewees from Santo Domingo via purposeful sampling, although a few individuals were contacted via the snowball technique. I did not purposefully select the participants from El Caño, however. I was part of a group that went to listen to a town hall meeting on nationality deprivation in that batey and I consequently ended up informally interviewing five of the attendees (all women). Two additional interviews were conducted in New York City with two other members of OSJI earlier in 2012 on the subject of statelessness in the Caribbean.

In all cases, with the exception of the email interview response from the Bahamian Ministry of Foreign Affairs, I recorded and transcribed the interviews. Since I am interested in the participants' experiences with, and knowledge of statelessness, noncitizen rights, and state membership practices, the interviews were semistructured. I did not constrain our conversations solely to the interview questions that I had, but was open to the interviewee leading the dialogue in other directions. This often allowed me to discover information that I had not originally thought was important or pointed me to new directions of inquiry. The semistructured interview approach therefore allowed me to collect a series of responses to common questions, but also added a richness to the narratives that I perhaps would not have been able to capture otherwise. Such an approach, I believe, is appropriate for examining the lived realities of exclusionary state membership practices and their effects upon people's sense of belonging and ability to access rights in practice.

Besides the fifty-five semistructured interviews, I engaged in participant observation in a number of settings in the Caribbean and the United States as a means of assessing how individuals engage with each other on questions surrounding statelessness, migration, and human rights. In 2009, I attended the Second Annual Youth Conclave, sponsored by the United Haitian Association of The Bahamas, which addressed problems of discrimination and ways to empower the Haitian-descended youth in the country. Many of the young people present had faced obstacles growing up in The Bahamas and felt ostracized.

In 2012, I attended a *coyuntura* (town hall meeting) on the effects of Dominican migration law at the Centro Bonó[48] in Santo Domingo where members of the public, Dominican lawyers, and migration experts from the International Organization for Migration discussed the effects of Dominican migration law upon persons of Haitian descent. I also witnessed an impromptu celebration at the Centro Bonó when a group of Dominicans of Haitian descent, deprived of their citizenship documents, came to the organization to thank it for the legal assistance it had provided to them. Also in 2012, I attended an event commemorating the life and work of Dominican activist Sonia Pierre[49] at Columbia University in New York City, listening to the stories that her children, close friends, and colleagues shared with the audience.

In 2013, I attended a panel discussion on statelessness hosted by the Sociocultural Movement for Haitian Workers (MOSCTHA-USA),[50] also at Columbia University, and participated in an invitation-only symposium hosted by the Centro Bonó, the Mesa Nacional para Migrantes y Refugiados (MENAMIRD), the Red de Encuentro Dominico-Haitiano Jacques Viau, and the Observatorio Migrantes del Caribe (OBMICA) in Santo Domingo. Both events focused on the right to a nationality in the Dominican context and included speakers from the Dominican government and civil society.[51] I took part in a similar, but public, conference on statelessness at the College of The Bahamas in 2012[52] and listened via the internet to the follow-up conference that took place in 2014.[53] At the invitation of the Norwegian Refugee Council, I was also part of the civil society team that took part in the Caribbean subregional deliberations in Cayman for UNHCR's Cartagena +30 process, from which a regional Plan of Action for the Americas resulted that includes a chapter on statelessness.[54]

As a Bahamian, I have spent many hours in The Bahamas informally chatting with "citizens" and "noncitizens" at supermarkets, retail stores, religious venues, and in their homes about Bahamian membership practices, Haitian migrants, and discrimination. I have thus had multiple opportunities to hear diverse viewpoints on citizenship denial and deprivation, the issues associated with statelessness, and the efforts that have been, or should be, undertaken to alleviate the problem.

In addition to fieldwork, I use various primary and secondary sources to challenge the postnational claim of the decoupling of human rights from citizenship and to examine the ways in which democracies engage in forced displacement. I examine the nationality, migration laws, and constitutions of The Bahamas, the Dominican Republic, and Haiti—as well as legal assessments by experts on the latter country—to identify how individuals ought to be covered as nationals under a given law *in theory*. I stress "in theory" because, in practice, individuals may fall under the operation of a given state's law as a national, but in reality they do not possess said state's citizenship. Both The Bahamas and the Dominican Republic, for example, deny that statelessness is an issue on their territories. They point to Article 11 of the Haitian Constitution, which declares that any person born of a Haitian mother or father who has not renounced her or his Haitian citizenship is also a Haitian at birth (Government of Haiti 2011). These governments' position is that the offspring of Haitian migrants born on their soil are Haitian citizens through their parents. It therefore does not matter whether or not they have Bahamian or Dominican citizenship.

Yet, as UNHCR's Handbook on Protection of Stateless Persons makes clear, determining whether an individual is stateless "requires a careful analysis of how a State *applies* its nationality laws in an individual's case *in practice*" (2014g, 12; italics added). UNHCR asserts that "The reference to 'law' in Article 1(1) [of the 1954 statelessness convention] should be read broadly to encompass not just legislation, but also ministerial decrees, regulations, orders, judicial case law (in countries with a tradition of precedent) and, where appropriate, customary practice" (12) when determining whether a person is stateless. Such an approach, they contend, "may lead to a different conclusion than one derived from a purely objective analysis of the application of nationality laws of a country to an individual's case" (13). Using such an approach, I find—and illustrate in Chapters 3 and 4—that many individuals of Haitian descent, born in The Bahamas or the Dominican Republic of Haitian migrants do *not* fall under the operation of Haitian law *in practice*. They are consequently forced into liminality—a place where they are denied or deprived of formal belonging to the country of their birth, but unable to enjoy effective nationality from their alleged country of nationality (Haiti).

I also assess the status of these countries' treaty ratifications regarding statelessness or the right to a nationality,[55] and the reports of various NGOs and the UN on the subject to understand what treaty obligations these states ought to have and whether they are fulfilling them in practice. I examine pertinent judicial cases in the Dominican context as well—such as the *Case of the Girls Yean and Bosico v. the Dominican Republic* (IACtHR 2005) and

Sentence TC/0168/13 (Government of the Dominican Republic 2013e)—to understand their impact on Dominican membership practices.

Using my interview data and these primary and secondary sources, I demonstrate that far from being an institution whose "limits" have become "inventively irrelevant" (Soysal 1994, 162), citizenship in a state is increasingly important to access and exercise rights, as well as corresponding freedoms and protections, especially for those who are noncitizens everywhere. Moreover, states continue to jealously guard their sovereign right to demarcate and defend these limits, even if under the cover of seemingly neutral laws or bureaucratic procedures. This results in a form of forced displacement that is just as injurious as the forced displacement that we typically associate with movement under crisis or conflict conditions.

Because I find that citizenship continues to be a necessary status to hold in our allegedly postnational era, I move from theory testing to theory building in the final part of the book and offer a just membership framework for addressing statelessness. I contend that interpreting statelessness through such a framework is crucial in a world where states engage in arbitrary and discriminatory membership practices under the cover of law and where a large gap exists between the operation of said law and practice.

Book Overview

In order to make the case that the stateless face a peculiar and injurious form of forced displacement, even as they remain physically rooted in the countries of their birth, the book is divided into three parts. This first section, "Reconsidering Forced Displacement," discusses the debate over the relevance of citizenship in an era of human rights and the alleged waning of state sovereignty. It situates my argument in the existing scholarship on citizenship, noncitizenship, statelessness, and forced migration, describing why statelessness is an issue of global, regional, community, and individual import. This section underscores the lack of attention that has been paid to the stateless (those who do not cross borders but who are nevertheless "noncitizen") and illustrates how the focus on mobility within forced migration studies, especially as a result of conflict, persecution, or crisis, has served to make the plight of these populations largely invisible. It also draws attention to the ways liberal democracies around the world have engaged in practices that render people liminal subjects or make noncitizens out of citizens in the post-9/11 environment. This book thus speaks to broader questions of belonging, democratic regime behavior, and human rights access globally.

The second part, "Democracies as Engines of Forced Displacement," forms the empirical backbone of the book. Herein I provide support for the argument presented in the first section that liberal democracies are engaging in practices of forced displacement against those they consider "Other" within. While human rights and postnational scholarship tend to portray liberal democracies as those that allow for a person to enjoy rights, freedoms, and protections without formally belonging to the state, I use data gathered from the aforementioned original field interviews, supported by other primary and secondary sources, to demonstrate how the developing world democracies of The Bahamas and the Dominican Republic are forcibly displacing Bahamian- and Dominican-born persons of Haitian descent into liminality or making them become Haitian nationals against their will.

It should be noted that while the stateless have occasionally been referred to as liminals—or some such similar term—no work to date has used anthropologist Victor Turner's work on liminality to assess whether the stateless are indeed liminals. I use Turner's markers of "invisibility," "impurity," "rightlessness," and "reflection," which describe the liminal's condition and state of mind during liminality, to examine how liminality affects the stateless. While the stateless face varying degrees of invisibility and rightlessness, as well as treatment as "impure," unlike Turner's liminals, they do not share the ability to return to society (or the communities of their birth) on their own terms and with a new identity (citizenship in the case of the stateless). They thus remain displaced in the realm of the "betwixt and between."

The final portion of the book, "Noncitizen Insiders and the Right to Belong," explains the effects of forced displacement in situ upon people who are "noncitizen insiders" (Belton 2011); that is, those who are neither migrants nor citizens of the country of their birth and residence. Drawing on the detailed findings of my case studies, I demonstrate how rooted displacement affects these people's sense of identity, as well as their ability to enjoy human rights and be self-determining agents. It is here that I conclude that the greatest "calamity" to befall the stateless is not that they lack the "right to belong to some kind of organized community" (Arendt [1948] 2004, 377), but that they lack the right to belong to the *specific* communities of their birth. I therefore propose a "human right to belong" and justify it over the conventional understanding that states alone should determine their membership.

Chapter Summaries

Chapter 2 provides an overview of statelessness beginning with Arendt's experience and ending with its contemporary development. It describes the many ways in which a person may become stateless, the problems associated with this condition from an individual, community, and state vantage point, and international efforts to address it. The chapter demonstrates that exclusion from an "organized [political] community," as in Arendt's time, continues to be problematic in the twenty-first century. In contradistinction to Arendt's time, however, Chapter 2 shows that statelessness is not a "Europe-only" phenomenon, one of cross-border movements, or one that is necessarily generated by conflict, crisis, or persecution. Stateless people are found globally, within all regime types, and are generally physically rooted in a place, even though displaced in other ways.

Chapters 3 and 4 bring the discussion of global statelessness to the state level with case studies of The Bahamas and the Dominican Republic, respectively. These chapters detail how democracies can forcibly displace people under noncrisis and nonconflict situations via legal, political, and bureaucratic means. Specifically, Chapter 3 explains how seemingly neutral citizenship laws, when situated within a politicized citizenship-granting process and combined with bureaucratic inefficiencies, work together to displace Bahamian-born persons of primarily Haitian descent[56] into liminality or into the category of Haitian national, often without confirming that said persons are Haitian nationals in practice.

Chapter 4 continues the analysis of how the human right to a nationality is implemented in practice by examining the ways in which the Dominican state erects boundaries of belonging against the racialized "Other" within its borders. Via constitutional amendment, the retroactive application of laws, and arbitrary bureaucratic procedures, the chapter demonstrates how people can be turned into foreigners in their own country. Both chapters thus illustrate the precariousness of belonging under state-defined conditions and the ways in which individuals can be forcibly displaced while remaining "in place."

Whereas Chapters 3 and 4 demonstrate how two democracies of the developing world are engaging in forced displacement within their territories, Chapter 5 examines the effects of forced displacement in situ from an individual perspective. Using Victor Turner's analysis of liminality as a basis, the chapter illustrates how statelessness affects an individual's sense of belonging, his or her ability to access human rights, and prospects of being a fully self-determining agent. It thus demonstrates that the consequences of not being a citizen of somewhere in practice has ramifications far beyond the legal realm and it directly challenges the postnational claim that human rights have decoupled from citizenship.

The sixth and final chapter takes into account the forced nature of the stateless' displacement, making the case that the fulfillment of the human right to a nationality and the resolution of statelessness are matters of global distributive justice (GDJ). It is here I argue for a human right to belong that is predicated upon individual agency and choice and is less statist in orientation than current membership practices. For noncitizen insiders, this right consists of formally belonging to a specific place from birth—the state in which one was born—and the right to choose to continue to belong at maturity.

In conclusion, *Statelessness in the Caribbean* asks that we move our gaze inward to evaluate the effects of practices of citizenship deprivation and denial enacted upon those who come from within our own polities. As individuals who try to make their life within the state of their birth, even as it excludes them, the stateless suffer a form of forced displacement that is not unlike that faced by other types of forced migrants. They, too, are susceptible to human rights violations and face significant limitations on their ability to carry out key life projects. They are, in effect, displaced even as they remain rooted in the communities of their birth.

CHAPTER 2

Statelessness

A stateless person is someone who is like a ghost—they
are invisible to all the things we take for granted.
—UNHCR Goodwill Ambassador Barbara Hendricks

Historical and Contemporary Statelessness

Statelessness is not a new phenomenon. People have been displaced from formal belonging in the state in various ways since the 1800s. In nineteenth- and early twentieth-century Europe, individuals were rendered stateless as a form of punishment for criminal activities or because they were deemed threats to social order.[1] Even today, many countries' laws allow for denaturalization of an individual if he or she is deemed a threat to "social order." It was not until the twentieth century, however, that statelessness became a group, as opposed to an individual, problem.[2] With the dissolution of the Austro-Hungarian and Ottoman empires, groups of people found themselves stateless when they were prevented from acquiring citizenship in the newly formed states. Hannah Arendt, herself a stateless person for many years, called this group the *Heimatlosen*, the "oldest group of stateless people" ([1948] 2004, 353).[3] Jews were the primary group affected by these events, although other minority groups, such as Armenians and Roma, were also affected.

The establishment of totalitarian regimes of different persuasions added to the growing number of stateless persons in Europe during the early to mid-twentieth century. "Denationalization became a powerful weapon of totalitarian politics" (Arendt [1948] 2004, 343). Individuals fleeing Communism in the wake of the 1917 Bolshevik Revolution, for example, were summarily denationalized and many of those fleeing Fascist Italy, Japan, and Germany were also rendered stateless (Torpey 2000, 124–26). While Jews and Armenians "showed the highest proportion of statelessness" from such discriminatory denationalization procedures during this time (Arendt [1948] 2004, 358; see also 367), "Trotskyites," Spanish Republicans, and other political enemies were also targeted (343). In fact, Marc Vishniak lists the following groups as affected by statelessness during this period:

> Armenians who had escaped from Kurdish and Turkish massacres; Russians who had fled from the Soviet Union; the inhabitants of the Saar who had voted for France or for the League of Nations at the time of the Saar plebiscite; the Assyro-Chaldeans and Assyrians who had left Iraq after the massacres in that country; the Jews, democrats and socialists who had fled Nazi Germany; Austrian Jews, monarchists, democrats and socialists; Rumanians who opposed the dictatorship, and Rumanian Jews; anti-Fascist Italians and Italian Jews; Spanish Republicans, Czechoslovakian democrats, etc. After the outbreak of the war Poles, Norwegians, Netherlanders, Belgians, Frenchmen, Yugoslavs, Greeks, Estonians, Lithuanians and others joined their ranks. (Vishniak 1945, 34)

During this time of economic decline, "disintegration" and "hatred" (Arendt [1948] 2004, 342), statelessness became a pervasive, and serious, problem. Arendt likened statelessness to being expelled "from humanity altogether" (377). Once individuals no longer belonged formally to some state through citizenship, they became "outlaw(s)" (360, 363) and "barbarians" (384) whose only way of escaping from their political and legal nonexistence was either to commit a crime or to demonstrate some sort of genius (364). In a world of sovereign states, premised as it was and continues to be on individuals belonging formally to some state, Arendt argued that the stateless represented a possible regression from civilization (382). They were—and still are—liminal subjects, caught in the space of the "betwixt and between" that lies outside states' nationality classifications.[4]

Although the exact number of stateless persons during this period is unknown, and although the stateless were a diverse lot, Arendt's account describes certain commonalities among them. First, statelessness was largely the result of denaturalization and denationalization campaigns. That is, individuals became stateless because they were stripped of citizenship ([1948]

2004, 353–54, 365, 577), often on political grounds, not because they were born into statelessness, as occurs in The Bahamas, the Dominican Republic, and elsewhere today.

Second, also in contrast to the present era, statelessness was associated with border-crossings. The stateless were arrivals from elsewhere (Arendt ([1948] 2004, 341, 352, 356) and therefore had a country of origin: "Nonrecognition of statelessness always means repatriation, i.e., deportation to a country of origin" (355). As I illustrate in this book, however, the stateless today do not necessarily have a country of origin to which to be deported and the majority do not cross international borders to escape persecution.

Third, loss of citizenship entailed the loss of rights: the right to a home (Arendt ([1948] 2004, 372), the right to government protection and a legal status (373, 577), the right to an identity (364–65), the right to belong to a community (375, 377) and, in some instances, the right to life (375). Without citizenship, they "lost all other qualities and specific relationships—except that they were still human" (380).[5] Of all the rights violations that the stateless suffered during this time, Arendt felt that the loss of a community to which to belong was the gravest, as it led to the deprivation of all other rights. "The calamity of the rightless is not that they are deprived of life, liberty, and the pursuit of happiness, or of equality before the law and freedom of opinion . . . but that they no longer belong to any community whatsoever" (375).

As noted in Chapter 1, Arendt consequently insisted on the "right to have rights," which comprised the "right to belong to some kind of organized community" where one's opinion and actions mattered and one's rights could be guaranteed (376, 377). It was because Arendt believed that human rights rested not on some sort of inherent human dignity,[6] but rather on belonging as an equal to a political community,[7] she insisted that "man as man has only one right that transcends his various rights as a citizen: the right never to be excluded from the rights granted by his community" (628).

While much has changed since Arendt wrote *The Origins of Totalitarianism* more than sixty years ago—human rights have become part and parcel of international and local discourses, many governments incorporate such rights into their legislation and policies, and UNHCR has taken on the mandate of preventing and reducing statelessness globally—statelessness persists. UNHCR's Statistical Online Population Database has data on just over 3.49 million stateless people in seventy states (UNHCR 2015b), but the agency estimates that more than ten million people are de jure stateless worldwide (2012b). It admits, however, that it has a "tough task determining the true number of stateless people" (2012b n. pag.) and others surmise that the problem of "*de jure* statelessness is overshadowed by an even greater crisis of *de facto* statelessness" (Adjami and Harrington 2008, 107).

UNHCR defines de facto stateless persons as those who are "outside the country of their nationality who are unable or, for valid reasons, are unwilling to avail themselves of the protection of that country" (Massey 2010, 61). Other perspectives exist, however. For instance, in some cases de facto statelessness is described as the condition of being unable to prove one's nationality. This may result because an individual's birth is never registered, or because he or she is an undocumented migrant or a trafficked person, or because identity documents are purposely destroyed.[8] In other cases, de facto statelessness is defined as the lack of "effective" citizenship, which can mean a lack of government protection[9] or the inability to enjoy rights.[10] Additionally, in the more recent climate change work on statelessness, UNHCR asserts that those people who lose their state of citizenship due to rising sea levels could be rendered de facto stateless (Park 2011, 14).[11] The number of stateless persons, de jure and de facto, therefore, may be very high globally at present (and in the future).

Although I focus on the Caribbean in this book, stateless people are found in all areas of the world: from Central Asia to Western Europe and the African Great Lakes. The majority of stateless persons are found in Eastern Europe, the Middle East, and South and South East Asia, however (see Figure 1). The number of known stateless populations in these latter areas ranges from hundreds of thousands to millions and includes individuals of Russian descent in Estonia and Latvia, certain national minorities in the Russian Federation, Bidoon in Kuwait,[12] Palestinians in Syria and Lebanon, highland tribes in Thailand, Rohingya[13] in Myanmar, and Lhotshampas in Bhutan, among others.[14] Figure 1, which does not capture the stateless populations in states for which data are unavailable (such as Australia, The Bahamas, Canada, or South Africa), presents the scope of UNHCR's known stateless populations.

Causes of Statelessness

When statelessness became a prominent international concern during the World War II era, it was in the context of geopolitical upheaval, war, and genocide. Groups of people, once recognized as nationals of a given state,

Figure 1. De jure statelessness, 2012. Migration Policy Institute Data Hub, 2015.

were stripped of their citizenship, often on a discriminatory basis. Stateless-ness as a result of arbitrary denationalization policies did not vanish when the war ended or when the UDHR proclaimed in Article 15 that everyone has a right to a nationality and not to be arbitrarily deprived of it, however. In fact, the "Deprivation or denial of nationality based on discriminatory practices, particularly against racial, ethnic or religious minorities . . . is per-haps the most important cause of statelessness worldwide" today (Manly 2007, 256). In Chapters 3 and 4, I explain how statelessness is generated on these grounds in the specific contexts of The Bahamas and the Dominican Republic.

Many of those who are denied or deprived of citizenship on discrimina-tory grounds are found in democratizing regimes or in newly formed states that are still in the process of nation building. For example, democratization has had the "effect of triggering an obsession with belonging" in Africa (Geschiere 2009, 6). Consequently, from Côte d'Ivoire and Cameroon to Zam-bia and Zimbabwe, people have been turned into "foreigners" in their own country because they are not deemed "autochthonous" to the state.[15] The pro-cess of denationalizing citizens often occurs around election time. Thus, in

Cameroon, "Belonging has become a choice weapon for manipulating elections" (52). The NGO Citizenship Rights in Africa, a group that seeks to end statelessness on the continent, records how black Africans in Mauritania, Nubians in Kenya, and various groups in Côte d'Ivoire have been denationalized around election time because they represent political competition.[16] Similarly, OSJI observed that "the advent of multi-party democracy in many African States in the 1990s heightened the political significance of distinguishing citizens from noncitizens, and led to a marked increase in attempts to denationalise political opponents or even entire ethnic and social groups" (cited in Kanengoni 2008, 4).[17]

Statelessness can also be "a by-product of entrenched discrimination and social exclusion," which is "often closely related to incomplete nation-building" (Manly 2007, 257). Juan Linz and Alfred Stepan observe that democratizing or transitioning regimes often suffer from a "stateness" problem. That is, regimes that are attempting to leave behind a previous authoritarian structure often face a crisis wherein "profound differences about what should actually constitute the polity (or political community) and which demos or demoi (population or populations) should be members of that political community" become problematic (Linz and Stepan 1996, 16). When "profound differences" exist "as to who has the right of citizenship in that state . . . a 'stateness' problem" occurs (16).

The creation of "strangers" and an upsurge in nationalism thus purportedly go hand in hand with democratization processes (Snyder 2000; Geshiere 2009). Many of the groups identified as "strangers" in the nation-building exercise are rendered stateless. For instance, with the exception of Lithuania, the Baltic states excluded ethnic Russians from their understanding of the demos; the Bengalis excluded the Biharis; the Myanmarese omitted the Rohingya; the Bhutanese targeted the Lhotshampa; the Congolese excluded the Banyamulenge; and the Kuwaitis rejected the Bidoon.

This exclusion is often made formal through restrictive or discriminatory citizenship laws. Claude Cahn and Sebihana Skenderovska (2008) observe how many post-Communist states created laws to restrict citizenship, and the concomitant privileges of voting and running for office, to a particular "national" group. Consequently, Serbs and Roma have been excluded from citizenship in Croatia and ethnic Albanians and Roma have been disenfranchised in Macedonia.[18] Brad Blitz (2006) discusses the "erasure" of Slovenes shortly after post-Communist independence and Igor Stiks similarly observes how citizenship laws were manipulated in Slovenia "to eliminate a certain number of citizens from the political, social and economic life of the new state" (2006, 492).

Outside of these cases, which clearly violate the UDHR's Article 15 prohibition on the arbitrary deprivation of nationality, states retain the right to denationalize individuals on other grounds.[19] For example, a person may be denationalized for converting to another religion, for failing to renew his or her passport, or for not adapting to a state's "customs." As in the early twentieth century, denationalization may occur for residing abroad without permission, committing a crime, or engaging in an act deemed "threatening" or "disloyal" to the state. A person may also be stripped of citizenship if he or she acquires citizenship or seeks asylum in another state. Moreover, denationalization on these and other grounds is not peculiar to democratizing regimes or illiberal states. Developed democracies can and do strip individuals, particularly naturalized persons, of their citizenship.

Whether it is through laws that allow for the denaturalization of those deemed (or suspected) terrorists, those who have committed acts against national security,[20] or the revocation of citizenship from those born on the territory "without warning or judicial approval" (Ross and Galey 2014 n. pag.), developed world democracies also engage in practices that force those they consider unworthy of citizenship into liminality or deprive them of membership without consent. In the UK, for instance, people can be stripped of citizenship on these grounds without ensuring they are nationals of another country in practice, rendering them stateless (Bennhold 2014a, b).

In 2014, Canada adopted Bill C-24 (Parliament of Canada 2014), which amends the Canadian Citizenship Act such that dual citizens, or those who have "the possibility of dual citizenship" may be denationalized "for a criminal conviction in another country, even if the other country is undemocratic or lacks the rule of law" (Georgia Straight 2014). According to the Canadian Association of Refugee Lawyers (CARL), "Bill C-24 eliminates any type of hearing in most revocation cases, and *replaces it with an administrative procedure* that gives citizens in revocation proceedings less protection than permanent residents who are found inadmissible on grounds of misrepresentation" (2014, 7; italics added). CARL adds that "The result of this law is to remove citizenship and *render the person a foreign national*" (8; italics added). It is then up to the person concerned to prove she or he is not a citizen of another country in order to avoid statelessness (8).

In 2015, the Australian Parliament passed a similar act to Canada's Bill C-24. The Australian Citizenship Amendment (Allegiance to Australia) Act

(No. 166) declares that a dual national who "acts inconsistently with their allegiance to Australia by engaging in conduct" related to terrorism or foreign recruitment effectively "renounces" her or his Australian citizenship (Parliament of Australia 2015, Section 33AA, para. 1). This provision not only applies to naturalized Australians, but also to those dual nationals who became Australian citizens at birth (para. 8).

According to the act, the minister in charge of denationalization or denaturalization of the Australian dual national does not have to give notification of said person's citizenship deprivation if the minister "is satisfied that giving the notice could prejudice the security, defence or international relations of Australia, or Australian law enforcement operations" (para. 12). Furthermore, it is at the minister's discretion or "determination" to decide whether to exempt a person under the act's effects (para. 14) through consideration of "the person's connection to the other country of which the person is a national or citizen and the availability of the rights of citizenship of that country to the person" (para. 17f). A person could, therefore, be potentially rendered stateless should the minister choose not to exercise his or her power under paragraph 14.[21]

While not a case of denaturalization or citizenship deprivation, the state of Texas in the United States has recently been the site of a practice that is almost tantamount to citizenship denial. For several years the Texas Department of State Health Services refused to provide birth certificates to children who were born to undocumented parents in its territory. This affected hundreds of children, primarily of Mexican descent or whose parents were from Central America (Hennessy-Fiske 2016). The result was the creation of Americans "without the papers to prove it" (Blitzer 2015 n. pag.) with repercussions that ran the gamut of being unable to re-enter the United States and problems enrolling children in school and receiving healthcare (2015 n. pag.; and Hennessy-Fiske 2015).[22]

The affected families sued Texas in federal court and reached a settlement with the Texas Department of State Health Services wherein the latter agreed to accept an expanded list of documents as proof of the immigrant parent's identity (for example, foreign voter cards, U.S. utility bills and residential leases, or library cards). Juanita Valdez-Cox, executive director of La Unión del Pueblo Entero in Texas, called the settlement "a critical victory for immigrant families, but it is also a victory for the constitutional rights of all of us. . . . Questioning the citizenship of U.S.-born, citizen children of immigrant parents erodes our constitutional freedoms and protections, causes instability for parents and children, and undermines the guarantee that all of our children will unquestionably be citizens" (cited in Hennessy-Fiske 2016 n. pag.).

These are but a few examples that illustrate the tenuous nature of formal belonging in developed democracies, even for those who are so-called "birthright" citizens (that is, they acquired citizenship at birth through the authorized channels). What makes the cases of denationalization and denaturalization especially troublesome in the Canadian and Australian examples—as opposed to the blatant document denial in the Texas case—is the surreptitious way in which the process may be carried out while the citizens concerned are overseas (thereby preventing their reentry and greatly hindering their ability to pursue legal recourse).

While states have come a long way in reducing gender bias in laws related to property and nationality rights compared to one hundred years ago, statelessness still results from outright gender discrimination. For instance, twenty-seven states prevent their female citizens from passing on their citizenship to their children the same way their male counterparts do: The Bahamas, Bahrain, Barbados, Brunei, Burundi, Iran, Iraq, Jordan, Kiribati, Kuwait, Lebanon, Liberia, Libya, Madagascar, Malaysia, Mauritania, Nepal, Oman, Qatar, Saudi Arabia, Sierra Leone, Somalia, Sudan, Swaziland, Syria, Togo, United Arab Emirates (Global Campaign for Equal Nationality Rights 2016).[23]

In many of these countries, a citizen woman who gives birth to her child while overseas cannot automatically pass on her citizenship to her child. This is not a problem if the father is a citizen of a state that allows for the jus sanguinis transmission of nationality or if the child is born in a country that grants citizenship through jus soli. If neither of these conditions holds, however, or if the father is stateless, the child can be rendered stateless. Many examples exist of children becoming stateless due to conflicts in nationality laws because there is no overarching framework at the international level for regulating citizenship acquisition. It also bears pointing out that developed democracies are not immune to creating stateless persons via gender discrimination either.[24]

Thus, although "reliance upon the accident of birth is inscribed in the laws of all modern states and applied everywhere" (Shachar 2009, 4) through jus soli and jus sanguinis citizenship transmission, states differ in how they qualify the acquisition of this status. For instance, some states, such as the Dominican Republic, grant citizenship via jus soli as long as one of the parents is a citizen or a legal resident, while other states do not have such a stipulation. In other cases, citizenship through jus sanguinis is limited in application through the first generation born overseas if the parents are no longer residents of their state of citizenship. Other states have different conditions depending on whether a child is born to a mother who is married or is born out of wedlock.

Female citizens are also at risk of denationalization in some states because of the prevailing marriage and divorce laws of their state of origin or state of residence. That is, some states stipulate that a woman will lose her birth citizenship and acquire the citizenship of her foreign husband upon marriage. If the marriage dissolves, the woman may be rendered stateless if the state of her former husband's citizenship no longer recognizes her as a national or if her state of original citizenship does not reinstate the citizenship she held at birth. These and many other cases of conflicts, or protection gaps, in nationality laws force people into liminality, or statelessness.[25]

Even when laws are nondiscriminatory in principle, they may be arbitrarily applied in practice. As I demonstrate in Chapters 3 and 4, people may become stateless when civil servants, or those individuals authorized to act on behalf of the state regarding the provision or renewal of citizenship and identity documents, fail to provide such documents, intentionally or not. As Bronwen Manby, discussing the case of statelessness in Africa, explains, civil servants have been known to deny birth certificates on discriminatory grounds or to delay the granting of a passport to a legitimate, but "nonnative" citizen.

In practice, individual Africans far more often face the practical impossibility of obtaining official documentation than an explicit denial of nationality. Yet something as simple as a failure to register a birth or an indefinite delay in obtaining a national identification card . . . can have consequences just as damaging and permanent as if denationalization had been enacted in the law. (2009, 115)

Such problems are not confined to Africa. In various places around the world, minority citizens face obstacles in obtaining or retaining their identity documents. As Chapter 4 explains, the Dominican Republic has generated much attention in recent years because civil registry officers have denied birth certificates, and consequently proof of citizenship, to children born of

Haitians in the country who, according to the law prevalent at the time, should have been recognized as Dominican nationals (Wooding 2008, 370; Goris 2011).

While possession of a birth certificate or other forms of state-issued identity documentation does not necessarily mean that a person falls under the operation of a state's law as a citizen,[26] such documents are still the primary means by which a person who is struggling to establish or retain citizenship is able to make a claim to this formal status. This is one of the reasons why trafficked persons, as well as undocumented or irregular migrants, are susceptible to statelessness (van Waas 2008, 165–87). Children whose births go unregistered often find themselves in the same predicament.

Despite the fact that the majority of states around the world have signed the Convention on the Rights of the Child ([CRC] UN 1989), which explicitly asserts in Article 7 that "The child shall be registered immediately after birth," the UN Children's Fund (UNICEF) estimates that the births of approximately 290 million children are unregistered globally (UNICEF 2014a). Unable to prove to whom (citizenship acquisition via jus sanguinis) or where one was born (citizenship acquisition via jus soli) places a child at risk of not having their right to a nationality fulfilled—a clear violation of Article 7 of the CRC. The problem is of such magnitude that UNICEF considers birth registration one of its key child protection issues:

> Apart from being the first legal acknowledgement of a child's existence, birth registration is central to ensuring that children are counted and have access to basic services such as health, social security and education. Knowing the age of a child is central to protecting them from child labour, being arrested and treated as adults in the justice system, forcible conscription in armed forces, child marriage, trafficking and sexual exploitation. . . . In effect, birth registration is their "passport to protection." (UNICEF 2014a n. pag.)

Lack of birth registration occurs for various reasons. Some states simply do not have the resources to establish civil registries in remote locations, while others have endured serious political or environmental events that destroy existing registries. In still other cases, parents fail to register the birth of their child in the appropriate institution or do not have the means to pay for the transportation or administrative costs to obtain a certificate. Most of the cases of unregistered births occur in South Asia and Eastern and Southern Africa where an estimated 61 and 62 percent of children under five years old are unregistered, respectively (UNICEF 2013, 43).[27]

Beside issues surrounding conflicts in nationality laws, inadequate application of existing nationality laws by state bureaucrats, outright discriminatory policies, and problems obtaining birth registration and documentation, statelessness can also result from state dissolution. Just as in the early twentieth century, when the Austro-Hungarian, Ottoman, and Tsarist polities disintegrated, the former Yugoslavia, Czechoslovakia, USSR, and Sudan are all states that have either dissolved or have had a portion of their state secede and create a new state over the past few decades. In several of the European successor states, certain minority peoples were denied their right to a nationality and remain stateless today.

UNHCR, for example, has official figures on stateless people in Armenia, Azerbaijan, Belarus, Bosnia and Herzegovina, Czech Republic, Estonia, Georgia, Kazakhstan, Kyrgyzstan, Latvia, Lithuania, Montenegro, Republic of Moldova, Russia, Serbia, Slovakia, Turkmenistan, Tajikistan, the former Yugoslav Republic of Macedonia, and Ukraine. These populations range from as few as 206 known stateless persons in Armenia to 262,802 in Latvia (UNHCR 2015b). Controversies over citizenship have similarly come to the fore between Sudan and the Republic of South Sudan and consequently placed thousands at risk of statelessness (Reynolds 2012; Sanderson 2014).[28]

Human Rights Repercussions

As the previous section illustrates, statelessness may result for many different reasons and is not a condition that affects a particular age group or just one region of the world. A person can be born into statelessness or become stateless later in life, and statelessness is not a problem particular to authoritarian or transitioning regimes. Democracies also create and harbor stateless populations. Despite the wide range of people affected and the diverse ways of becoming stateless, stateless people are everywhere excludable because they belong nowhere. Without citizenship, a stateless person may have to deal with the refusal of identity documents and licenses,[29] forced labor[30] and enslavement,[31] the denial of private sector employment,[32] inadequate housing and healthcare,[33] as well as the violation of other economic and social rights like social security and education.[34] Stateless persons are also susceptible to family separation,[35] torture,[36] trafficking,[37] and indefinite or unnecessary detention,[38] while being denied adequate access to judicial procedures.[39]

Due to the obstacles that stateless people face in accessing various human rights, stateless populations often face higher degrees of chronic illness and unemployment, both of which can affect community development. For example, the poor conditions in which many stateless people live either generate or exacerbate health-related problems. The camps and settlements where stateless people live often lack adequate sanitation facilities and running water. Maureen Lynch describes the situation of the Biharis of Bangladesh:

Lack of water and co-habitation with animals, combined with poor drainage and sanitation systems, contribute to a variety of medical problems, including skin disease, water-borne illness, upper respiratory infections and gastro-intestinal disorders. In one camp, only two working wells supply water to 650 families. In Mirpur's Millat Camp, there was only one latrine for 6,000 people. Few medical clinics exist, and several camps have no health care at all, leaving entire families susceptible to both medical and related financial hardship. (2005, 15)[40]

The stateless are also susceptible to other health problems that can run the gamut of chronic illness, sexually transmitted diseases, and drug abuse to psychological issues such as depression, which sometimes results in "alcoholism, domestic violence and suicide" (Sokoloff 2005, 22). Stateless people are often prohibited from receiving government subsidized healthcare and insurance or in other instances do not receive complete coverage akin to their citizen counterparts,[41] which results in higher percentages of stateless people suffering from treatable health conditions, such as tuberculosis, high blood pressure, and diabetes.[42] Vulnerability to trafficking,[43] as well as lack of education and access to health care services, also results in what may be "epidemic" proportions of HIV/AIDS among some stateless groups (Ehna 2004, 5).[44] The problem is often compounded when the stateless are directly or indirectly denied access to antiretroviral drugs.[45]

Children are especially susceptible to HIV exposure from their stateless mothers who cannot always access government-provided HIV/AIDS services or prenatal care generally. Additionally, stateless children may also suffer from malnutrition and treatable illnesses. Lynch notes, for instance, that "Children without birth certificates cannot be legally vaccinated in at least twenty countries and over thirty countries require documentation to treat a child at a health facility" (2008, 12). Such limitations on these children's ability to access health care can have far-reaching consequences: from the inability to obtain medicines for curing preventable or treatable illnesses to higher rates of malnutrition and even death.[46]

Beside health-related issues, the stateless often lack access to favorable labor conditions. Studies illustrate that the stateless are regularly channeled into "3-D jobs"—those that are dirty, dangerous, or degrading. Constantin Sokoloff explains, for example, how the Rohingya are forcibly employed by the Myanmarese army, without pay, "for construction and maintenance of [the army's] facilities, as well as for a variety of other tasks required by the authorities" (2005, 21).[47] The denial of opportunities to own land or property and the inability to access credit or obtain business licenses also affects their ability to work.[48] As Laura van Waas notes in the case of Syria, "stateless Kurds cannot obtain property deeds, register cars or businesses, open a bank account or obtain a commercial driver's license and in Bahrain, Bidoon have been prohibited from buying land, starting a business or obtaining a government loan" (2010, 25). Moreover, many states forbid noncitizens from holding certain public sector jobs such as that of teachers or medical professionals. These are just some of the possible problems that a stateless person may face within their state of birth or residence.[49]

Since international law deems citizenship the formal vehicle by which states extend protection to their populations when they are outside their own state's territorial confines, the stateless also lack such protection. Moreover, although Article 13 of the UDHR affirms that everyone has the right to leave any country and return to his or her own country, the stateless often face great hardship when trying to reenter the state that they consider to be their "own" country because the latter does not recognize them as citizens under the operation of its law.[50] Movement, both within a state and across borders, can therefore be highly problematic, resulting in one of the ironies of statelessness—those who lack a formal membership bond to any state through citizenship are among those with the most severely restricted mobility on earth.

This section has illustrated that stateless people, in general, are bound in numerous ways. Although the stateless are not forced to flee their homes in the same way that other kinds of forced migrants are, they suffer many of the same effects of forced displacement. They are, in Lubkemann's words

(2008), immobilized as their ability to carry out "key life projects" has been involuntarily—and severely—disrupted. Thus, while the issue of statelessness may not be at the forefront of humanitarian agendas or among the stories of the forcibly displaced that have come to our attention in recent years, it is clear that the stateless do suffer.

Macrolevel Repercussions

When one considers the domestic and international constraints faced by those without citizenship, it becomes apparent why international jurists, such as Hersch Lauterpacht, would consider citizenship to be an "instrument for securing the rights of the individual in the national and international spheres" (quoted in van Panhuys 1959, 236), and why citizenship is often considered "not one right but a bundle of rights" (Odinkalu 2008, 14). The violation of the human right to a nationality does not simply have individual-level repercussions, however. Its effects can also be felt community-wide.

For example, statelessness can affect regime stability in various ways. Earlier it was noted that democratization processes may sometimes have negative effects for certain minority populations when they are denationalized or denied citizenship for political gain. The flip side to this phenomenon is the inability of a state to consolidate a democracy. As Linz and Stepan assert, "The greater the percentage of people in a given state who were born there or who had not arrived perceiving themselves as foreign citizens, who are denied citizenship in the state and whose life changes are hurt by such denial, the more unlikely it is that this state will consolidate a democracy" (1996, 33). Virginia Leary likewise adds that "the exclusion of a group of people who reside within a given regime and who have little hope of regularizing their status and becoming citizens can be destabilizing domestically and challenge any regime's ability to transition fully to a democratic status" (1999, 257).

Some interviewees for this study fear that the legal, political, and social exclusion of Bahamian- and Dominican-born persons of Haitian descent will escalate into a large-scale social problem in the countries of their birth. "We will have pockets of the population that are going to then enter into crisis," says Francisco Henry Leonardo of the Centro Bonó. "They're going to enter into a crisis and search for their own identity. Because, look, they feel

Dominican, but they are rejected. So, 'What is our identity?' They are going to start a process of differentiation." Altair Rodríguez, a Dominican social scientist, agrees: "It's a time bomb. We're creating a bomb. There's thousands of kids being raised in bateyes without access to education, without access to basic rights. . . . So we're creating a social bomb that's going to explode."[51]

These fears are echoed in the Bahamian case. Bahamian lawyer Dexter Reno Johnson proclaims that the situation "is a keg of dynamite, a source of potential social unrest of mammoth proportions"; "a critical problem that makes most other problems pale into insignificance since unless properly handled, this one could threaten the peaceful existence of the Bahamas, as we know it at any time, and for the foreseeable future" (Johnson 2008, 71, 72).[52] An anonymous interviewee adds that the Bahamian government's exclusionary citizenship laws are "creating more liabilities than assets"[53] for the country and Mark Desmangles, born of Haitian descent in The Bahamas, observes how statelessness "affects economics. Because this is a group of people who cannot participate economically in the banking system, in the work force to give toward the economic well-being and the betterment of the community."

Another anonymous Bahamian interviewee, discussing the problems associated with denying citizenship to children born of noncitizens until age eighteen, declares that "What you do in fact do is frustrate and alienate that person for 18 years. How does that serve the public good?"[54] The Bahamas Constitutional Commission, which made recommendations to alter the Bahamian Constitution in diverse areas, including nationality, also emphatically asserts that it:

> cannot overstate the enormous psychological, socio-economic and other ill-effects that result from leaving large groups of persons *in limbo* in relation to their aspirations for Bahamian citizenship. Not only are the affected individuals badly damaged and marginalized, *the entire society is put at risk and its future compromised* by having within its borders a substantial body of persons who, although having no knowledge or experience of any other society, are made to feel that they are intruders without any claim, moral or legal, for inclusion. Such feelings of alienation and rejection are bound to translate into anti-social behavior among many members of what is, in effect, a very large underclass in our society. (Government of The Bahamas 2013b, 96–97; italics added)

Additionally, the combination of poor living conditions, limited employment prospects, and social stigma sometimes leads to communal tension in
the states where the stateless reside. As UNHCR points out, the "Denial of
basic human rights [to stateless persons] impacts not only the individuals
concerned but also society as a whole, in particular because excluding an
entire sector of the population may create social tension and significantly
impair efforts to promote economic and social development" (2010b, 4).
During the past few years, for example, significant violence has erupted between Buddhists and stateless Rohingya in Myanmar, with hundreds of
people being killed and thousands of homes destroyed.[55] Banyamulenge,
who have struggled for citizenship recognition in the Democratic Republic
of Congo, continue to face "discriminatory treatment and ethnic tensions"
(UN HRC 2008b, 17), and "excessive force" has been used by the Kuwaiti
authorities against Bidoon who have been peacefully protesting for citizenship recognition in that state (Al Jazeera 2012; Reynolds and Cordell 2012, 2).

The problems associated with statelessness are not limited to one state's
borders either. States that refuse to grant citizenship to stateless persons may
be providing grounds for these people to "seek full national legal identity
elsewhere" (Batchelor 2006, 10). This is problematic because international
law does not allow one state to "release itself from the international duty,
owed to other states, of receiving back a person denationalized who has acquired no other nationality" (McDougal et al. 1974, 951). That is, states are
not permitted to allow stateless people to become "charge[s] on other States"
(951). While most stateless groups do not cross borders (they are "noncitizen
insiders"), the Rohingya are a prime example of a stateless group that has
crossed borders—leaving Myanmar for Bangladesh, Thailand, Saudi Arabia,
Pakistan, and the Gulf States—in the hopes of finding a home elsewhere.

The Bidoon of the Gulf region, European Roma, and Banyamulenge are
also cases of stateless people who have crossed state borders, whether forcibly or voluntarily. Conflict between states may arise when they do not agree
on the origin of stateless people or on which state should be granting citizenship to them, especially when resources are scarce. As Andrew Shacknove
remarks, "The potential for international conflict is increased when ambiguity exists about the allocation of, and responsibility for, either territory or
populations of forced migrants" (1993, 527).

The issue of deciding who belongs where, and how a given minority population should be treated, can be a particularly politically sensitive regional
issue when a state has to deal with stateless persons on its territory who also

happen to belong to a recognized minority population in a neighboring state. For instance, the stateless Lhotshampas are allegedly straining Nepal's resources. Nepal has asked Bhutan, the ethnic "origin" state of the Lhotshampas, to sort out the latter's nationality status (Khan 2001, 24–25). India, being the regional power, has the clout to negotiate an agreement between Nepal and Bhutan concerning this stateless group, but will not do so because of the huge number of ethnic Nepalis within its own borders. "India is no longer particularly anxious to be associated with Nepali minority rights movements in third countries for fear of its own vulnerability on the matter" (21). Thus, the Lhotshampas end up in a protracted stateless situation. Relatedly, many Roma have found it difficult to obtain citizenship in the states that succeeded the USSR because those states tried to pass them off as residents of a neighboring state at the time of independence.

Surrounding states may also act as staging grounds for stateless persons to engage in activities aimed at overthrowing a particular regime. As Peter Mutharika notes, "Where political enemies have been expelled and denationalized, they may continue to engage in activities aimed at overthrowing the ruling elite" (1989, 17). He adds that neighboring states may "even be drawn into attempts by some stateless persons to subvert the state of origin" (19). Statelessness is thus not only a human rights issue, but a matter of regional security as well.

International Activity Around Statelessness

Since statelessness is a pressing issue from an individual, community, state, and regional perspective, UNHCR and the Inter-Parliamentary Union have encouraged UN member states to accede to the 1954 and 1961 statelessness conventions as a means of "bolster[ing] national solidarity and stability" and "improv[ing] international relations and stability" (UNHCR and IPU 2005, 49). UNHCR has been actively campaigning for statelessness treaty accession since 2011. As Figure 2 illustrates, there has been a sharp increase in the number of states ratifying the two statelessness conventions since the turn of the century.

Former UNSG Ban Ki Moon also engaged in increasing activity on the issue of statelessness, publishing several reports on the arbitrary deprivation of nationality (UN HRC 2009a and b, 2011, 2013b), another report on discrimination against women under nationality law (UN HRC 2013a), as well

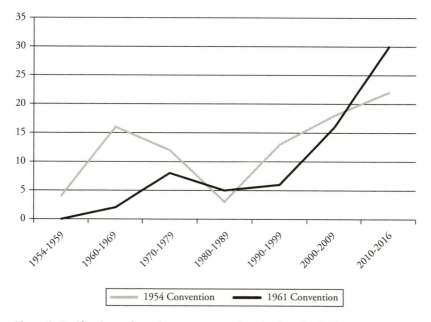

Figure 2. Ratifications of statelessness conventions by decade, 1950s-present.
UN Treaty Collection 2016.

as a Guidance Note on "The United Nations and Statelessness" (UNSG 2011).
The former Secretary General made clear in the latter report that the UN
"should tackle both the causes and consequences of statelessness as a key
priority within the Organization's broader efforts to strengthen the rule of
law" (3).

While the UN considers statelessness a rule of law issue today, when international concern around statelessness first surfaced in the aftermath of
WWII it was primarily tied to another group of forcibly displaced persons—
refugees. UNHCR, the body created for the protection of refugees in 1950,
did not acquire its second mandate over stateless persons until more than
twenty years later through General Assembly Resolution 3274 (XXIX) (UN
1974).[56] Since that time, UNHCR's mandate on statelessness has expanded
through a series of other resolutions (UNHCR 2014a). Prior to the establishment of the agency's second mandate, however, the UN had already produced
the two aforementioned statelessness conventions.

The Convention relating to the Status of Stateless Persons (UN 1954)
delineates the rights and duties of stateless persons in their states of residence.

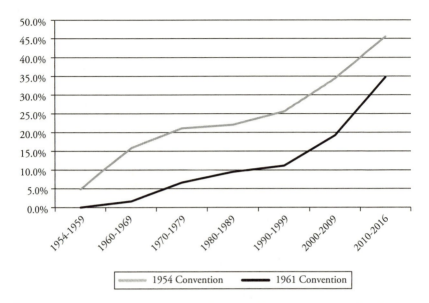

Figure 3. States parties as a percentage of UN membership over time, 1954–2016.
UN Treaty Collection, 2016.

It asks signatory states to treat the stateless as well as "aliens generally in the same circumstances" regarding the rights of property, association, gainful employment, housing, and freedom of movement and to treat them as well as nationals regarding artistic and scientific rights, access to the courts, elementary education, public relief, and labor legislation. The Convention on the Reduction of Statelessness (UN 1961), which followed a few years later, asks contracting states to offer citizenship to children on their territories who would otherwise be stateless, provide an expedited naturalization procedure to stateless people, avoid denationalizing a person arbitrarily, and to ensure that an individual has access to another nationality before being denationalized, among other stipulations. Although more than a half century has passed since these conventions were issued, and despite the fact that there has been an uptick in the number of ratifications since the early 2000s, the statelessness conventions are among the most poorly ratified human rights treaties of the UN system.[57] At the time of this writing, and as Figure 3 reflects, of the 193 UN member states, eighty-eight (46 percent) are party to the 1954 convention and sixty-seven (35 percent) are party to the 1961 convention (UN 2016).

While fewer than half the UN membership have ratified either of the statelessness conventions as of December 2016, the current UNSG, António Guterres, believes there has been "a real breakthrough, a quantum leap . . . in relation to the protection of stateless people" (UNHCR 2011b) over the last few years. For example, a High Level Ministerial Meeting was held in Geneva in 2011 where more than 150 state representatives attended and more than sixty made pledges regarding statelessness: from committing to improve birth registries and acceding to one or both of the statelessness conventions to reducing statelessness on their territory (UNHCR 2012d).

Additionally, in 2010 and 2011 three international expert meetings were held on statelessness. They addressed de jure and de facto statelessness, SSD procedures, and protecting stateless children, respectively. A fourth expert meeting was held in 2013 on interpreting Articles 5 through 9 of the 1961 statelessness convention.[58] From this series of meetings and other work, UNHCR was able to issue a series of guidelines on statelessness, which culminated in their Handbook on Protection of Stateless Persons (2014g). Within this document UNHCR defines a stateless person under the 1954 convention, articulates the rights and status of stateless persons under international law and provides advice on how governments can create statelessness status determination procedures, among other guidelines and clarificatory points. In effect, this Handbook, along with Guideline No. 4 on a child's right to a nationality (UNCHR 2012c), can be used to assist a wide array of actors in identifying, and addressing the needs of, the stateless.

Moreover, whereas UNHCR previously admitted that it was "not doing enough" to address statelessness (UNHCR 2007), the organization "has more than tripled its expenditure on statelessness—from USD 12 million to USD 36 million in 2013" (UNHCR 2014e, 6) and "The number of UNHCR operations planning statelessness activities more than doubled between 2009 and 2011, from 28 to 60" (UNHCR 2012a, 45). The activities carried out by UNHCR teams center upon the agency's four areas of responsibility, including the identification and protection of stateless persons and the prevention and reduction of statelessness. As such, UNHCR has provided technical assistance to states, such as Nepal, Sri Lanka, and Bangladesh, so that their nationality laws can be modified to prevent and reduce statelessness. It has carried out campaigns, conducted workshops and education programs, and provided mobile birth registration units as well (Manly and Persaud 2009).

UNHCR's most ambitious campaign to date, however, is the aforementioned #IBelong Campaign to End Statelessness by 2024. Launched in 2014 in partnership with United Colours of Benetton (UCB),[59] the Campaign's central message is that every person on the planet has the right to belong through citizenship. In order to achieve its articulated goal of ending statelessness by 2024, UNHCR published the Global Action Plan to End Statelessness: 2014–2024 (GAP) (UNHCR 2014e).

The GAP contains ten Actions—and fifteen associated goals—that fall within UNHCR's mandate to resolve and prevent statelessness (Actions 1–5, 7, 9) and to identify and protect stateless persons (Actions 6, 8, 9, 10). These include activities that require political will—such as state ratification of the two statelessness conventions and their grant of protection status to stateless migrants. Other actions demand economic and personnel resources—such as better data collection of stateless populations and the ability of governments to issue ID documents to all those who should hold them. Still other actions demand that governments operate in a transparent and nondiscriminatory manner, especially in the grant, denial, or deprivation of citizenship.[60] Although I elsewhere critically evaluate the transformative potential of the #IBelong Campaign, and its ability to end statelessness via the GAP by 2024 (Belton 2016), it is important to note here that the Campaign is an ambitious project the likes of which has not been seen since the international community first came together to create the statelessness conventions in the aftermath of World War II.

Beside UNHCR's latest activities, the Human Rights Council, which has long been silent on the issue of statelessness, has passed multiple resolutions on the right to a nationality in recent years (UN HRC 2008a, 2009c, 2010, 2012b, 2014). These resolutions encourage states to become parties to the statelessness conventions and to amend their national legislation with an eye to addressing statelessness. They also ask for cooperation among UN bodies on statelessness data collection, among other activities. The HRC also passed another resolution on birth registration (UN HRC 2015) and issued the OHCHR-UNSG report on the arbitrary deprivation of nationality via legislative and administrative means, with a special focus on childhood statelessness (UN HRC 2013b) during its 23rd Session.

The UN's recent upsurge of interest in statelessness is also reflected regionally.[61] The OAS, of which both The Bahamas and the Dominican Republic are members, held an International Meeting on Refugee Protection, Statelessness and Mixed Migratory Movements in the Americas in Brazil in 2010[62] and adopted the ensuing Brasilia Declaration on the Protection of

Refugees and Stateless Persons in the Americas (UNHCR 2010a). This declaration, although primarily focused on refugees, resolves:

7. *To urge* countries in the Americas to consider acceding to the international instruments on statelessness, reviewing their national legislation to prevent and reduce situations of statelessness, and strengthening national mechanisms for comprehensive birth registration.

8. *To promote* the values of solidarity, respect, tolerance and multiculturalism, underscoring the non-political and humanitarian nature of the protection of refugees, internally displaced persons and stateless persons, and recognizing their rights and obligations as well as their positive contributions to society. (UNHCR 2010a, 3; italics in original)

The regional intergovernmental organization has passed several resolutions on the "Prevention and Reduction of Statelessness and Protection of Stateless Persons in the Americas" as well (OAS 2010, 2011, 2013b, 2014). In these resolutions, the OAS General Assembly, akin to the UN Human Rights Council, encourages member states to ratify the statelessness conventions and to amend domestic legislation to prevent and reduce statelessness. Highlighting the importance of regional education on statelessness, the OAS issued a more comprehensive resolution on statelessness, AG/RES.2826 (XLIV-O/14), in which it calls for continued training of member states representatives on the issue of statelessness. In addition to reiterating its calls to amend domestic legislation in line with international law relating to statelessness, this 2014 resolution also asks states to strengthen their civil registry systems,[63] amend nationality laws to prevent and eliminate statelessness, and draft regional guidelines on the protection of stateless people. Interestingly, the OAS declares statelessness "a serious global humanitarian problem" in this resolution as well (OAS 2014, 1).

In keeping with its effort to educate governments on the issue of statelessness, the organization has created spaces for government functionaries and interested stakeholders to come together and discuss ways to move forward in addressing regional statelessness. For example, the OAS recently held a workshop on the "Fundamental Elements for Identification and

Protection of Stateless Persons and Prevention and Reduction of Statelessness in the Americas," which served as "an opportunity for participants to
strengthen their awareness on the phenomenon of statelessness, as well as
to [sic] the legal tools available to identify and provide protection for stateless persons, and to prevent and reduce statelessness" (OAS 2012, n. pag.).

Heeding resolution AG/RES.2826 (XLIV-O/14)'s call to draft regional
guidelines on statelessness, member states of the OAS recently came together
in a series of subregional meetings to revisit the Cartagena Declaration on
Refugees (OAS 1984) as part of UNHCR's Cartagena +30 process.[64] From
this series of meetings, the Brazil Declaration and Plan of Action for the
Americas (UNHCR 2014c) was issued. Significantly, the Brazil Declaration
addresses statelessness more expansively than its regional predecessor declarations, with an entire section devoted to solutions for eradicating and preventing statelessness. While it reiterates calls for member states to accede to
the statelessness conventions, it also encourages them to establish SSD procedures, engage in community outreach regarding birth registration, and to
restore nationality in cases where it has been arbitrarily removed, among
other measures. In solidarity with the #IBelong Campaign, participating
states also openly declare that they are committed to eradicating statelessness globally by 2024 (5).

While these are necessary actions to eradicate statelessness in the region
(and elsewhere), there are some aspects of Chapter VI on statelessness within
the Brazil Plan of Action that perhaps too closely associate statelessness
with migratory movement. For example, the introductory paragraph to that
Chapter says, "At the end of the next ten years, we hope to be in the position
to affirm that the countries of Latin America and the Caribbean succeeded
in . . . protect[ing] stateless persons *arriving in* their territories" (UNHCR
2014c, 17; italics added). It then later declares that states should "Adopt legal
protection frameworks that guarantee the rights of stateless persons, in order to regulate issues such as *their migratory status*" (17; italics added). Finally, it calls on states to confirm the nationality of those who need it, noting
that "cases of people who may require having their nationality confirmed
frequently arise in situations of irregular migration or when people live in
border areas" (17).

Although statelessness may arise in the context of migration, as I note
earlier—and as I explain in Chapters 3 and 4—the majority of stateless persons are noncitizen insiders. They have not migrated from elsewhere. They
may be the descendants of migrant parents or grandparents, but they are

born and continue to reside in the countries of their birth, even though formally excluded. Associating a migratory trajectory to their predicament without clearly specifying that most stateless people are not migrants thus obfuscates the peculiar type of forced displacement they face and ignores the fact that for many of these persons, they know no other home.

Despite these promising international and regional activities around statelessness, the fulfillment of a human right to a nationality remains elusive globally. Exclusionary state practices of citizenship denial and deprivation continue to make people's access to rights, freedoms, and protections as precarious as they were during Arendt's time. In distinction to her time, however, the creation of stateless populations is not necessarily linked to crisis, conflict, or persecution. Thus the humanitarian element of their predicament is far from obvious to many. Furthermore, and in contrast to Arendt's time, practices of citizenship deprivation and denial are not limited to authoritarian regimes. As I demonstrate in the next two chapters, even allegedly democratic states can act in arbitrary and discriminatory ways to forcibly displace people in situ.

PART II

Democracies as Engines
of Forced Displacement

CHAPTER 3

The Bahamas: Neither Fish Nor Fowl

> The social reality is that we have a very large number of
> persons in this society of Haitian extraction who have a
> very dubious status in The Bahamas; neither fish nor
> fowl. They don't qualify for Bahamian citizenship
> constitutionally and conversely there are issues as to
> whether they have retained Haitian citizenship.
> —former governmental official; personal interview

When we think about forced displacement, the Caribbean is not necessarily the first place that comes to mind, even though hurricanes and earthquakes do forcibly displace people within their island homes. Instead, we tend to think of the region as a prime tourist destination, a place where we can relax on the beach, play in the casinos, hike through tropical forests, visit wetlands, and an array of other such similar activities. "Paradise." Yet for an untold number of people, this paradise has become an inferno. Far from a world of blurred boundaries, flexible citizenships, and denationalized rights, these stateless—or at risk of statelessness—populations find walls erected against their belonging at nearly every turn. Unable to secure any effective citizenship, their rights are highly precarious and they are displaced in situ.

While states have created an intricate web of domestic laws to distinguish who has membership in the polity, the right to belong formally to a state via citizenship is conditioned by other factors as well. Political practices, bureaucratic procedures, and discrimination also play their part in determining who belongs. The fulfillment of one's human right to a nationality is thus far more complex in practice than simply determining to whom (jus sanguinis citizenship acquisition) and where one was born (jus soli citizenship acquisition).

Through the case study of The Bahamas, this chapter illustrates how exclusionary citizenship laws, electoral politics, bureaucratic inefficiencies, and cronyism work together to displace Bahamian-born persons of Haitian descent
into liminality or into the category of Haitian national without consent.

Situating the Case Study

The Bahamas is a chain of over seven hundred islands and cays off the coast
of Florida. Its northern tip, located in the Abacos, reaches as far north as
West Palm Beach, Florida, while its southern land mass extends as far as
southern Cuba. Great Inagua, the most southerly island in the archipelago,
lies less than eighty-five miles from Port-de-Paix, Haiti. Despite their geographical closeness, The Bahamas and Haiti could not be more distant in
terms of economic, political, and human development. With a Gross National
Income (GNI) of $21,280 per capita, The Bahamas is considered a high-income
developing country (UNCTAD 2012, xii, xvi; World Bank 2013a). Haiti, on
the other hand, is considered a "heavily indebted poor country" (UNCTAD
2012, xv), with a GNI of only $760 and with more than 75 percent of its
population living in poverty (World Bank 2013b). Although The Bahamas'
unemployment rate is high at nearly 13 percent (Government of The Bahamas 2016, 17), it pales in comparison to the estimated 70 percent or higher
unemployment rate in Haiti (Bergdahl 2012 n. pag.).

    In comparison to the peaceful transitions of power in The Bahamas,
Haiti has undergone numerous political challenges since the 1950s.[1] From
political violence and the dictatorships of the Duvaliers to coups d'état and
environmental catastrophes—such as the 2010 earthquake that destabilized
much of the country and left hundreds of thousands internally displaced—
Haiti is far from the "Pearl of the Antilles" that it once was. Due to The Bahamas' proximity both to Haiti and to the United States, its stronger economy,
and the fact that it outranks Haiti in education, healthcare, sanitation, and
other measures of the UN Development Programme's Human Development
Index (UNDP 2013b),[2] it is unsurprising that Haitians migrate to The Bahamas, whether temporarily or permanently, in search of a better life. In fact,
and noted in Chapter 1, The Bahamas is one of the top three destinations for
irregular Haitian migration (IOM 2013, 23).[3]

    Although the precise number of irregular Haitian migrants in The Ba-
hamas is unknown, hundreds, if not thousands of Haitians are speculated

to migrate to the country each year through irregular or unauthorized channels. Many of these migrants remain in The Bahamas. According to the latest census numbers, 11 percent of the Bahamian population[4] is made up of
Haitian nationals[5] (Government of The Bahamas 2012, 89 and 90, Table 9.0),
but this figure does not capture the undocumented population,[6] which is no-
toriously difficult to enumerate. Many of these migrants have children in
The Bahamas, some of whom are at risk of becoming stateless.

The Legal Context

Bahamian nationality law is neutral in theory. Thus, while Dawn Marshall
argued that The Bahamas Independence Order of 1973 "further restricted
the possibilities for children born of Haitian parents in the Bahamas to claim
Bahamian citizenship" (1979, 127), neither the Bahamian Constitution,
nor any of The Bahamas' Acts addressing nationality—such as Chapter 190/
Bahamas Nationality Act and Chapter 191/Immigration Act—specifically
target Haitian migrants or their descendants when it comes to the acquisition of Bahamian citizenship. The qualified nature of the jus sanguinis and
jus soli provisions of the Constitution applies equally to all persons born of
noncitizens on the territory.

Nationality acquisition is qualified in the following ways: a child born
in The Bahamas may only become a Bahamian citizen if one of his or her
parents is a Bahamian citizen (Government of The Bahamas 1973a, Article 6).
This Article is not specific to any particular race or ethnicity. Those individuals born in the country, neither of whose parents is a Bahamian citizen, are permitted to apply for Bahamian citizenship through registration
within twelve months of turning eighteen (Article 7), but there is no
guarantee they will obtain Bahamian citizenship. As a former Free National Movement (FNM) official makes clear, "it's not an automatic entitlement."[7] Statelessness is therefore a possibility if the child does not
possess another nationality. Those who miss the eighteen- to nineteen-
year-old application window must go through the regular naturalization
procedure, a more involved, time-consuming, and costly process than registration. It is of note that being born in The Bahamas does not provide
any benefit in expediting the naturalization process for those who miss
the one-year registration window. As an official from the Ministry of Foreign Affairs (MFA) makes clear, "*The fact that the individual was born in*

The Bahamas has no bearing on the application for naturalization" (italics added).[8]

The Bahamian Constitution states that only the governor-general is able to deprive a Bahamian national of citizenship (Government of The Bahamas 1973a, Article 11), but adds that Parliament has powers to deprive and bestow citizenship on persons by means that are not addressed in the Constitution (Article 13). Chapter 190/Bahamas Nationality Act (1973b) provides more extensive details regarding the acquisition and loss of Bahamian citizenship and also discusses the provision of nationality to non-Bahamian adopted children and minors generally. It details the reasons for loss of Bahamian citizenship, which include acquiring Bahamian citizenship through fraudulent means, committing a crime within five years of obtaining said citizenship, or demonstrating disloyalty to the country, among other criteria, if a naturalized citizen or a citizen via registration (Article 11.2). Again, in none of these cases are individuals of Haitian descent—or of any other particular ethnicity—specifically targeted.

What is of note is that the Nationality Act provides extraordinary leeway and power to the minister in charge of naturalization and immigration, which today falls under the portfolio of the minister of foreign affairs. In a thirteen-page act, not including the final two pages that deal with schedules of different types, the phrase "the Minister may at his discretion" appears ten times. The minister may thus grant and revoke citizenship at his or her discretion, often without having to confer with any other governmental body. Even when the minister is supposed to refer a case of citizenship deprivation to a "committee of inquiry," which then recommends whether or not said deprivation should take place, the minister is under no obligation "to act upon or in accordance with any such recommendation" (Article 11.8). Moreover, any decision of the minister regarding citizenship acquisition or deprivation is not subject to judicial review:

> The Minister shall not be required to assign any reason for the grant or refusal of any application or the making of any order under this Act the decision upon which is at his discretion; and the decision of the Minister on any such application or order shall not be subject to appeal or review in any court. (Article 16)

In practice, however, questions regarding the grant of citizenship are typically performed by cabinet, which consists of the ministers of the executive branch of government, and not by the minister "in charge of naturalization and immigration." As one former minister of the FNM government explains, a citizenship application "goes before Cabinet, and Cabinet considers it" or the citizenship application goes to the minister of foreign affairs who "prepare[s] a Cabinet brief" and then sends that brief to cabinet to consider.[9] The entire cabinet then decides on the basis of consensus whether to grant or deny citizenship to an individual. Alfred Sears, former attorney general of The Bahamas (2002–2006) and former minister of education, science, and technology under the Progressive Liberal Party (PLP) administration admits that such a procedure often "takes up a lot of cabinet time" because each application is dealt with individually, making it a "cumbersome" process.[10] It remains, however, that these cabinet citizenship decisions are not subject to judicial review. As I illustrate, this is highly problematic given that the practice of granting Bahamian citizenship is highly politicized and fraught with bureaucratic inconsistencies.

The Political Context

In "Client-Ship and Citizenship in Latin America," Lucy Taylor explains how clientelistic practices and charismatic leaders have shaped Latin American politics. Clientelism, she explains, "is not about equality but inequality . . . it is not about rights but about favours . . . it is not about democracy but about negotiated authoritarianism . . . [and] Finally, it is not about formal relationships but personal ties" (2004, 214). Her comments are applicable to the broader region, including the Caribbean. While The Bahamas is far from being an authoritarian state—as I explain in Chapter 1, it is considered a democracy—favoritism and the use of personal ties (cronyism) to achieve a particular good or political gain has plagued much of its post-Independence history, infiltrating the realm of citizenship determination.

Sir Lynden O. Pindling, the individual who led the country to Independence and who became the country's first prime minister, is heralded as the "Black Moses" among many Bahamians. "I just remember people worshiping him. . . . He was always this grand myth to me," says Travolta Cooper, the writer and director of the "Black Moses" documentary on Sir Pindling (Nicolls 2013). Sir Pindling's PLP government, which lasted twenty-five years (1967–1992) was accused of corruption and cronyism from many sectors of society, both Bahamian and abroad (Dahlburg 1982; Freedland 1992). As

Frederick Donathan explains, "The government's tentacles spread very far. . . . You got accustomed to thinking, 'I better vote for the old regime, in case they get in again'" (qtd. in Freedland 1992). When Hubert A. Ingraham, the then leader of the opposition FNM became the second prime minister of The Bahamas in 1992 he vowed to create a "government in the sunshine" where transparency and fairness would reign (Freedland 1992; see also I. Smith 2012).

A "government in the sunshine" never transpired, however, and accusations of corruption and cronyism continue to the present day. The PLP is once again in power and former prime minister Ingraham recently lambasted the party for "victimising" civil servants and removing them from their jobs because they are not PLP supporters (Evans 2012). Current FNM leader, Dr. Hubert Minnis recently published a statement on the PLP government's "Unadulterated tribalism, cronyism and out-and-out nepotism!" (*Bahamas Weekly* 2012 n. pag.). The PLP has also issued its fair share of corruption and cronyism accusations against FNM administrations as well (S. Brown 2013).

Just as Taylor finds that a "goods-for-power" deal operates in many Latin American countries, wherein "People support a certain patron because they gamble that to do so will improve their own or their family's prospects" (2004, 215), Bahamian politics seems to be infused with such a mentality. When it comes to Haitian migrants and their descendants, the "good" is citizenship and no matter the party in power (PLP or FNM) this good suddenly becomes more readily available prior to a general election.

Study participants, Haitian and non-Haitian alike, remark that the number of citizenships awarded to foreigners escalates around election time. As one anonymous interviewee laments, "There's the issue of the politics of citizenship in terms of who gets it. How is it awarded? It's a cabinet decision—there is just so much room for abuse, with so much room for timing it to coincide with elections. It's a seriously flawed approach."[11] Gwendolyn Brice-Adderley, a lawyer for the Nationality Support Unit[12] in Nassau, adds that "I know around election time some of those applications are fast forward."[13] While Harry Dolce, a Bahamian-born police officer of Haitian descent who went through the citizenship registration process, explains how "you'll have certain times during the election period" where "they'll hold your citizenship—no matter if you've applied three years ago, two years ago. But when it comes time to election, [they say], 'Okay, we're gonna give you your citizenship. Okay, you're a Bahamian.'"[14] George Charité, a medical doctor of Haitian descent on the island of Abaco, similarly affirms that "It could take elections" for individuals' citizenship applications to be considered. "They normally get up around election time," he says, "they make them citizens. So pray to God and thank God for elections. Election coming up. . . . Most likely you'll get [citizenship]."[15] Such allegations are not limited to study participants either. The *Bahama Journal* (2013) cites Lovy Jean, a Bahamian-born student of Haitian descent who spoke before the Bahamas Constitutional Commission,[16] stating that difficulties exist in getting Bahamian citizenship unless "you're lucky during a general election [and] you'd get it right away."

Newspaper articles and letters to the editor also report on the regularization of "hundreds" of Haitian nationals as Bahamian citizens prior to elections as a means for the ruling party to increase its vote share.[17] The *Nassau Guardian*, for example, states that "a monthly average of 31" citizenship applications were approved "between May 2, 2007 and June 30, 2010" for a total of "1,144 citizenship applications" (McCartney 2011). This number more than doubled to "a monthly average of about 75" applications "between November 18, 2011 and January 13, 2012"—less than four months prior to the 2012 general election (2011). According to then deputy prime minister Brent Symonette of the FNM party, the increased number of citizenship approvals was due to "improved efficiencies" regarding "applications that had been languishing for many years" within the Department of Immigration (DoI) (2011)[18] and not because of politically motivated reasons.

Archival data I obtained from the Haitian Embassy in Nassau point to an increased number of Haitian nationality renunciations in the years prior to the 2007 and 2012 general elections (see Table 1). This is of note because, as part of the Bahamian citizenship application process, a person must renounce his or her current nationality in order to be eligible to be sworn in as a Bahamian citizen. Table 1 demonstrates that 359 Haitian nationals renounced their nationality in 2006, or an average of 29 individuals per month. This number increases to an average of 41 renunciations per month in the period of January through April, 2007, just prior to the May 2 general election. In relation to the aforementioned statistic provided in the *Nassau Guardian* article—1,144 Bahamian citizenship conferrals in the period May 2007 through June 2010—the data in Table 1 illustrates that 543 persons renounced their Haitian nationality during this period.

Without data from the Department of Immigration listing the number of former Haitian nationals who obtained Bahamian citizenship during this time, there is no way to know whether these 543 individuals (47 percent of

Table 1: Haitian Nationality Renunciations by Year, 2003–2011

	2003	2004	2005	2006	2007	2008	2009	2010	2011
Janvier	2	21	1	20	39	13	30	20	38
Février	10	11	2	3	26	16	22	17	25
Mars	4	5	2	16	66	20	18	15	60
Avril	5	4	39	15	33	38	12	7	24
Mai	3	12	74	29	21	9	9	7	26
Juin	1	4	32	33	13	10	7	24	14
Juillet	1	7	14	66	10	9	12	27	13
Août	2	2	10	40	16	14	9	21	28
Septembre	5	1	17	51	17	12	3	34	60
Octobre	41	4	15	28	24	10	6	32	74
Novembre	16	4	16	35	9	19	3	38	119
Décembre	16	2	7	23	3	27	12	25	73
Total	**106**	**77**	**229**	**359**	**277**	**197**	**143**	**287**	**554**

Source: Original printout provided to the author by Ambassador Rodrigue, Haitian Embassy, Nassau, Bahamas, October 31, 2012. Total of 2,229 renunciations.

the 1,144 persons) obtained Bahamian citizenship or what the nationality was of the other 53 percent of Bahamian citizenship recipients.[19] In email correspondence from the Ministry of Foreign Affairs, the MFA notes that the Department of Immigration "does not have statistics on the number of applications for citizenship each year. However we do have statistics on those persons who are sworn in as citizens. On average, between 265 and 400 such persons are sworn in each year since 2007." If we assume that these 543 persons in Table 1 obtained Bahamian citizenship, it appears that Haitian nationals make up a large proportion of naturalized Bahamians during this three-year period. This is not surprising, however, given the aforementioned statistic that Haitians make up 11 percent of the Bahamian population, which is the largest foreign presence in the country.

Whether former Haitian nationals are the recipients of the majority of these grants of Bahamian citizenship, it appears—in the words of Haitian ambassador Antonio Rodrigue—that "The question of citizenship is very political here [in The Bahamas]."[20] As Ambassador Rodrigue observes, pointing to the data in Table 1, the trend of Haitian nationality renunciations prior to general elections holds regardless of which political party is in power (see Figure 4 for a graphic depiction of the preelection peaks):

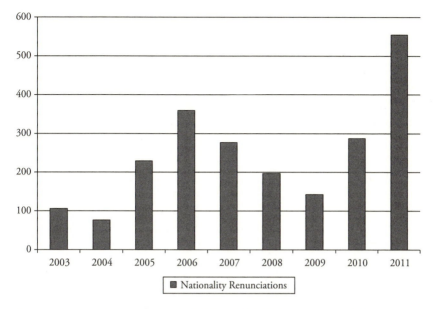

Figure 4. Renunciation peaks before 2007 and 2012 Bahamian general elections.

When you are close to the election, it [the number of renunciations] rose. After the election, here, the number is almost close to zero a month. And when you go getting close to the election, there's a peak. There's a peak. In this formulation of 2002, 2007, and 2012 you can see that. So each government . . . before the election, they issue a lot of citizenships.

The politicized nature of Bahamian citizenship bestowal is not merely reflected in data held at the Haitian Embassy or in Bahamian newspaper articles, however. As the study participants make clear, obtaining Bahamian citizenship is often predicated on knowing someone in the Department of Immigration or elsewhere in government who can do you the "favor" of granting you citizenship. Formal politics and informal personal connections thus have an equally significant influence on citizenship decisions in The Bahamas.

Bureaucratic Failures

Describing the reality of Latin American politics, Taylor states that "the only way to get anything done is to 'pay an extra fee' or ask a 'friend' to cut through the red tape on your behalf" (Taylor 2004, 213). Taylor may as well have been writing about the Bahamian case as her quote aptly captures one of the problems associated with bureaucratic failure in The Bahamas: going through official channels, and following the rules to acquire the "good" of citizenship does not necessarily translate into the most efficient way to obtain Bahamian citizenship. As artist Bernard Petit-Homme explains, he applied for Bahamian citizenship when he turned eighteen, but it took him three years to acquire citizenship, despite being born in the country and meeting all the requirements. He thinks it probably would have taken longer to acquire Bahamian citizenship if he had not run into a former high-ranking government official who had a friend in the Department of Immigration who was able to act on Petit-Homme's application. "They called me the following week to say it is ready. So that's how I got it," he says.[21]

Desmangles similarly observes that "It's all about networking and who knows who in some instances." He adds that in his case, "it came to a point where I had to think for myself, 'Who do I know out there? Who can assist me? Who can make this possible?'"[22] Bianca Zaiem, born of noncitizen parents in The Bahamas, also remarks that "a lot of people get citizenship by doing favors for other people. And I feel like that's hurt us over the years. So normal people like me who want to do it the right way are pushed aside for somebody who's getting a favor done by somebody else."[23] Natacha Jn-Simon, a College of The Bahamas student, adds that sometimes these "favors" take on a more sinister tone:

You know what they have the Haitian kids subduing to? It's like okay, I'm a female, right, and you're in Parliament or [you're] someone who is connected with government. And let's say you see me on the road or something, and you see that I look nice. And people have to realize that just as they say poverty is like a state of mind, you feel encapsulated, wherever you see a way out, it's what you're gonna do. So when these young ladies see these men [who say], "Oh, I'm gonna help you. I'm gonna do this for you. I'm gonna help you do this." That's how a lot of them get their citizenship you know. This guy said, "Okay, well, just be my friend." You understand? "I have

Table 2: Participants Born to Noncitizens in The Bahamas

Participant	Born in The Bahamas?	Applied at age 18?	Length of time to acquire Bahamian citizenship
Mark Desmangles	Y	Y	1 year
Harry Dolce	Y	Unsure[a]	3 or 4 years
Luzena Dumercy	Y	N[b]	2 years
Gillard Louis	Y	Y	3 years
Bernard Petit-Homme	Y	Y	3 years
Natacha Jn-Simon	Y	Y	Currently under consideration
Marie St. Cecile*	Y	N	8 years
Bianca Zaiem	Y	Y	14 years

*Name changed to protect anonymity, as per interviewee's request.
[a]Dolce says, "I think I applied at 18," but is unsure as he "wasn't kind of interested anymore" because of the way the Department of Immigration was treating him at the time. He admits, however, that "at a certain point you say, 'Listen here, okay, I am going to do it.' You have to comply and complain afterwards."
[b]Dumercy began the process at eighteen but due to a number of complications submitted her application three days after she turned nineteen. As a result, she had to begin the process again, but under a new procedure—naturalization—with additional requirements and costs since she had missed the one year window in which to apply via registration.

friends, I know people in immigration. I could get your stuff out." It's sad.[24]

As illustrated in Table 2, most Bahamian-born participants of noncitizen parents waited several years to hear back from the Department of Immigration on their citizenship application. Desmangles believes this is not uncommon. He thinks maybe one out of a hundred applicants will acquire their citizenship three to six months after they apply for it, but the other "99 of them, they're gonna have to wait until five years to get it." Ambassador Rodrigue notes that if a person applies for citizenship after the one-year mark beginning at age eighteen then "It can take up to 12 years. I've had people say they were waiting for 12 years. It can take 5 years, 8 years, 10 years. Because now you are going through another type of process. Between 18 and 19, it's like almost a natural or normal process to get it. But after 18, after 19, I don't know."[25]

While in Nassau, I was able to read an award of citizenship letter from the Bahamian government that was dated May 21, 2012. The person to whom the letter was addressed had applied for Bahamian citizenship on May 2, 1997. It took a decade and a half for the Department of Immigration to make a decision on that individual's application.[26] Whether or not this is an example of an extreme situation, Marie St. Cecile, born in The Bahamas to Haitian parents, remarks that her parents were able to acquire Bahamian citizenship before she did. St. Cecile did not apply for Bahamian citizenship at eighteen because "I basically didn't know that I should, that you should apply at 18 at that time. So I applied late."[27] She adds that she thought that "once I applied, I would automatically get it because of my age and all that stuff," but that this was not the case. She had to wait eight years for the Bahamian government to give her citizenship and, in that time, her Haitian-born parents obtained Bahamian citizenship:

> my dad got it a year before me and my mom afterwards because my dad gave my mom residency because they were married and he got his own before me. . . . And you know, even though that's my dad, I was saying, you know, I don't understand the system. How come he could get his own [Bahamian citizenship] first and I could get mines afterwards? So that really made matters worse.

St. Cecile adds that she even approached a person whom she knew at the Department of Immigration to explain to her why her Haitian-born parents obtained Bahamian citizenship before she did: "they could not explain that. 'I don't know. I really can't tell you.' He [my dad] knew someone there and he got his own before me."

In addition to the clientelism displayed by some public officials and civil servants in the citizenship application process, a second bureaucratic failure is the inefficiency with which citizenship applications are processed. Beside Marie St. Cecile, who did not apply for citizenship within the one-year time frame, the duration of Zaiem's case for Bahamian citizenship stands out because she did apply during the requisite period. As Zaiem, who applied for Bahamian citizenship in 1999, explains, she received a phone call from the Department of Immigration the day after the PLP obtained power in 2002, "saying that they don't have my paperwork. It's lost. So, every time I called before that, they were 'dealing with it,' they were 'dealing with it.' 'These things take time.' 'There's a huge list of people'" and then, all of a sudden, her file went missing.

Once she received the call that her application was lost, Zaiem began the application process again. In fact, she states that she "ended up having to do the whole process. . . . Three times" because the paperwork for her application was again lost by the Department of Immigration. Jn-Simon, currently in the process of applying for citizenship, explains how her brother faced a similar situation when the Department lost his application documents. "They always lost a birth certificate. 'Bring it again.' They always lost something. 'Bring it again.'" Two years into the application process, the Department of Immigration is still requesting additional documents from her brother.

Dolce was constantly told to come back with other documents when he tried to apply for citizenship at eighteen. "They tell you, 'Listen here, we need this document.' They keep turning you around and sometimes you get discouraged." Dumercy agrees, stating that even when you provide them with all the documentation required on the citizenship application form, "every time you come, they ask you for these other documents. . . . They say, 'Oh, you need this and that.'" She says that the additional documents are not always "easily, readily available" or are "not on the [application] form. So why didn't you tell me that [I needed these documents] the first time? [And] why are they asking for that?" She reveals that this kind of bureaucratic inefficiency causes many potential applicants to "just give up" and she almost did, too. Whether or not it is the intention of some persons within the Department of Immigration to discourage persons from completing the citizenship application process—hence the "lost" documents and requests for additional documents—the process does appear arbitrary in nature and provides ample leeway for some persons to engage in discriminatory acts under the guise of bureaucratic inefficiencies.

Even when documents are not lost or "extra" documents are not requested, a few interviewees lament the lack of communication they received from the Department of Immigration regarding their application status. Petit-Homme relates,

There is no communication between you and the Department of Immigration. You know, no one updating you to say what you might be missing or what other things are necessary. It's just that you go up there, or you follow them and they say, "Well, it's not been approved as of yet." They're "still looking at it," which never makes sense to me, you know. There's not a definite time to respond [to applicants].

Gillard Louis, a College of The Bahamas student, states that "there was no run-around in terms of missing documents. However, there was a back-and-forth for me in terms of checking. I had to keep a constant check. It got a bit frustrating at a point. It was a bit frustrating because my thing is, don't give me a date to come back and then tell me when I reach that, you know, it's not ready or come again."[28]

In some cases the problem was not only that documents were lost or that individuals were told to come back at another time with additional documents that were not part of the original application, but that once approved for Bahamian citizenship, it took them an inordinate amount of time to actually be sworn in as a Bahamian citizen. Dumercy explains that her Bahamian-born sister's application for Bahamian citizenship was approved in less than a year—"one of the quickest [turnarounds] I've known thus far"—but it took more than a year for her sister to be sworn in. When asked why it took so long, Dumercy says, "They didn't have any swearing in going on" or, if they did, "they just didn't let her know."

Zaiem's story is once again extraordinary in this regard. After finally receiving her letter of citizenship approval from the Department of Immigration, she "was told that within three weeks[29] I'd get a phone call stating when to come in to get sworn in. That didn't happen for about a month and a half, and me still calling every week. You know, they're 'checking on it.' 'They're checking on it.' I'm straight. It's just the next one [swearing-in ceremony] I'm gonna be in." Finally Zaiem "got a phone call saying, 'Be here' . . . [The DoI employee] said, 'Two o'clock on Thursday.' She told me what to wear. She told me to be there 45 minutes early. I show up, this was in July. Yeah, I show up, and they have a note on my file saying, 'Could not be contacted.' And they said, 'Well, we tried these numbers'" and the numbers they had called were from her second application, "the one that they had lost. So, it was from my job that I worked at like ten years ago. So I told them somebody did contact me. 'It's too late. You're not on the list' [they said]."

Zaiem had reached her breaking point. She had now been without any citizenship for six months, having already renounced her former nationality as part of the application process, and she had shown up at what was supposed to be her swearing-in ceremony, only to be denied entry because of bureaucratic errors within the Department of Immigration. A month later she was finally sworn in as a Bahamian citizen in the country of her birth. "The only reason" she believes that she made it onto "that list was because at this point, which is really stupid of me, I should have done this ten years ago,

I involved somebody." She called a family friend who knew the then director of immigration who ensured that she was included in the next ceremony and was sworn in as a Bahamian citizen.

In addition to the clientelism and bureaucratic inefficiencies, a third reason that allows for the politicization of the citizenship application and bestowal process in The Bahamas is the lack of transparent or clear guidelines regarding the process. I interviewed several people who were involved in the citizenship application process within the highest echelons of the Ministry of Foreign Affairs and the Department of Immigration. None of these persons was able to provide me with a definitive answer on how long it takes for a person to be sworn in as a Bahamian citizen after receiving his or her approval.

One participant from the Department of Immigration stated that individuals are sworn in "right away. Right away. We don't hold up with that. If you renounce [your original citizenship] today—it's been approved by cabinet last week—you renounce today, in the next swearing in exercise, we ensure that you are on the list."[30] This individual was unsure, however, as to how many swearing-in exercises had occurred for the year or how long the average wait time was to be sworn in. Another participant, who worked in the MFA, declared that it was "a matter of days" for a person to get sworn in,[31] while a third admitted that "we try to do it quickly"—and when asked what the average of "quickly" was, stated, "I'd say a few weeks."[32] Comments such as these, along with the absence of official, publicly available data on citizenship processing, belie a lack of standardized procedures that results in inefficiency and undue personalization of the citizenship application process.

These comments from government officials stand in stark contrast to the aforementioned stories given by the Bahamian-born interviewees of noncitizen parents. Beside Dumercy's sister and Zaiem, Dumercy had to wait four months between renunciation and Bahamian citizenship acquisition. Louis thinks it was closer to "two months" in his case and Petit-Homme recalls it "happening in a matter of months." Dolce, while unable to remember how long it took for him to be sworn in as a Bahamian citizen, tells the story of his friend "who recently gave up her Haitian citizenship and it took her like up to, I would say, two or three months." He says that others also "wait for two months, three months. I know it doesn't take days. I know [that] for sure."

Email correspondence from an administrator at the MFA—as opposed to the aforementioned quotes from elected officials—is more in line with the interviewees' experiences. This official notes that "The time between the submission of the [renunciation] documents and the swearing-in ceremony can range on average between three (3) and six (6) months."[33] Thus despite the fact that government officials contend that individuals are quickly sworn in as Bahamian citizens once approved by cabinet, the experiences of the interviewees born to noncitizen parents in The Bahamas contradicts this assertion.

Beside the arbitrariness in the waiting period to be sworn in as a Bahamian citizen and the inefficiencies in communicating when a person is to come in for a swearing-in ceremony, ceremonies are sometimes cancelled as well. This is particularly problematic for individuals who live in the Family Islands and who have to make a special trip—and all the costs associated with that trip—to Nassau for the ceremony. Dumercy, for example, traveled from Abaco to Nassau for her swearing-in ceremony only to receive a call from the Department of Immigration that it had been cancelled once she "was already in Nassau." If an individual does not have family or friends with whom to stay, or if the next swearing-in ceremony is a week or longer away, the cost of waiting in Nassau can be prohibitive in terms of employment, living expenses, and personal time commitments.

It is important to emphasize that in all these cases, during the interim between renunciation of one's former nationality and the acquisition of Bahamian citizenship, the individual is de jure stateless. He or she is *not* formally covered under the operation of any state's law, whether in theory or in practice. For as the approval letter from the MFA states, "At the time of registration, you will be required to take an oath as prescribed by Regulation 7 of The Bahamas Nationality Act, 1973 and thereupon *from the date of registration you will be a citizen of The Bahamas*" (italics added). Statelessness is thus a very real possibility in The Bahamas.

Statelessness

As noted in the previous section, as part of the process of acquiring Bahamian citizenship, an individual must renounce any citizenship that he or she holds and provide proof of this renunciation to the Department of Immigration. Although this is the last part of the process—an individual is not required to give up his or her citizenship until said person receives the approval letter to become a Bahamian citizen from cabinet via the Department of

Immigration—the participants' aforementioned experiences demonstrate that a person can be without the citizenship of any state for several months, and in some cases up to a year. This is a highly problematic position for someone to be in, as I demonstrate in Chapters 2 and 5.

Although a DoI official admits that persons could fall into the category of de jure stateless during this time, he contends that it is "a priority of ours" to ensure that such instances rarely occur:

> Let me say this—if there is a need for a person to be sworn in, if there's an emergency or there's an urgency, we swear them in separately outside of an established or arranged swearing-in. So it's [the formal acquisition of citizenship] not limited to a swearing-in. Let's just say a person has to go off to college or they say, "This being *de jure* stateless is a problem" for any reason, for any number of reasons . . . we would move to have a single swearing-in when necessary. We don't have anything cast in stone or in law what says you have to wait for a grouping.[34]

While further investigation is needed to corroborate this statement, one of the primary problems appears to be precisely that the Department of Immigration lacks "anything cast in stone" when it comes to establishing transparent deadlines, rules, and procedures regarding the citizenship application process. This adds to the politicization of applying for and receiving Bahamian citizenship because an applicant cannot easily point to a rule or a procedure and ask to be treated in a fair manner based upon said rule or procedure. Additionally, it is revelatory that the three officials, all of whom should be on the "same page," or at least have a more defined idea of the timing between renunciation and Bahamian citizenship acquisition, offer inconsistent explanations on the nature and duration of the citizenship acquisition process.

One of these individuals, who was in the best position to answer questions dealing with the citizenship application and approval process given the nature of his professional duties, readily admits that he does not know what happens when there is "a pregnant woman" who has renounced her original citizenship as part of the citizenship application process. "She's about to give birth and the child's nationality is dependent upon the mother. And the woman gives birth. What happens to the child? That's a good question that you may want to follow-up [on]."[35] If people at the highest levels of the Department of

Immigration and the Ministry of Foreign Affairs are unsure of procedures and timelines in the citizenship application and approval process, it is unsurprising that the Bahamian-born interviewees faced the types of obstacles that they did on their path to becoming Bahamian citizens for "the functionaries of the state themselves find the practices of the state to be illegible" (Das 2004, 234). The system for awarding citizenship in The Bahamas is dysfunctional and statelessness consequently arises.

Beside the cases of de jure statelessness that exist during the interim between the renunciation of one's original citizenship and being sworn in as a Bahamian citizen, the risk of statelessness is heightened in The Bahamas for other reasons as well. The Bahamian Constitution does not accord its female citizens the same rights as their male counterparts when it comes to passing on their Bahamian citizenship.[36] A child born outside the country to a Bahamian father becomes a Bahamian citizen at birth (Article 8), but a child born outside the country to a Bahamian mother does not have this same right if the mother is married to a foreigner.[37] Her child is entitled to apply for Bahamian citizenship at eighteen, alongside those who are born in The Bahamas to noncitizen parents. The only difference is that the child born overseas to a Bahamian mother has until age twenty-one to register as a Bahamian citizen (Article 9).[38] In this case, the child born overseas to a Bahamian mother is susceptible to statelessness if the child is born in a state that does not automatically grant citizenship via jus soli and there are restrictions on the ability of the child's father to pass on his citizenship via jus sanguinis.

In a much-anticipated referendum, Bahamian voters were asked in 2016 to: 1. allow Bahamian women married to foreigners to pass on their citizenship to their children when the latter are born outside the country; 2. permit the foreign spouses of Bahamian women to apply for Bahamian citizenship; 3. allow Bahamian men to pass on citizenship to their children born outside of marriage; and 4. to amend the Constitution so that "sex" becomes a prohibited ground of discrimination.[39] Each proposed bill stood or fell on its own, yet all four proposals were resoundingly rejected by the Bahamian electorate.[40] This was the second time in less than twenty years that such an initiative failed, the first referendum on gender equality being held in 2002. Thus formal belonging, or the fulfillment of a human right to a nationality, also has a gendered component in the Bahamian case.

Lack of parental documentation is one of the primary problems among irregular migrants and another reason for potential statelessness in the country. Individuals who are unable to prove who they are and where they are from via documentation—such as birth certificates, passports, driver's licenses and so forth—often pass on this insecure status to their children. The Haitian Embassy in The Bahamas cannot provide Haitian citizenship to those who are unable to provide proof of their parent's Haitian nationality or who cannot produce two witnesses to attest to the citizenship of the child's parents.

Lack of parental documentation is often particularly pressing for children born to parents from rural parts of Haiti, such as the Northwest, where most Haitian migrants to The Bahamas come from. As one Haitian official states, "Don't forget you're dealing with a poor country where governance is a big problem, particularly at the level of the Registrar['s] office. [Because] the main archive is in Port-au-Prince [and] because of poverty, many people give birth to their children and they do not go to the Registrar['s] office to register their children. That's a big problem."[41] Ambassador Rodrigue supports this assertion, describing how many parents "cannot get a birth certificate [from Haiti]. That's the big thing. The big, big, big problem" when it comes to obtaining Haitian citizenship for their Bahamian-born children.

This issue is not unique to children born of irregular Haitian migrants in The Bahamas. As I note in the previous chapter, lack of birth registration is one of the reasons that individuals are placed at risk of statelessness globally. While a high-ranking official at the Office of the Registrar in The Bahamas asserts that it is "very rare" for a child born in The Bahamas not to be registered and receive a Bahamian birth certificate, a former Haitian official discusses how many children born in The Bahamas end up being repatriated with their parents:

And now suddenly, when they are 16, 18, and they want to come here to get their citizenship that's a big problem because there's no way to prove that [they were born in The Bahamas]! The reason there is no way to prove that [is] you [were] born, [but] before leaving they don't even think about having an official document here. They cannot have a passport, but at least they could have a travel document. They did not. Then no vaccination, nothing; how you going to prove [birth in The Bahamas]?

The number of undocumented Bahamian-born children of Haitian parentage in this situation is unknown but as the official at the Office of the Registrar made clear, a parent must have a "valid government issued picture identification" in order to register the Bahamian-born child.[42] Brice-Adderley provides an account that supports the official's assertion:

> We have a case where that was brought to my attention. The father was born in The Bahamas. He's from Haitian parentage. He is 32-years-old. I think he may have submitted his documents for citizenship, but they haven't come through as yet, for whatever reason. The mother was an illegal immigrant, but she came here somehow and stayed for two years, met him, had a child. But two months ago she was detained and repatriated. But before, in between being detained and being repatriated, they called me in to see if I could assist her because she had a young baby. The young baby was not documented. . . . So the mother was the one who would have taken the child to be registered, but because she was illegal for whatever reason, she did not have any ID. So she couldn't do anything for the child. . . . She couldn't get the notice of birth from the hospital because she didn't have an ID.

Without such a valid ID, the ability of the child to acquire a Bahamian birth certificate and then apply for Bahamian citizenship at eighteen is placed in jeopardy. Such children are exposed to an obvious risk of statelessness, having no proof of where they "officially" belong.

A former employee at the Ministry of Foreign Affairs under the FNM administration also notes that children who are born in The Bahamas but who "go back to Haiti" with their mothers at "the age of two or three, or whatever" face difficulties in securing Bahamian citizenship for a different reason: "There's no connection with The Bahamas until one day before their 18th birthday, which they just happen to come back to Nassau just to file this piece of paper and then leave again. That puts a different spin on it [the citizenship acquisition process] in that they haven't been here for that length of time, etc., etc."[43] What exactly the "spin" is, given that no transparent rules and procedures exist for acquiring Bahamian citizenship, is unclear. However, the MFA's previous response that birth in The Bahamas does not facilitate an individual's ability to acquire Bahamian citizenship leads one to surmise that residency may play a large role in whether a person born of noncitizens in The Bahamas is able to acquire citizenship in these circumstances.

It is also unclear how many individuals fall into the situation of being repatriated with their mother to Haiti and then returning to The Bahamas at eighteen to apply for Bahamian citizenship. Dr. Charité, who offers his medical services in various Haitian communities in Abaco, believes that "We have quite a bit [who] are put in that situation. A lot of them go and come back when they're 18, 19" and those who come back are "a large enough number to affect a community."

According to Ambassador Rodrigue, however, even undocumented persons of alleged Haitian nationality are able to obtain a letter from the Haitian Embassy that "serves as an ID because we put a picture on it and that person, we request he or she bring two witnesses who can identify her and say, 'Yes, this is so and so.'" This letter is then accepted at the hospital as "valid government issued picture identification," allowing that individual's child to obtain his or her Bahamian birth registration. But if the undocumented parent does not come to the embassy for such a letter, and does not possess his or her own Haitian birth certificate, then that becomes, in the words of Ambassador Rodrigue, a "big, big, big problem," especially if "The parent dies. The parent dies and that kid doesn't know anything. . . . We have cases like that."

However, this ID letter, which serves as a form of identification for a pregnant woman who lacks a Bahamian government issued ID cannot, according to the ambassador, be used to acquire Haitian nationality: "But that document or that letter we give is used only for that [as ID at the hospital]. They cannot use it [to] afterwards come and say, 'I have that from you. I need to have a passport.' Because no matter what, for the passport we need a birth certificate."

As part of the Bahamian or Haitian citizenship application process for their Bahamian-born children, Haitian nationals must obtain a certified copy of their birth certificate ("extrait"). The Haitian Embassy in The Bahamas is unable to provide this service to Haitians despite having tried to convince the Haitian government to allow them to do so.[44] Haitians must therefore either return to Haiti—a voyage that few undertake—or solicit the services of a person or agency to acquire the certified copy of their birth certificate for them. Says Ambassador Rodrigue,

Some service they call it, where people can go and that person . . . tr[ies] to get those document[s] for them. At that point you give your information: born here, born this day, in what city, etc. And that person tr[ies] to get that information [the birth certificate] for them. But sometimes the person just hires someone to give them [a] false document. And when that person bring[s] that document here at the Embassy, we verify it's not authentic. We have to tell them, "I'm sorry. We cannot legalize the document."

The ambassador adds that sometimes a person goes through the process multiple times, paying individuals to obtain a certified copy of their Haitian birth certificate only to find out that the document is not genuine and cannot be accepted by the embassy in Nassau. "When they come the third time and you say, 'No, it's not good,' the problem is you. The problem is the embassy because 'I paid all that money' and we refuse to take it. 'You are blocking me from doing this or doing that.'" This is why, in the words of another former Haitian official, "if you go outside of the embassy, talking to the people in the yard, the embassy is not popular."[45] This same individual notes that fraudulent documents are not the only problem the Haitian Embassy in Nassau faces when trying to authenticate the Haitian nationality of an individual; a black market for Bahamian birth certificates also exists.

That is, the birth certificate of a deceased child born in The Bahamas is sold to another person who attempts to use the deceased's birth certificate for his or her purposes. The former Haitian official states that "I think the Bahamian government has a big problem to solve" in this area and that "You have a lot of cases like this. . . . Sometimes they even steal document[s]." The Haitian Embassy cannot provide a Haitian birth certificate or passport to individuals under such circumstances. "If you come to the consular section and ask me for a passport, if you cannot prove [to] me beyond any doubt that you [are] Haitian, I'm not going to give you the passport. I'm not going to issue the passport. You have to prove me that. Okay? That's why you may find many Haitian[s] who left Haiti to come here . . . they're coming to the embassy for 2 or 3 years [and] they [still] cannot get a [Haitian] passport."[46]

The problem of false documents also affects these persons' ability to obtain Bahamian citizenship. Without the extrait, as Ambassador Rodrigue points out, "they cannot bring all what they need to bring to the immigration service. . . . So it's a challenge, it's a real challenge for the people." The former Haitian official also points out how "very often people try to blame the Bahamian government" for the inability of Bahamian-born children of Haitian descent to obtain Bahamian citizenship, "but the people also complicate the situation with fraudulent document[s], and we have to pay attention to that." Statelessness is thus a real risk to those children born to Haitian parents who are unable to secure Haitian citizenship from the embassy due to their lack of documentation or their use of fraudulent documents.

Another issue is that some Bahamian-born individuals are ignorant of their ability to go to the Haitian Embassy and obtain a Haitian passport. A few interviewees, for example, note that their parents did not know they could have taken them to the embassy to secure Haitian nationality documents. Whether this is due to ignorance or a deliberate act on the part of the parent(s), the children are at risk of statelessness because they lack Haitian nationality documents and are not yet able to apply for Bahamian citizenship. Ambassador Rodrigue explains how even though the Haitian Embassy provides Haitian birth certificates to children born in The Bahamas,

> when they get the birth certificate from the Bahamian authority, they are satisfied with that. And, as a matter of fact, they keep it preciously because that is the only thing that can prove they were born here [in The Bahamas] and that is going to give them the possibility, at 18 years old, to apply for [Bahamian] citizenship.

Although possessing Haitian identity documents does not affect a child's ability to apply for Bahamian citizenship at eighteen, many parents believe it does. Ambassador Rodrigue states, "They think if they come here at the embassy and get a Haitian birth certificate," it is "never going to happen that they get the Bahamian citizenship." They believe that "having a Haitian birth certificate . . . compromise[s] their chance or the possibility of becoming Bahamian." So, says the ambassador, "no one" comes to the embassy to obtain Haitian identity documents for their children. This again poses a real risk of statelessness for Bahamian-born children.

A former Haitian official concurs, adding that embassy personnel go to churches to explain to the Haitian congregations that having a Haitian passport or birth certificate does not hinder an applicant's ability to acquire Bahamian citizenship later on. "I invite them to come to the embassy to get [a Haitian] passport for their children. But they're still waiting for [the] Bahamian passport." An MFA official agrees, stating that

> Many persons born in The Bahamas to non-Bahamian parents, especially persons of Haitian descent *do not see themselves as Haitian nationals*[47] and therefore do not wish to claim Haitian citizenship and would rather have a Bahamian certificate of identity instead of a

Haitian passport. The Haitian Embassy willingly issues Haitian passports to persons born in The Bahamas to Haitian parents.[48]

These individuals—who have the ability to obtain Haitian nationality documents and choose not to—are not stateless according to Ambassador Rodrigue: "if you don't want to take it [a Haitian passport], I can say that's your problem. That's you. But you have the potential nationality . . . if for any reason you say, 'No, this [passport] I don't want it.' No one put you in the position to have no nationality. You are the one." The MFA official adds that "It can be contended that there are cases of *de facto* statelessness" in The Bahamas, but that such "cases are due to choice of the individual and not by any discriminatory practice of the Bahamas government."[49]

It is important to emphasize, however, that the responses of the ambassador and the MFA official do not hold for Bahamian-born children because they are unable to undertake citizenship and passport application procedures themselves and cannot, therefore, make active choices one way or the other. Moreover, and in the words of Open Society Foundation program officer Sebastian Kohn, "Having a right to a nationality is not the same as actually having a nationality."[50] They are thus once again vulnerable to statelessness, even if it is because of the inaction or choice of their parents.

Despite the predicaments generated by Bahamian nationality law—both for children born of noncitizens in the country and for children born abroad to Bahamian mothers married to foreign men—the government of The Bahamas has not ratified either of the two statelessness conventions and denies that statelessness is an issue in the country. If it does exist, in the words of a former high-ranking MFA official, it "is not necessarily stateless here, but it's a statelessness of their country";[51] meaning that if persons are found stateless in The Bahamas, it is a result of problems in the laws and procedures of other countries, not of The Bahamas. An anonymous official from the MFA asserts that "It is believed that there are no cases of de jure statelessness in The Bahamas. . . . Persons born in The Bahamas to non-Bahamian parents are considered under Bahamian law to be the nationals of the country of their parents."[52] In the case of children born of Haitian parents, therefore, the assumption is that the children are covered under Article 11 of the Haitian Constitution,[53] which states that any person born of a Haitian mother or father who has not renounced his or her Haitian citizenship is also a Haitian at birth.

This chapter demonstrates, however, that many such persons are unable to claim and acquire Haitian citizenship in practice. Beside the cases provided above, Marselha Gonçalves Margerin and Melanie Teff (2008) point out that children born to undocumented parents or parents seeking asylum do not acquire Haitian citizenship at birth and Wooding adds that "The reality is that under the Haitian Constitution and Haiti's 1984 law on nationality, there are several groups of people of Haitian origin born outside Haiti who do not have automatic access to Haitian nationality" (2009, 24). UNHCR goes further to observe how

> complying with the documentary requirements to demonstrate descent from a Haitian national is very difficult and costly for those outside of Haiti. An additional problem is the lack (to UNHCR's knowledge) of clear, concise written consular regulations on interpretation of the law. For example, in a 2008 survey conducted by UNHCR of four Haitian consulates in locations with the highest numbers of Haitians and their descendants living abroad, consular officials disagreed on how far, i.e. to which generation, lineage rights could extend to grant nationality. (UNHCR 2011a)

Alarmingly, it appears that Haiti may not consider such persons "Haitians" either. When former Haitian president Michel Martelly visited The Bahamas in 2012, for instance, he referred to the "stateless" people of Haitian descent living in The Bahamas, asserting that it "could be considered as a crime" that they are denied citizenship in The Bahamas and repatriated to Haiti. This resulted in a public outcry and then Prime Minister Ingraham declared that "Such persons are not stateless; they have the nationality of their parents" (K. Rolle 2012b).[54]

Where then do these Bahamian-born persons of Haitian descent belong? Not only has The Bahamas not ratified the two statelessness conventions, which could potentially improve their situation, but it also has no statelessness status determination procedures in place. Without any SSD procedures or provisions to address statelessness within its nationality or immigration laws, The Bahamas is unable to accurately and transparently verify whether the "potential [Haitian] nationality" of which Ambassador Rodrigue speaks is actually enjoyed *in practice* by the Bahamian-born individuals in question, exacerbating the potential for statelessness in the country.

Although no SSD procedures exist, the aforementioned MFA official affirms that "The Department [of Immigration] seeks confirmation of citizenship from the assumed country of citizenship in writing or by asking the
individual to apply for a national passport."[55] Based on the above testimony
from the former Haitian official and the current ambassador, however, the
Haitian Embassy cannot provide a Haitian passport or a written letter attest-
ing to the nationality of those who either lack the requisite identity documents from Haiti or who cannot produce two Haitian witnesses to verify
their Haitian nationality. It is thus not apparent that the Bahamian government's alleged reliance on written letters is sufficient for establishing the nationality of all persons born in The Bahamas of noncitizen parents.

Moreover, asking people "to apply for a national passport" as "confirmation" of their nationality is not proof that they are nationals. An application
for a passport is not the same as actually possessing a passport as proof of
citizenship. What happens to those individuals whose parents lack identifying
nationality documents is thus unclear. Once again, it seems that the current
operating procedures of the Bahamian government expose Bahamian-born
persons of noncitizen parents to the risk of statelessness, the government's
denial notwithstanding.

As Figure 5 illustrates, Bahamian-born children of Haitian descent are
at a heightened risk of statelessness in the country through a combination of
factors. Protection gaps in Bahamian law,[56] bureaucratic inefficiencies, obscure citizenship decision-making rules and practices, and the politicized
nature of citizenship bestowal place them at risk of statelessness on the Bahamian side; while parental inability or refusal to obtain Haitian identity
documents for themselves or their children place them at risk on the Haitian side. As former attorney-general Sears points out, "When someone has
no evidence of another nationality, has never applied for a Haitian passport,
has never had a Haitian passport . . . because they've never had any documentation to evidence a Haitian nationality . . . this is where the issue of
statelessness comes in." Another former Bahamian government official similarly notes that

the social reality is that we have a very large number of persons in this
society of Haitian extraction who have a very dubious status in The
Bahamas; neither fish nor fowl. They don't qualify for Bahamian citizenship constitutionally and conversely there are issues as to whether
they have retained Haitian citizenship. . . . In any case, there is a very

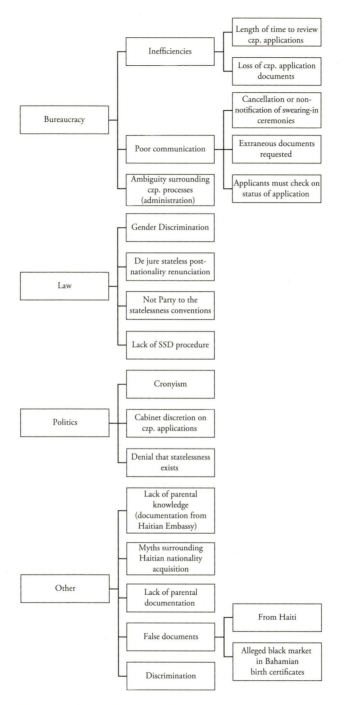

Figure 5. Risk factors for statelessness: Bahamas.

great question as to whether we do not unwittingly have within our borders a very large number of people who may possibly be stateless or who may become stateless at a certain point in time.[57]

When these Bahamian-born persons are not relegated into liminality, they are—as explained above—assumed to be Haitian under Article 11 of the Haitian Constitution. In 2014, Bahamian authorities sought to make this assumption a reality by forcing Bahamian-born persons of Haitian descent to acquire Haitian nationality documents. When I interviewed participants of Haitian descent for my 2012 fieldwork, the Bahamian government had purportedly begun a practice of trying to make these individuals obtain "Haitian" nationality documents at a critical time in the Bahamian citizenship application process. According to Dumercy, the Bahamian government at the time was failing to renew travel documents at eighteen for those who had not gone to the Haitian Embassy to acquire Haitian identity documents. A travel document, which is a Bahamian-government issued Certificate of Identity, used to be issued to children born of noncitizen parents in The Bahamas. It was a crucial document that served as an ID and allowed children born of noncitizens on Bahamian soil to travel abroad and reenter The Bahamas as well. According to the MFA official,

> The certificate of identity is issued at any age up to the 18th birthday. The expiry date therefore varies, and does not automatically expire on the 18th birthday. The last certificate of identity will be issued on the eighteenth birthday and is valid for five (5) years enabling the holder to remain in The Bahamas, and re-enter The Bahamas during the processing of the application for registration as a citizen.[58]

As Dumercy explains, however, it used to be that you could go to the Department of Immigration to get a letter stating that the travel document could be renewed at age eighteen. But "Now they stopped doing that." Instead, "what they're making the kids do" is "go and apply to the Haitian Embassy in Nassau . . . in order to get a valid ID." On November 1, 2014, Dumercy's account received corroboration when the Department of Immigration put into effect a new policy, which "*forces them* [noncitizens born on Bahamian soil] to apply for a passport from their parents' country of origin" (Robles 2015; italics added). As part of this new policy, Certificates of Identity are no longer issued to noncitizens born on the territory (Mitchell 2014). Dumercy is certainly right that the Bahamian government is "sending a mixed, confused message" if they are refusing to renew Bahamian-issued travel documents and forcing these Bahamian-born persons to acquire Haitian identity documents at eighteen. Age eighteen is, after all, when they can apply for Bahamian citizenship, as per Bahamian law.

Conclusion

This chapter illustrates that determining who belongs where is no simple endeavor. It is not merely a matter of identifying whether an individual falls under a given state's law as one of its nationals. In order to establish whether a person's human right to a nationality is fulfilled in practice, we must examine the political practices and bureaucratic procedures of states to see how laws are implemented in reality. As this chapter shows, a large gap exists between what Haitian law says regarding the acquisition of Haitian nationality and what actually occurs in practice for those born of Haitian migrants in The Bahamas. The offspring of such migrants are exposed to statelessness because the country of their birth, The Bahamas, denies them citizenship for at least the first eighteen years of their life and because they do not possess nationality documents from the country of their parents' alleged nationality (Haiti).

While Bahamian government representatives claim that statelessness does not exist, I demonstrate in this chapter that de jure statelessness exists, especially during the Bahamian citizenship registration or naturalization process. Although the Ministry of Foreign Affairs official asserts that discrimination plays no role in engendering statelessness in The Bahamas, without publicly available data on the number of persons who are denied or granted Bahamian citizenship by national origin, we have no way of corroborating this statement. What is known, and what I illustrate in this chapter, is that the obscureness, arbitrariness, and politicization surrounding the grant of Bahamian citizenship provide ample cover for the government to defend a position of neutrality, even if the experiences of the Bahamian-born noncitizens demonstrate otherwise.

That the majority of study participants, both citizen and noncitizen, remark on the prevalence of Bahamian-born persons of Haitian descent among those at risk of statelessness also speaks to a problem of discrimination. As James Goldston points out, "Indirect discrimination—also known as de facto discrimination or disparate/adverse impact or effect—occurs when a practice, rule, requirement, or condition is neutral on its face but impacts particular groups disproportionately, absent objective and reasonable justification" (2006, 328). Whether it is because they are the largest foreign-descended population (and consequently by their sheer numbers will have more affected persons) or because of discrimination, Bahamian-born persons of Haitian descent do appear to be disproportionately affected by The Bahamas' exclusionary citizenship laws. They are either thrust into the liminal space of statelessness or assumed to take on the nationality of a state with which they have no effective ties—a state whose former leader contends that they are not Haitian nationals.[59]

Unlike the postnational world of blurred boundaries then, these Bahamian-born noncitizens come up against the very real boundaries of formal belonging to the Bahamian state. Rejected by the country of their birth for at least the first eighteen years of their life and assumed—or made—to hold a nationality that they feel does not belong to them,[60] these individuals are forcibly displaced into the realm of the "betwixt and between." They know all too well that "belonging to the community into which one is born is no longer a matter of course" (Arendt [1948] 2004, 376). This situation is not unique to The Bahamas, however. Only a few hundred miles to the south, in the Dominican Republic, the precariousness of belonging is exposed in a far more overtly discriminatory manner.

CHAPTER 4

The Dominican Republic:
Foreigners in Their Own Country

A history teacher asked . . . what would we want to
change if we were to be born all over again. I said if I
were born again, I'd be born in a country where they
don't deny me my nationality.

—Felix Callo Marcel

Whereas in The Bahamas, Bahamian law clearly denies persons born of non-citizens Bahamian citizenship at birth, in the Dominican Republic the negation of belonging has not always been so clear-cut. While the DR has engaged in various exclusionary membership practices toward individuals of Haitian descent for several years now, it was not until September 2013 that mass denationalization was judicially sanctioned. In Sentence TC/0168/13 (Government of the Dominican Republic 2013e) the Constitutional Court ruled that civil registry officers were not acting unconstitutionally when they refused to issue citizenship and identity documents to persons whose parents' residency status was unclear or illegal when they were born in the country. In one fell swoop, the Constitutional Court paved the way for tens, and possibly hundreds, of thousands of Dominicans of Haitian descent to be stripped of their citizenship and forced into liminality (Archibold 2013; Edmonds 2013; Rojas 2013).[1]

As I explain in further detail below, Sentence TC/0168/13 is only the culmination of a series of exclusionary membership practices carried out by the Dominican state. As in the Bahamian case, legal, political, and bureaucratic factors work together to preclude Dominican-born persons of

Haitian descent from enjoying the fulfillment of their human right to a nationality in practice. What distinguishes the Bahamian and Dominican cases
is the prevalent anti-Haitianism that exists in the Dominican Republic and
the fact that those born in the country of Haitian descent were once Dominican citizens, as per Dominican law. This chapter thus illustrates how people
are being turned into foreigners in their own country (see Chapter 2) and
being "forced to be Haitian."[2] The chapter therefore demonstrates that in a
seemingly postnational world, the state continues to erect clear boundaries
of belonging and to deny citizenship to those it feels should have no place
within them.

Situating the Case Study

The Dominican Republic is the second largest country in the Caribbean.[3]
Located on the island of Hispaniola, it shares a 223-mile border—and a long
history—with Haiti. Although both Haiti and the DR served as colonies for
European powers, slavery and plantation-style agriculture were most prominent in Haiti. The brutality of this system led to black slave revolt and the
eventual overthrow of the French in Saint Domingue (Haiti), with Haiti declaring its independence in 1804. Less than twenty years later its eastern
neighbor declared its independence as well. The Republic of Spanish Haiti's
(DR's) independence was short-lived, however. The once-colonized became
the colonizer as Haitian president Jean Pierre Boyer led some 10,000 troops
into the country as a means to unify the island.[4]

While Haitian rule only lasted twenty-two years, its legacy in the Dominican Republic lasted far longer. Many, especially those of a nationalist
persuasion, fear the threat of another "Haitian invasion" akin to what occurred during Haiti's rule of the country.[5] This particular "invasion" takes
the form of Haitian migration, with the "illegal" Haitian being the primary
source of concern, although Dominican-born descendants of Haitian migrants
also generate unease. It is thus not uncommon, as Franciso Henry Leonardo
points out, to read newspaper headlines that glare: "'Immigrants mobilize
to demand they be given their documents'; 'Haitians demand they be given
their documents'; 'Judge in San Pedro orders Haitians be given their documents'"[6] when the subjects of these stories are neither immigrants nor Haitians, but Dominicans of Haitian descent.

Even though the Dominican economy is weaker in comparison to other Haitian migrant destinations (such as The Bahamas or the United States) it is nevertheless much stronger than that of Haiti, and the quality of life that a person can enjoy is higher as well.[7] Thus many Haitians migrate to the Dominican Republic in the hopes of finding more secure and profitable employment in the construction, agricultural, and private security sectors. Although debate exists regarding the number of Haitian nationals and Dominicans of Haitian descent in the country, a recent survey conducted by the country's National Office of Statistics (NOS)[8] determined that 87.3 percent of the immigrant population is Haitian-born (Government of the Dominican Republic 2013c, 29), while 86 percent of the immigrant-descended population is made up of individuals of Haitian descent (30). Despite increasing alarm at the Haitian presence, the total number of Haitians is estimated to be less than 5 percent of the Dominican Republic's overall population (62). Given the country's recent political and judicial moves to denationalize and potentially render stateless hundreds of thousands of citizens of Haitian descent, however, this percentage is likely to increase.

The Legal Context

The Dominican Republic has historically been a country of jus soli where the transmission of nationality occurs through birth on Dominican territory. The two exceptions to this form of citizenship acquisition were that a child born to a diplomat or a person "in transit" through the country did not receive Dominican citizenship. A person was "in transit" if he or she remained in the country for ten days or less (Government of the Dominican Republic 1939). Until 2010, this understanding of citizenship acquisition held throughout various revisions of the Dominican Constitution, even if it did not always apply in practice. In 2010, however, the DR amended its Constitution to state that children born to parents who reside illegally on Dominican territory are also excluded from jus soli citizenship acquisition (Article 18, Government of the Dominican Republic 2010b). A rather expansive definition of "in transit" was also promulgated, dismissing the temporal element and instead equating "in transit" status with not being legally present in the country (Government of the Dominican Republic 2013e, 62–63). As Indira Goris of the Open Society Justice Initiative observes, "it didn't really have anything to do now with how long you were in the country, it became a matter of proving that you were legally in the country."[9]

This broad understanding of "in transit" found its official formulation in Ley 285-04, which establishes the distinction between resident and nonresident noncitizens (Government of the Dominican Republic 2004). According to this law, resident noncitizens may be either "permanent" or "temporary." The former enter the Dominican Republic with permission from the relevant authority and with the intention of permanently residing within it; the latter only reside for a limited time (Articles 29 through 31) and are considered "in transit" (Article 36). They allegedly have no intention of making the DR their home (Article 32). Groups that fall within this temporary resident noncitizen category include tourists, students, business people, in transit passengers, temporary workers, and border crossers engaged in petty commerce. As Goris's OSJI counterpart in the Dominican Republic, Liliana Gamboa, points out, "migrants [who] come here from Haiti fall into almost all those categories."[10]

This particular interpretation of the "in-transit" clause has caused much consternation in the migrant and human rights communities in the Dominican Republic, especially since it affects large numbers of individuals of Haitian descent, many of whom have been residing in the DR either for all their lives or for decades (Beaubrun 2008, 21). Edwin Paraison, former minister of Haitians living abroad and current executive director of the Zile Foundation, argues that "in no way can you consider people who have been living [in the DR] for 25 or 30 years 'in transit.'"[11] Leonardo similarly states that "it is absurd to consider a person, who has spent many years living in the Dominican Republic, even if undocumented, as being 'in transit.' It doesn't make sense." In 2005 the Inter-American Court of Human Rights (IACtHR) also ruled on the matter in the *Case of the Girls Yean and Bosico v. the Dominican Republic* (herein *Yean and Bosico*; IACtHR 2005).

In its ruling, the court argued that when the Dominican Republic denied birth certificates to Dilcia Yean and Violeta Bosico, children born on Dominican soil of Haitian descent, it was violating their rights to a nationality, a juridical personality, a name, and equal protection before the law (IACtHR 2005). Moreover, the IACtHR held that the DR's interpretation of "in transit" was deficient according to its own migration law since a person could only be "in transit" if he or she were passing through a state's territory, which, as previously noted, the 1939 statute stipulated was ten days or less. Regardless what interpretation the Dominican state wanted to give to "in transit" then, the IACtHR held that it should be a "reasonable temporal limit" that kept in mind "that a foreigner who develops connections in a State cannot be equated to a person in transit" (62). Moreover, the court stated that the mothers of Yean and Bosico were Dominican and that the girls were consequently not "in transit." They therefore had the right to a Dominican nationality and all the concomitant rights and protections associated with it.

While the DR ended up paying the fine established by the IACtHR and providing Yean and Bosico their birth certificates, the Dominican Supreme Court of Justice (SCJ) found in that same year that the state had not acted incorrectly by equating "in transit" with being a nonresident or an illegal. Thus, in a strange twist of logic, the SCJ argued that if a child born to a legally resident diplomat does not acquire Dominican citizenship according to the law, then a child born to an illegal resident certainly should not receive Dominican citizenship (Government of the Dominican Republic 2005; see also Government of the Dominican Republic 2013a, 5–6). It therefore contended that Ley 285-04 was not unconstitutional. The SCJ also ruled that individuals were not being rendered stateless because they were covered under Article 11 of the Haitian Constitution, which, as noted in Chapter 3, declares that any child born to a Haitian mother or father who has not renounced his or her Haitian citizenship is a Haitian.

Not only did "the category of 'non-resident' [become] conflated with the concept of 'in transit' status" (UN HRC 2008c, 18) because of Ley 285-04, but this law also paved the way for the creation of a separate birth registry system for children born to "non-resident" mothers. Thus, according to Article 28 of Ley 285-04, health centers must issue an official declaration of birth ("constancia de nacimiento") to resident and nonresident mothers alike, but nonresident mothers must be given "pink," as opposed to "white," birth declarations and go to their respective embassies to actually obtain a birth certificate.

Health centers are thus charged with performing an immigration task as they decide who should be issued a white birth declaration and who should receive a pink one. "And that's why people were so upset about the pink certificate," says Gamboa. "Because it left at the discretion of hospitals to decide who were entitled to which documents. Because once you received the one at the hospital, then you were screwed if you didn't get the right one . . . I mean, at the hospital it was made the decision whether you would get the actual document for a [Dominican] birth certificate or not." Additionally, Goris adds that she "believe[s] that the rate at which the Dominican government hands out this pink birth certificate does not match the rate of children born to Haitian migrants, Haitian non-residents." Such children are therefore left without proof of their birth and at risk of statelessness.

Article 28 of Ley 285-04 also requires health centers to inform the Junta Central Electoral (JCE)[12] and the Ministry of Foreign Affairs of these births to nonresident mothers so that the Ministry can know who is and who is not a national and so that the mothers can inform their respective embassies that one of their nationals has been born on Dominican soil, thereby allowing the embassy to begin the process of providing citizenship to the child.[13] Yet, as a UN HRC officer based in the country observes, "it never occurs. It never happens. It hasn't really worked, the mechanism."[14] Gamboa adds that although embassies are supposed to receive notification from the Ministry of Foreign Affairs on the birth of a child to one of their nonresident nationals, "it never worked with embassies. . . . The Haitian Embassy says that it never received a copy of anything [from] the government." Bridget Wooding, director of the Observatory on Migration and Development in the Caribbean[15] in the DR, agrees, stating that

> It's not quite clear that they've actually been receiving any of these papers, or quite what they've been doing with them. If you actually ask them, "Have you seen a pink paper? What do you do with it?" It's less than clear. So this pink paper system, it's not clear that they exist in all the hospitals. It's not clear that, even if they exist in the hospitals, people know how to fill them in. . . . So the evidence so far is that this pink paper system, at least insofar as Haitian residents are concerned, has not been very functional.[16]

Moreover, it is highly problematic to expect mothers who have just given birth to visit their respective embassy or consulate to register the birth of their child and obtain a birth certificate, especially if the process is, as Gamboa says, "never explained to people. So people never really understood that they are to go to the embassy" to register their child and acquire a birth certificate. This places these Dominican-born children of Haitian descent in a vulnerable position since, as I explain in Chapter 2, birth registration is the first and primary means by which a person is able to obtain the necessary proof to secure a nationality.

Despite the fact that the Inter-American Court of Human Rights found the Dominican Republic in violation of international law in this and other areas in 2005, Dominican authorities passed Resolutions 02-2007 and 12-2007,[17] which have further disenfranchised an untold number of Dominicans of Haitian descent. Thus what used to be sporadic individual "rogue registry officers" engaging in racially motivated denationalization acts in the country has become "a concentrated State policy to deny and deprive entire ethnic groups of nationality."[18] Resolution 02-2007 creates a foreigner's book or "Registry of Births to Foreign Non-Resident Mothers in the Dominican Republic"[19] (Government of the Dominican Republic 2007a). Local civil registry officers are required to record all births to foreign nonresident mothers.

The Junta Central Electoral applauds the enactment of this resolution because it fulfills a child's right to a name and birth registration, regardless of the mother's legal status in the country and regardless of whether or not she took in her pink birth declaration to her specific embassy (Government of the Dominican Republic 2014a). Critics argue, however, that it provides a means by which Dominican authorities can deny citizenship to people of Haitian descent born on Dominican soil prior to the 2010 constitutional amendment. Gamboa thinks that it may also simply be a means of "shut[ting] up NGOs in terms of registration because there's an argument that people should be registered and there's a whole campaign in the Americas about the right to registration."

Furthermore, Gamboa wonders if this foreigner's registry book does not serve to further confuse parents on their child's right to a nationality: "it doesn't necessarily mean what nationality [a child has], but [it] just [means] to be registered. And there's an argument of nationality rights as a right. So to go into that direction and say, 'Well, we have registered [the children], we are not leaving them unregistered' may not be a fair position." She wonders whether

maybe purposefully, maybe not, [the] underlying intention was to confuse people. I mean, we're talking about migrants who a lot of the time are not even literate. [They] don't necessarily know what's going on with the laws. . . . I mean, it's complicated for us to understand everything that has happened and how laws have been changed and, you know, how you can challenge them and what you have [a] right to. Imagine for migrants who haven't even heard about this.

Paraison, an early proponent of the pink birth declaration and foreigner's book, concedes that the system has not worked as he had initially hoped, but, unlike NGOs who see it as a form of discrimination and a means of denying Dominican citizenship to individuals of Haitian descent, he believes that it still serves as a basis from which these children can mount claims in the future. "It is going to be more difficult to fight for one's rights without having anything [registered in a book]. And for us, it's better to be mentioned in that [foreigner's] book so that in the future we have a place [to go to that states] where that child was registered." It is not enough, therefore, to be present in the country of one's birth to engage in rights-claiming. One's personhood must also be documented.

Allegedly, some persons who were born on Dominican soil prior to the 2010 constitutional amendment—and who are, therefore, Dominican by law—are being deregistered from the registry of legal resident births and transferred to this foreigner's book. As Leonardo points out, this is being done without these individuals' consent.[20] Gamboa adds that this action "is a new development and we haven't analyzed the impacts or necessarily the consequences of it." She explains how the Open Society Justice Initiative of the DR received a case wherein a child born prior to the 2010 constitutional amendment "had a birth certificate [registered] in one book" and when she went to get a certified copy of this certificate, "they told her it was her only copy and it was for judicial purposes only, and [the civil registry officer] said that it was registered in a foreign book, number 1 page 1—it was a completely different registration" from the one she previously held. These children are therefore being forcibly displaced from the book that registers allegedly "legitimate" Dominican births to one that is for foreigners only.

Simultaneously with the implementation of the pink registration system/foreigner's book, the Dominican authorities passed resolution 12-2007 (Government of the Dominican Republic 2007b). This resolution effectively placed thousands of Dominicans, primarily of Haitian descent, in legal limbo as it ordered all civil registry officers to provisionally suspend the issuance of all vital records and documents to individuals suspected of originally obtaining such documents in an "irregular" manner. Vital records include, among others, a Cédula de Identidad y Electoral (cédula/national ID)—akin to a voter registration card—and a certified birth certificate. The latter, as noted earlier, is one of the primary documents for obtaining a nationality (i.e., it provides proof of where one is born and to whom), while the cédula is needed to perform almost any function in the Dominican public realm.

As a UNDP officer explains, "Under the Dominican legal system, an identity card is indispensable for the exercise of certain rights. . . . If you do not have an ID, you cannot open a bank account. . . . [You] cannot cash a check, get a credit card, enter into a contract."[21] Leonardo agrees that in order to exercise one's rights as a citizen you have to have a cédula. Without the cédula or a birth certificate, "you do not exist under the law."[22] Furthermore, the cédula or ID generates a sense of security. As Eddy Tejeda, a member of the Latin American Faculty of Social Sciences in the DR, says, "You need it [the cédula] for everything. If I don't have my ID card with me, I feel afraid you know. You feel more secure if you have your ID with you here with the police."[23] And, according to Gamboa, a person can "be arrested for up to 30 days for not having a cedula [sic]" (Gamboa 2010, n. pag.).

These problems of document denial and the consequent inability to exercise citizenship rights all came to a head in the judicial realm in 2013. In Sentence TC/0168/13 (Government of the Dominican Republic 2013e) the Dominican Constitutional Court heard the case of Juliana Deguis Pierre who claimed that when she had tried to obtain her cédula at her local JCE office they took away her birth certificate and told her that she could not have a cédula because she was not Dominican. The Constitutional Court, upon hearing the case, stated that Deguis's parents were "in transit" (nonresident) at the time of her birth and she did not, therefore, satisfy the requirements for Dominican jus soli citizenship acquisition (29–30).[24]

Deguis was born in the Dominican Republic in 1984 to Haitian nationals, well before the creation of Ley 285-04 and the 2010 constitutional amendment. In order to register her birth, her parents used fichas (a work permit generally issued by the owners of sugarcane estates to temporary foreign sugarcane workers). According to Gamboa, at different times in the Dominican Republic's labor history, these fichas could be used to acquire residency status and Dominican identity documents, while at others they were merely considered cards that granted permission to work for a given company:

There were periods in which being here, working with one of those cards also meant being an actual resident and Migration would give you identity documents, too. The civil registry office would provide you with all identity cards that were for foreigners. So even though it sounded like modern things now, it existed back in the day, too.

Gamboa continues that sometimes it was not clear how the ficha was used and "State versus industry or company-owned identity documents were a lot of the time just mixed all together." Nevertheless, these fichas "were sufficient for registration. So civil registry officers received those documents as a proof of an ID, of an identity. . . . [And] these identity documents were enough for people to register their children and so a lot of the children of migrants were registered" in this way "And got Dominican citizenship and grew thinking that they were Dominicans." William Charpantier, coordinator of MENAMIRD, agrees, stating that civil registry officers considered the ficha to be a valid ID document, "the photo and name of the person was there."[25]

Despite the fact that fichas were used to register the births of Haitian workers' Dominican-born children in past decades, the president of the JCE, Roberto Rosario, states that children born to foreigners who registered them with fichas or "other documents not permitted or authorized by law" are "irregularly" registered as Dominicans (Government of the Dominican Republic 2013a, 7; author's translation). The Constitutional Court has taken this position as well, finding that Deguis's parents lacked the requisite ID to be able to declare her birth as a Dominican (Government of the Dominican Republic 2013e, 36) as they were temporary workers or "nonimmigrant foreigners" (55). The court therefore held that Deguis's parents fell under the "in transit" clause of the 1966 Constitution (65), which was in operation at the time of Deguis's birth.

According to the court, even then, as per various laws, persons were considered "in transit" if they lacked a legal residence in the Dominican Republic or if they lacked a legal residency permit. Consequently, the court held, it was not possible for persons in Deguis's situation to argue that they were being denied Dominican citizenship as it was "legally inadmissible to establish an entitlement from an unlawful situation in fact" (Government of the Dominican Republic 2013e, 66). Furthermore, the Constitutional Court argued that the IACtHR had interpreted Dominican law incorrectly when giving its opinion on the "in transit" clause (70) and that persons in Deguis's situation were not being rendered stateless because they were covered under Article 11 of the Haitian Constitution.

Leonardo and others take umbrage at the argument that the ficha did not serve to legally register a child born in the Dominican Republic. According to Leonardo,

One of the fallacies that they have sold from a political vantage point is to say that they are dealing with, that all those who are registered, those records are illegal because the parents were undocumented and they [the children] should never have been registered. And that's not completely accurate. In the first place, even if the parents were undocumented, according to the law in force at the time they were born, they could have been registered. Secondly, the majority of these people were children of immigrants whose admission into the Dominican Republic was authorized by the Dominican State. They were hired by this very State to work as sugarcane workers. And the private sector employed them with the consent of the Dominican State. So one cannot claim that they entered the Dominican State through unauthorized means. They entered with State permission and the ficha is proof of this.

Despite what Leonardo and others think, or the fact that the Inter-American Court of Human Rights already found the DR in violation of international law when it came to discriminatory practices against individuals of Haitian descent in its civil registry system, the country has continued to engage in practices that are deemed arbitrary and that, arguably, forcibly displace persons entitled to Dominican citizenship into liminality.

The Political Context

As the Constitutional Court recognizes, issues surrounding nationality are "a particularly sensitive issue for all sectors of Dominican society" (Government of the Dominican Republic 2013e, 74). Human and migrant rights NGOs emphatically believe that the Dominican government, no matter which political party is in power, deliberately discriminates against people of Haitian descent when it comes to citizenship acquisition or retention. Goris contends that nowhere else in the Caribbean or Latin America is there "a concentrated state policy to deny and deprive entire ethnic groups of nationality" as occurs in the Dominican Republic. Rodríguez agrees, noting that the discriminatory nature of the country's treatment of Haitians in particular has been "driven—it hasn't happened by chance, of course—it's been an intentional, deliberate effort from the elites." Leonardo adds that as

each day has passed, "it became clearer that we were dealing with a deliberate policy on the part of the State that had clearly discriminatory overtones."

Akin to Rodríguez, Leonardo believes that the current Dominican "worldview, all of it, is a construction of an elite that has had politico-economic
control from colonial times." This worldview consists of embracing its Spanish heritage, while ignoring, if not denying, its black heritage. As Leonardo
explains, the Dominican "national identity that people have constructed [is
one in which] we are not black. We are indios. My complexion is indian.
They think as if they were a Hispanic from Spain, as if they were Spanish.
And they assume Spanish aesthetic standards as their own." Rodríguez agrees,
explaining how the cédula or national ID does not allow for the category of
black as a race. You are either white or indio.[26] "I have india on my ID," she
shows. She believes that the cédula only gives these options because Dominicans want to think of themselves as "white, Spanish, Catholics; as opposed
to Haitian, black, voodooist." Goris concurs, "I think in the Dominican Republic, the Dominican identity is in a large part, not a large part but an important part of what it means to be Dominican when you are talking about the
island of Hispaniola is to say, 'Well, we are Dominican. We are not Haitian.
We are not black.'"

Allegedly the blackness of one's skin is often enough to find oneself deported to Haiti, even if not a Haitian. Human Rights Watch claims that "the
Dominican Republic has deported hundreds of thousands of Haitians to
Haiti, as well as an unknown number of Dominicans of Haitian descent"
(2002, 11)[27] and "Suspected Haitians are targeted for deportation based on
the color of their skin, and are given little opportunity to prove their legal
status or their claim to citizenship" (3). Samuel Martínez, an anthropologist
who provided an expert affidavit in the *Yean and Bosico* case, explains how
"deportations generally do not follow the process stipulated by Dominican
law. Generally, people determined at the point of arrest to be Haitian, on the
basis of their appearance or accent, are quickly transferred without legal proceedings to buses for transportation across the Haitian border" (2011, 60).

One's appearance or last name also has important ramifications when a
person is present at a local JCE office. In the Deguis case, Deguis claims
that the local civil registry officer confiscated the copy of her birth certificate
on the mere grounds that she had a "French" (meaning "Haitian") last name.
This is not unusual, as Rodríguez states, "Your last name and how you look
often determines whether you are deemed Dominican or not." Gamboa
agrees, describing how when it comes to the JCE and the issuance of identity

documents, if a person's "last name sounds like someone of Haitian origin, then it starts an investigatory process" and that is where "the whole discrimination and racial profiling comes in." Charpantier also believes that Circular 17 (OHCHR 2008),[28] which was issued to examine irregularities among all holders of Dominican identity documents, was mainly applied to "those persons who have a strange last name. When they have a strange last name it is a French-sounding one—like Pierre, Jacques."

Some contend that the above quotations illustrate that a deep strain of anti-Haitianism exists in the country. Anti-Haitianism is "a set of perceptions, attitudes and negative stereotypes toward Haitians and Haiti" (Sagás 1998, 128; author's translation).[29] Paraison contends, along with Leonardo and Rodríguez, that the anti-Haitianism present in the Dominican Republic emanates from the political elite and that they are "systematic[ally]" critical of Haiti, whereas Haitian elites do not exhibit the same hostility toward Dominicans. He laments what he considers to be the biggest problem facing the Haitian diaspora in the DR: "the denial of their very existence. For the anti-Haitian groups in the Dominican Republic to help the Haitian community is to put—in their minds—is to put Dominican national sovereignty in jeopardy. Thus they do not even want to accept that we exist."

Although the Dominican government firmly denies that racial discrimination exists, that it violates the human rights of migrants or that it is rendering Dominican nationals stateless,[30] the retroactive application of laws, the creation of a special registry that checks immigrant status from 1929 onward, and the Dominican government's failure to comply with all the 2005 IACtHR decision, undercut this position. Ley 285-04, which, as noted earlier, defines the distinction between a resident and nonresident immigrant and equates nonresidency with an "in transit" status, is being retroactively applied to those who were recognized as Dominican citizens prior to 2004.

As previously mentioned, many Dominicans of Haitian descent who go to their local JCE offices to obtain certified copies of their birth certificates or their IDs are being denied such documents on the grounds that they were irregularly registered. That is, their parents did not provide the appropriate documentation—such as a residency permit or a cédula—to prove that they were authorized to be in the country. As such, the Dominican government contends that these children should never have been recognized as citizens. Although the Dominican government is not actively denationalizing such persons through a specific law, it is administratively doing so. As Goris explains:

There are very few cases of the Dominican government going after an individual in court, as they should, and saying, "We don't think that you're a Dominican citizen, so we're going to follow all the procedural steps to officially withdraw recognition of you as a Dominican." There are very few cases of that. So what you have is, sort of denationalization by default because you don't give these people these documents. And it's true, when you refuse to give them these documents, it's not like they give you a letter saying, "You are no longer a citizen." They are saying, "No, we understand that you don't have a right to these documents because of this law" [Ley 285-04]. . . . And you have entire generations of people that were once recognized as Dominican citizens, but are no longer [recognized] because the government has decided to retroactively apply this 2004 migration law.

The practice of denationalizing Dominicans via administrative means occurs even though the 2010 constitutional amendment is clear that all those who enjoyed Dominican citizenship prior to 2010 are Dominican citizens (Government of the Dominican Republic 2010b, Article 18). Moreover, akin to the Bahamian case, seemingly neutral laws and policies appear to have a more significant impact upon individuals of Haitian descent than any other group. We thus appear to be faced with a case of institutional racism:

When apparently neutral requirements for recruitment or routines affect certain ethnic groups more than others, or more generally when certain rules, instructions or everyday practice within an institution have systematic intended (or unintended) discriminating consequences . . . we may talk about institutional discrimination. (Burns 2011, 157; see also Delanty et al. 2011, 5)

Although the Dominican government claims it is only applying its own law, the present understanding of "in transit," which is the root of the government's justification for its actions, was only officially delineated in law in 2004 (OSJI and CEJIL 2012, 4). It is thus unfair to use a contemporary understanding of "in transit" to that which operated prior to 2004. As Justice Katia Miguelina Jiménez Martínez makes clear in her dissenting opinion in the Deguis case, the common understanding of "in transit" until 2004 was that it was a ten-day period (Government of the Dominican Republic 2013e, 118). Furthermore, Justice Ana Isabel Bonilla Hernández, also dissenting, argues that "to equate the condition of a foreigner in transit with an illegal foreign resident violates the legal principle of retroactivity" because prior to the 2010 constitutional amendment, the Constitution "was silent with regard to illegal foreign residents and nationality" (114).

In another demonstration of what Leonardo would call the politicized nature of the high courts,[31] the Constitutional Court decided in the aforementioned Sentence TC/0168/13 that the JCE should perform an audit of all birth registry books as far back as 1929 to identify all the foreigners therein listed and then create another list that names all those who were irregularly registered. Such persons, who should not have been given Dominican citizenship according to Sentence TC/0168/13, must be placed in special birth registration books, based on the year they were born, that identify them as foreigners. The Ministry of Foreign Affairs must then notify such persons (and their embassies/consulates) of their transferal from the regular Dominican civil registry of births to the special foreigners' book (Government of the Dominican Republic 2013e, 100).

The Constitutional Court also ordered the JCE to send the aforementioned *List of foreigners irregularly registered in the Civil Registry of the Dominican Republic* to the minister of the interior and police, "who presides over the National Council on Migration," so that the latter body can create a National Plan for the Regularization of Foreigners in an irregular migratory situation (hereafter, "National Plan"; Government of the Dominican Republic 2013e, 100). The Constitutional Court then instructed the executive branch of government to implement this plan. In a matter of months, the Dominican government has already taken steps to fulfill the orders given to it by the Constitutional Court. It has thus established a National Regularization Plan for Foreigners in an Irregular Situation, which consists of forty Articles elaborating where, when, and with what documents each person is to come forward to begin the process of regularizing their presence on Dominican soil (Government of the Dominican Republic 2013d).

The speed with which the government is implementing the orders given to it by the Constitutional Court in Sentence TC/0168/13 stands in stark contrast not only with the slow pace of processing citizenship claims (also discussed in the Bahamian case in Chapter 3), but also with the delay in implementation of those court decisions that do not mesh well with the political stance of the government. These can be local court decisions mandating that JCE offices give birth certificates or IDs to specific people, which are often ignored, or they can be the orders of the Inter-American Court of

Human Rights. Thus, as Wooding explains, in the above-mentioned *Yean and Bosico* case,

> there's been a partial implementation of the Yean and Bosico sentence. Whereas certain cosmetic things were done—there was some compensation given to the people involved, there was a publication of the sentence—but the more important things (in terms of creating a clear, nondiscriminatory civil registry system) that has not been obeyed. And on the contrary, there's been a backlash where the discrimination has been widened further against a particular segment, which is those people of Haitian descent.

Paraison agrees, stating that "the sentence was not applied. It was not respected by the Dominican State." Furthermore, he contends that

> nationalist groups in the Dominican Republic used the sentence all the time to say that when we [Haitians or individuals of Haitian descent] claim our rights, what we are actually doing is carrying out a campaign of denigration against the Dominican Republic. A defamation campaign.

Goris adds that "the politicians [are] going out there and saying, 'We don't believe in the legitimacy of this institution,' meaning the IACtHR. 'They're being manipulated by foreign NGOs that are trying to destabilize the country and ruining its reputation.'" The political backlash against the IACtHR's ruling in *Yean and Bosico* has therefore been harsh, with interviewees contending that discriminatory policies toward individuals of Haitian descent have become even stronger since the ruling. Thus, while Rodríguez believes that "It's good that we got sanctioned" at the IACtHR, "in the end, in the long view, it's been more negative in the sense that there's been now a very legal and concrete, determined policy to discriminate against Dominicans of Haitian descent. It wasn't like that before the ruling. It wasn't as concrete and as deliberate." Leonardo concurs, stating that the Dominican authorities' failure to implement the 2005 IACtHR decision shows that "The State was not committing errors, but that it was acting in a deliberate manner. And what it has done is reinforce its practice in the wake of the IACtHR decision."

This reinforcement has come in many ways. Even though international law is supposed to have the same legal status as domestic law within the country (Government of the Dominican Republic 2010b, Article 26), the Dominican Constitutional Court issued Sentence TC/0256/14 in 2014 (Government of the Dominican Republic 2014d), declaring IACtHR jurisdiction over it to be unconstitutional. This is a blatant attempt to invalidate the IACtHR's rulings in the 2005 *Yean and Bosico* case, the *Case of Expelled Dominicans and Haitians v. the Dominican Republic* (2014a)[32] and others. For its part, the IACtHR has emphatically denied that the Dominican Republic can withdraw from its jurisdiction (IACtHR 2014b).

Even prior to the Constitutional Court's 2014 ruling, the Dominican Republic had reinforced its alleged state practice of discrimination toward persons of Haitian descent—and disregard for the IACtHR's rulings, in other ways. The aforementioned Circular 17 and Resolutions 02-2007 and 12-2007, as well as the 2010 constitutional amendment, which included illegal immigrants and nonresident persons (with the new interpretation of "in transit") among those who are ineligible for Dominican jus soli citizenship acquisition, were all issued after the 2005 IACtHR decision in *Yean and Bosico*. The 2013 Deguis sentence is particularly troubling because it directly challenges the IACtHR's 2005 proclamation that the migratory status of one's parents has no bearing upon a child's migratory status. In Sentence TC/0168/13, the Constitutional Court argues that

> assimilating foreigners who lack permission to reside to **in transit foreigners** does not imply, in any way, that the migratory situation of the parents is being transmitted or transferred to the children, since the latter are not considered to be in an unlawful situation, they only lack the right to a Dominican nationality. (Government of the Dominican Republic 2013e, 75; bold in original)

Ordering the creation of special birth registration books that extend the reach of contemporary law as far back as 1929, and using this data to determine whether or not a Dominican was "irregularly" registered based on the documentation used by their parents or grandparents, demonstrates how a parent's—or even a child's grandparent's—migratory status *can* affect a child's current nationality status, however. Deguis, for example, was denied Dominican citizenship on these very grounds.[33]

Yet the Constitutional Court does not believe that it is allowing for discriminatory acts to be pursued against persons of Haitian descent via this Sentence. It asserts that while it is lamentable that it takes so long for civil registry officers to resolve individual citizenship cases and to issue identity documents, this is not due to a state policy of discrimination, but to "deficiencies in the [civil registry] system" instead (Government of the Dominican Republic 2013e, 89). Whether or not the Dominican Republic is deliberately discriminating against persons of Haitian descent, the fact is that citizenship issues are highly politicized and racialized in the country and this begs crucial scrutiny of government action in this area. That this politicization occurs in an environment of institutional weakness does not help those who find themselves at risk of statelessness either.

Bureaucratic Failures

In Resolution 12-2007, the Junta Central Electoral recognizes that institutional weaknesses plague the civil registry system and exacerbate many of the problems the country now faces when it comes to citizenship matters. The JCE itself admits that "The lack of supervision of Civil Registry offices and the complicity of quite a few of their employees, made it relatively easy for these unlawful acts [the giving of Dominican birth certificates and other identity documents] to occur" (Government of the Dominican Republic 2007b, 3; author's translation). Likewise, in Sentence TC/0168/13, the Constitutional Court acknowledges that the civil registry system "has been affected by unlawful issuances, forgeries, identity theft and falsifications of civil registry acts; as well as by deficiencies in the upkeep of the registry books," affirming that they *"are implementing a program of rescue and clean-up of the Civil Registry system in order to reinforce it against harmful and fraudulent actions . . . that have so long affected [it]"* (Government of the Dominican Republic 2013e, 9; italics in original).

The issue of documentation is an important one in the Dominican Republic. As I note earlier in the chapter, a cédula (ID) is needed to carry out many citizenship rights and functions, and a recently certified copy of one's birth certificate is necessary to obtain this ID. Without it, as a UNDP official makes clear, you are an invisible person. The problem of undocumentation not only affects individuals of Haitian descent, however. The UNDP participant explains how a census of Dominican school students carried out by the secretary of state for education found that more than 17,800 students were undocumented. "They do not have birth certificates," he says. "They are not going to be able to attend high school." While a 2001 survey found that 25.4 percent of Dominican children under five are not registered (UNICEF 2014c), according to the UNDP participant, this problem of un-documentation or "citizen invisibility affects almost 20% of the Domini-can population."[34] It is for this reason that UNDP-DR has been focusing on strengthening the civil registry system.

In 2007–2012, the UNDP worked with the JCE in a project entitled "strengthening the civil registry system."[35] The goals were to improve the JCE's institutional capacity and to provide identity documents, especially birth certificates, to those who lacked them. The UNDP used mobile civil registry units, engaged in door-to-door awareness raising in specific neigh-borhoods, and established a methodology by which future birth registrations could take place.[36] According to the UNDP interviewee, at the time of the interview more than 13,000 of the 17,000 plus students identified as lacking documents in the initial census conducted by the Ministry of Education have now received their birth certificates.

Unlike the UNDP's "strengthening the civil registry system" project, which did not focus on providing documentation for persons of Haitian de-scent, UNICEF has also been active in the area of birth registration and works with the JCE and other organizations, both Dominican and interna-tional, to ensure that as many children are registered as possible. In the first phase of the "Register My Birth and You will Open Many Doors for Me"[37] campaign, UNICEF and other organizations engaged in a mobilization ef-fort to educate specific sectors of the Dominican population, which included the residents of particular bateyes, on the importance of birth registration. In its second phase, which it is currently in, UNICEF is disseminating regis-tration materials broadly with the aim of reaching all of Dominican society on this important issue.

Cognizant of registration problems, the JCE issued Circular 32-2011. This circular instructs civil registry officers to give individuals who are "born to foreigners," and have had their identity documents suspended while their citizenship status is under investigation, their birth certificates until such time that the JCE rules on their nationality status (Government of the Do-minican Republic 2011). Although this appears to be a positive step in en-suring that people whose citizenship status is being questioned are able to get on with their daily lives while being investigated, the Movement for a Civil Registry Free of Discrimination[38] contends that many civil registry offices are not complying with this order (MRCLD 2013, 2). Moreover, and as Gamboa explains, it is the JCE's own board of judges who make decisions on these cases when a person's citizenship is under investigation.

This board it's right now what the JCE is sort of holding onto to review these cases. So we [the JCE civil registry officers] find you suspicious. So we take you to investigation. Eventually we're going to take your case to our board and our board is going to make the decision on your case. And then it's going to notify all of the rest, like civil registry officers. So they are being, as I said, judge and jury of their own actions.

In what may prove to be just as questionable, civil registry officers are allegedly going to the homes of individuals who have brought claims to the lower courts concerning the issuance of their birth certificates and harassing them. In Sentence 259-12, for example, a judge from a Court of First Instance found the JCE in violation of the rights of twenty-eight Dominicans of Haitian descent because local civil registry officers had denied them their cédulas. The judge ordered the local civil registry officers to reinstate these individuals' IDs (Government of the Dominican Republic 2012, 23). As Leonardo points out, not only did the JCE not abide by the ruling, but "it is intimidating the claimants. It is hounding them; visiting them in their homes; interviewing them; asking them for documentation that is not found in the law." He adds that they are also making the claimants' parents sign blank papers.

Although Leonardo does not know why JCE representatives are asking the parents to sign blank papers, he surmises: "So putting myself in the shoes of the Central Electoral Board, the most likely reason for having them sign blank papers is to state that the children were not born in the country, or that they were 'in transit' when the child was born in the country." He says that the parents end up signing these papers because

You have to realize that most of these people, the parents, are illiterate. They don't have a high level of education and since they are undocumented immigrants, they are in a situation of extreme vulnerability. . . . They feel pressured and they think that if they don't sign whatever they ask them to sign, they are going to use it against them and repatriate them.

Whether or not this is an isolated and extreme example of JCE harassment, it appears more common that local JCE officers simply let languish irregular birth certificate cases that they are supposed to be investigating. According to Gamboa, the investigative process—which is generally triggered because a person's "last name sounds like someone of Haitian origin"—may last "up to three years, two years. Sometimes it is never resolved if there are too many cases and they don't get to yours." She adds that investigators "never actually in writing said, 'We're investigating your parents' residency status.' Cause they don't want to be really clear about it because they're afraid that they will be accused." Even the Constitutional Court in the Deguis case admits that "it is worrying . . . because it potentially threatens the fundamental rights of foreigners, even if they reside unlawfully in the country, that it takes many years to legally resolve the irregularities regarding their identity documents" (Government of the Dominican Republic 2013e, 89). The Constitutional Court goes on to say, however, that this problem does not just affect foreigners, but Dominicans as well. Thus, "it is not a matter of a discriminatory policy, but, simply, weaknesses in the system" (89).

Another weakness in the system, and one that is paralleled in the Bahamian case, is that individuals are not kept up to date on the status of the investigation into their documents or citizenship status; sometimes they are not even told that they are under investigation. Every one of the participants in Katerina Civolani Hischnjakow's study,[39] for example, said that "confusion and disinformation prevailed throughout the process [of trying to obtain documents from the JCE]" (2011, 48). Like their counterparts in The Bahamas, they are often required to bring numerous extraneous documents that are not part of the process to obtain a birth certificate or a cédula. "We observed the delaying tactics [of civil registry officers] and all of the excessive requirements that were demanded of those affected" (50).

It is thus a cumbersome process that does not always end with a person receiving his or her identity documents. Rodríguez explains, for example, how she tried to help a Dominican-born individual of Haitian descent obtain identity documents. She says that he had been multiple times to his local civil registry office for his cédula, but was constantly denied because his parents had registered him with a ficha. The local civil registry officers told him to go to the capital to get things sorted out. Rodríguez went with him to the main JCE office in Santo Domingo. There Rodríguez "ran into the mother of a friend that went to high school with me. I explained to her the situation. . . . She said, 'It's great that you're doing this, but he's not going to get a positive reply.'" The individual was never able to make any headway at the JCE after multiple attempts and Rodríguez heard that "he ended up buying a fake ID. You pay 5,000 pesos for a fake ID."

While in the Dominican Republic, and elsewhere in the developing world, "the apparently dry details of the rules for obtaining papers can hide an ocean of discrimination and denial of rights" (Manby 2009, 2),[40] the problems that Dominican-born persons of Haitian descent face in relation to documentation and their citizenship status is not only hampered by actions—or inaction as the case may be—on the part of Dominican authorities. As I describe in Chapter 3, acquiring nationality and identity documents from the Haitian government is also a challenge in many cases.

Although the UNHCR-DR official thinks "the willingness of the Haitian government to support its people . . . [is] amazing. They are really very cooperative,"[41] some interviewees are concerned that parents cannot perform a "late [birth] declaration" at the Embassy. As Gamboa explains,[42] "Only children under 24 months can be registered at the Embassy. This in turn, obviously, comes to be a practical problem that results in people not having a nationality." She continues, "It's not that by law they were prevented from having a Haitian nationality, it's just that because their parents are undocumented, they cannot travel freely back and forth. They probably do not have the means to go back and forth to Haiti, so probably that child remains without Haitian citizenship."

Council Minister Pierrot Delienne, who works at the Haitian Embassy in the Dominican Republic, denies that this is the case. He says that as long as the mother or father is Haitian "and can prove this," the child "will have the right to be [a] Haitian citizen," regardless of age. "There are no exceptions."[43] It is important to highlight, as I mention in the previous chapter, that Haitian citizenship is not automatically acquired via birth to a Haitian parent, Bahamian and Dominican government claims to the contrary. As Delienne points out: "He has the right to have [Haitian citizenship]. When I say the right, if he comes here with his papers, he will have it." But just because a child comes to the embassy "speaking Krèyol telling me he is Haitian, how can I tell he is a Haitian? He does not have a stamp on his head saying that."

The importance of documentation, and having the correct documentation to prove birth and parentage again stands out. Wooding notes, however, that "it's very difficult for people born here to acquire Haitian nationality" because of problems with documentation in Haiti.[44] The JCE agrees, stating that it is one of its biggest obstacles in trying to put its civil registry system in order (Government of the Dominican Republic 2013a, 7); while Charpantier, who is Dominican of Haitian descent admits, "we also have the problem that there isn't a culture of documentation on the part of Haitians in Haiti itself. That has to be said, too." Delienne again takes umbrage at this claim. He states that "it is not true" that "Haitians do not have documents" as "there are laws that facilitate their acquisition. . . . [I]f a person says that he does not have a birth certificate, my question is going to be, 'Where do you live?' Look, we have 550 rural sections in the country [Haiti] and each one has its own functionary to give documentation. This doesn't just happen in city centers."

Delienne thus argues that "No one in the world can tell me that the Haitian government is not going to give citizenship to its citizens. . . . But there are NGOs that are saying that the Haitian government does not want to give them citizenship. Look, they are in the business of talking poorly about officials and saying that I do not do my job because that's what they have to do to get money for their work." He then explains how the embassy—akin to its Bahamian-based counterpart—tries to reach out to those born in the country of Haitian descent who lack identity documents or birth certificates through mobile registration units every Saturday. He says, however, that he cannot force an individual to use their services: "it is the person who must first want to do it."

A publication by the Dominican Republic's National Office of Statistics contradicts the claims that Haitians are unable to acquire identity documents from Haiti and supports Delienne's assertion instead. In the "First National Survey of Immigrants in the Dominican Republic," NOS finds that 92.6 percent of those born in Haiti, living in the DR, have a birth certificate, while 51.9 percent of them possess a Haitian ID. It is those born in the Dominican Republic who lack documentation, with only 55.3 percent of such persons possessing a Dominican birth certificate and even fewer possessing a Dominican ID or passport (Government of the Dominican Republic 2013c, 31).[45] Thus, based on this study, the documentation issue lies on the Dominican side.

Several of the individuals whom I interviewed believe that the Dominican Republic readily violates the Convention on the Rights of the Child (CRC), which it ratified in 1991, because it deprives children of citizenship documents or denies citizenship to those born on Dominican soil because of the irregular status of their parents. Paraison, for example, says that "Many times they talk about how the parents arrived and stayed in an unlawful manner, but this argument clashes with the Convention on the Rights of the

Child that children cannot be responsible for the status of their parents."[46] Furthermore, the International Convention on the Protection of the Rights of All Migrant Workers and Members of Their Families (UN 1990) clearly stipulates in Article 29 that "Each child of a migrant worker shall have the right to a name, to registration of birth and to a nationality."

As noted earlier, in Sentence TC/0168/13, which gives constitutional weight to the government's practices of denationalization, the Constitutional Court holds that the migratory status of parents is not being transferred to children. Yet in this very Sentence the majority of justices find Deguis responsible for violating the Constitution by seeking a cédula. They state that she "cannot take advantage of her own fault and receive Dominican nationality through such an illegal act [initial 'irregular' birth registration]"[47] (Government of the Dominican Republic 2013e, 11). But it was Deguis's parents who performed the "act" of registering her birth with their fichas. Deguis was only trying to obtain her cédula for the first time, using a previously issued and approved Dominican birth certificate. She is thus being held responsible for the actions of her parents, which is clearly in violation of the Convention on the Rights of the Child.

Furthermore, it is interesting to note that the JCE, in Resolution 02-2007, does not focus on all of Article 7 of the Convention when explaining the function of the foreigner's registry book. Article 7 of the CRC states that "The child shall be registered immediately after birth and shall have the right from birth to a name, the right to acquire a nationality and, as far as possible, the right to know and be cared for by his or her parents" (UN 1989). In resolution 02-2007, the JCE only acknowledges that the CRC "established as a principle, that each child, regardless of the parents' migratory status, has the right to a name and to birth registration" (Government of the Dominican Republic 2007a 3). It mentions nothing about the right to a nationality, clearly illustrating the JCE's disregard for this right.

Worse still, three of the five study participants from El Caño were unable to register their child's birth, much less obtain a Dominican birth certificate or proof of citizenship for them because they had been the victims of identity theft. Whereas in The Bahamas an alleged black market exists for Bahamian birth certificates, in the Dominican Republic corrupt local JCE officers will purportedly sell someone's identity documents to another individual for the right price. Thus when these young women from El Caño went to their local JCE office to try and obtain their cédulas they were told that their cédula had already been issued to someone else. Unable to acquire their identity documents, these young Dominican-born women have been unable to register the births of their own Dominican-born children, placing them at risk of statelessness.

Part of the problem in the high number of unregistered persons may be that people do not know what they are supposed to do or where they are supposed to go in terms of registration because, depending on whether one was born prior to the 2010 constitutional amendment or not, a different set of laws is in operation with regard to the acquisition of Dominican nationality. As a UNHCR officer points out, "People are extremely confused on what legal framework applies to them. . . . What happens [is] mothers don't know anymore if they're supposed to register children in the civil registration offices or in the consulate." Gamboa adds that a "grey area" exists especially for those born in the Dominican Republic between 2004, when Ley 285-04 was passed, and the actual constitutional amendment of 2010. For this and the other reasons explained above, the risk of statelessness looms large in the Dominican Republic.

Statelessness

As I describe above, since the 2005 IACtHR decision in *Yean and Bosico*, the Dominican Republic seems to have changed its domestic legislation, and reinforced its political practices, in such a way that it increases the likelihood of forced displacement in situ in the country. With the current equation of "in transit" to illegality and nonresidency, and the JCE's refusal to grant Dominican birth certificates to many children born prior to 2010, individuals are finding themselves unable to enjoy their right to a Dominican nationality. Whereas it used to be that individuals born prior to the 2010 constitutional amendment were being rendered stateless via administrative fiat,[48] today denationalization has found judicial approval in Sentence TC/0168/13 of the Constitutional Court and is affecting tens, if not hundreds, of thousands of people.

The Dominican Republic is not alone in engaging in mass denationalization. The most prominent example, discussed in Chapter 2, is the denationalization of Jews and other minorities during the World War II era. In recent years, however, several states have engaged in mass denationalization. Mauritania confiscated the citizenship documents of, and then expelled, tens of thousands of its black, "non-Arab" citizens during the 1980s and 1990s

(Lynch and Calabia 2007; Manby 2009); Bhutan confiscated the citizenship cards of its ethnic Lhotshampa citizens (Bradley 2013, 198); Ethiopia summarily denationalized hundreds of thousands of its ethnic Eritreans at the end of the last century (Manby 2009; Campbell 2014); and, in the past two years, the Republic of Sudan denationalized those citizens who had involuntarily acquired the citizenship of the newly formed Republic of South Sudan (Sanderson 2014). The act of creating people who no longer formally belong is not, therefore, a relic of Arendt's dark times.

The Inter-American Commission on Human Rights, which visited the Dominican Republic in December 2013, found that "The violations of the right to nationality that the Commission observed during its last onsite visit, in 1997, continue, and the situation has been exacerbated as a result of Judgment TC/0168/2013 of the Constitutional Court." In fact, the Commission argues that this Sentence "denationalized a broad group of people born in the Dominican Republic between 1929 and 2010" and that this denationalization was both arbitrary and retroactive, leading to statelessness (OAS 2013a n. pag.).

The Dominican government claims that Sentence TC/0168/13 is not a means of denationalization, but a "regularization plan" (Kajouee 2014); and, along with The Bahamas, claims that these people are not stateless, but Haitian under Haitian law. In Sentence TC/0168/13, for instance, the Constitutional Court held that Deguis "has a full right to Haitian nationality because she is the daughter of Haitian parents" (Government of the Dominican Republic 2013e, 78) and that the Dominican government's refusal to give citizenship to the children of "in transit" foreigners "does not under any circumstances generate statelessness" (77). It bears stressing again, however, that just because a person has the potential to acquire a given nationality does not mean that the person is actually recognized as a national of a given state in practice.

Whereas Ambassador Rodrigue notes that individuals have a "potential" Haitian nationality in the Bahamian case, Delienne is careful to say that people have a right to Haitian citizenship, but that citizenship is not automatically granted just because an individual is born to a Haitian parent. The parent must have the appropriate documentation to prove Haitian nationality in order to pass it on to his or her child. Additionally, and as I note in Chapter 3, not all individuals born to Haitian parents have the right to Haitian citizenship. If a child is born outside Haiti to a Haitian mother but a non-Haitian father, for instance, Haitian law is clear that the child takes the nationality of the father until he or she reaches the age of majority and is then able to make a declaration at a district court in Haiti for citizenship (Beaubrun 2008, 16). In the eyes of Haitian law, then, the child of a Dominican father and a Haitian mother is a Dominican regardless of the residency status of the mother.[49] While Dominican law recognizes the child of a Dominican as a Dominican citizen irrespective of the legal status of their noncitizen parent (Government of the Dominican Republic 2013a, 6), it does not recognize the right to Dominican nationality of a child born on Dominican soil to noncitizen parents who are not legal residents or who are "in transit." Statelessness thus arises when the child is born to a Haitian mother who does not possess a cédula demonstrating legal residence and who cannot prove that her child's father is Dominican.

As Saint-Pierre Beaubrun observes, "But in reality, many of the children born of such unions are not registered. The Dominican father often abandons the mother even before the child is born and, without means or resources, and lacking documentation and facing marginalization, she has no opportunity to register her child" (2008, 22; author's translation). Confusion over where to register one's child further complicates the situation. As the UNHCR participant points out with regard to the pink birth declarations, "They don't know what those documents mean. So they think that if they register their children in the foreigner's book they are Dominican. But as you know, they become stateless."

Although, as described above, the Haitian Embassy makes an important effort to register its citizens who live in the Dominican Republic, it does not as readily accept as Haitian those children born on Dominican soil prior to the 2010 constitutional amendment. Leonardo asserts that while the Dominican state says these individuals are not Dominican because of the "in transit" status of their parents, "the Haitian State says they are not Haitian and that this is the Dominican Republic's problem."[50] Most recently, the Haitian minister of foreign affairs, Lener Renauld, confirms Leonardo's assertion. In an interview for CNN Español, Minister Renauld openly states that "We do not want to accept Haitians or foreigners who were born in the Dominican Republic whom the Dominican Republic wants to expel." He later reiterates, "We are not going to accept people that the Dominican Republic does not want" (CNN Español 2015, n. pag.; author's translation).[51]

Minister Renauld is referring to the deportation of Dominican persons of Haitian descent, which has been exacerbated by the expiration of Ley 169-14 (Government of the Dominican Republic 2014c). Ley 169-14 was created to mitigate the effects of Sentence TC/0168/13 by providing paths to regularization for those who had been denationalized. While not challenging the Constitutional Court's interpretation of how Dominican nationality should be acquired, the Dominican state recognized that it had to address the repercussions of this Sentence upon those born on Dominican territory between 1929 and 2007 to nonresident parents.

Consequently Ley 169-14 creates different classes of individuals and paths to Dominican citizenship dependent on whether a person was born to nonresident parents who registered them or not. Thus, the law provides for Dominican nationality and the issuance of a cédula to those whose parents registered them using documents that were allegedly not valid for registration at the time (such as the ficha). Individuals who meet this criterion fall into Group A. Those born on Dominican soil, but to nonresident parents who never registered them, must register in the foreigner's book. They are known as Group B. According to Ley 169-14, members of Group B have sixty days from the date of their registration in the foreigner's book to follow the instructions laid out in Decree No. 327-13, also known as the National Plan,[52] to regularize their status. Once their status is regularized, and after the passage of two years, they can then apply for naturalization.

According to Dominican authorities, in the eighteen-month period provided for persons to regularize their status, more than 350,000 people did so (El Caribe 2015). Of this number, approximately 12,000 were individuals who were irregularly registered by their "non-resident" parents between 1929 and 2007 and who have now received documentation that shows they are Dominican nationals. Just under 9,000 persons, born in the country to nonresident parents who did not register their births, are now registered in the foreigner's civil registry book and can eventually begin the process of naturalization (El Caribe 2015).

Although the Dominican government considers the regularization of so many individuals to be a success, Ley 169-14 and the National Plan have not been without criticism. James Goldston, executive director of the Open Society Justice Initiative, for example, remarks how

the new Law's [169-14] recognition of citizenship is based not on the fact of birth itself on Dominican territory, but rather on whether a birth was officially registered at the time. This creates continuing legal uncertainties. . . . [M]any Dominicans of Haitian descent, particularly those living in poverty, were either unable or actively prevented from registering births during the 1929–2007 period. As a result, they will still lose Dominican citizenship, and *may be rendered stateless.*

Secondly, the law lets stand the doctrine articulated by the Constitutional Tribunal that birth registration during the 1929–2007 period only bestows citizenship if the parents had formal status as migrants. However, much of the migration of laborers and their families from Haiti during the 20th century was informal. (Open Society Justice Initiative 2014, n. pag.; italics added)

The forced displacement of those whose birth was not registered prior to 2007 is glaringly apparent not only in that they lose the Dominican citizenship they once held via birth on the territory, but that they must also register as noncitizens. As Goldston states, "The process *forces* individuals who were legally Dominican to declare themselves to be foreigners, in the hope of eventually obtaining citizenship again" (Open Society Justice Initiative 2014, n. pag; italics added). The Robert F. Kennedy Human Rights Center similarly opines that the process "violate[s] their right to a nationality . . . as it *forces them* to declare themselves foreigners and does not reinstate their nationality in a fair and immediate manner" (2015, 2; italics added, author's translation). The center then remarks how numerous persons who fall into category B were unable to register in the foreigner's book:

they could not register due to lack of information, extremely complicated and costly application requirements, the many weaknesses in the implementation process on the part of the Government, and the time limit in which to do it. As a result, tens of thousands of Dominicans of Haitian descent are stateless and undocumented, without any ability to exercise their rights as citizens and extremely vulnerable to exploitation and illegal deportation. (Robert F. Kennedy Human Rights Center 2015, 2; author's translation)[53]

Thus, not only are persons being forcibly displaced and turned into foreigners in their own country, but some are at risk of being relocated to a place that they may have never even visited, much less lived in (Haiti).[54] Although the collective deportations that some envisioned would take place when the opportunity to regularize one's status expired in June 2015 have not occurred, allegations exist that Dominicans of Haitian descent are being deported. IOM, which carried out a country mission trip between June and July 2015, interviewed more than a thousand deported persons. Of this number, a third stated that they were born in the Dominican Republic (IOM 2015, n. pag.). Earlier in the year, Amnesty International similarly reported that Dominican-born persons were being deported "without due process to Haiti" (Amnesty International 2015, n. pag.).

Akin to their Bahamian counterparts, the situation of individuals of Haitian descent in the DR is further exacerbated by the fact that the Dominican government has not ratified either of the two statelessness conventions. It signed the 1961 Convention on the Reduction of Statelessness, but never instantiated the convention's provisions into domestic legislation via ratification. Based on current practice, it does not appear that the country will be ratifying either of these conventions any time soon either. Furthermore, the Dominican Republic has no statelessness status determination procedures, which means that it has no definitive way to identify who is and who is not a national in a transparent manner to ensure that those they are denationalizing are, in fact, Haitian nationals in practice. Statelessness, therefore, looms large. Figure 6 provides a graphic depiction of the risk factors that contribute to statelessness in the country.

Conclusion

This chapter shows that the maintenance of formal belonging, via citizenship, is not a guaranteed status. What can be given to you at birth, via the laws in operation at the time, can be taken away when laws are either retroactively applied (Ley 285-04, the Constitutional Amendment) or are interpreted in a different way (the "in transit" clause of the 1939 law). Although the Dominican Republic has engaged in exclusionary membership practices for many years, it was not until 2013 that such acts found judicial sanction by the country's Constitutional Court in Sentence TC/0168/13. Hundreds of thousands of people were summarily stripped of their Dominican citizenship and forced into a situation where "not belonging [to the community of their birth was] no longer a matter of choice" (Arendt [1948] 2004, 376). Figure 7 provides a timeline of the principal judicial cases and political

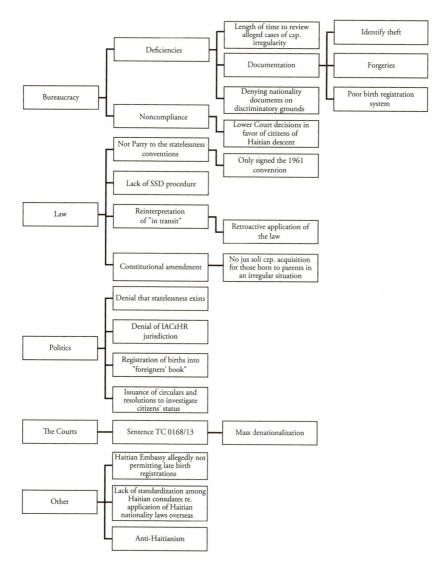

Figure 6. Risk factors for statelessness: Dominican Republic.

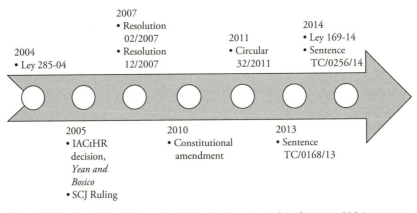

Figure 7. Timeline of Dominican Republic statelessness-related events, 2004–present.

processes that have affected the formal belonging of Dominicans of Haitian descent since 2004.

This chapter also reveals the many ways in which people can be forcibly displaced into liminality outside of the strictly legal sphere. Statelessness may occur through the application of policies and procedures such as the Junta Central Electoral's various resolutions and circulars that order local JCE officials to investigate the citizenship documents of "irregular" persons and then let languish the cases of such persons. Statelessness may take place because of outright document denial on discriminatory grounds or because of corruption, wherein one's citizenship documents are given to someone else. Additionally, statelessness may result because those who could qualify for Haitian citizenship are unable to obtain it due to the undocumented status of their parents, or because their parents chose not to get Haitian identity documents for them. As in the Bahamian case, Haitian parents sometimes "abstain from it [registering their child at the Haitian Embassy], whether because of ignorance or because they would like to bestow the enjoyment of the rights and privileges inherent in Dominican citizenship to their offspring" (Beaubrun 2008, 21; author's translation). Some of them may even "prefer to remain stateless instead of becoming Haitian" (22; author's translation).

That some of them would prefer not to be "forced to be Haitian"[55] is unsurprising since most of these individuals grew up "Dominican." Many were provided Dominican identity documents and were Dominican citizens until the retroactive application of Ley 285-04 and the implementation of resolutions 02/2007 and 12/2007. Unlike the individuals of Haitian descent born in The Bahamas, therefore, these persons once formally belonged to the state of their birth—in this case, the Dominican Republic.

Whereas this chapter and the previous one demonstrate how the forced displacement of persons into liminality or into the category of Haitian national can occur outside of conflict or crisis situations, the next chapter shows how the effects of The Bahamas and the Dominican Republic's exclusionary membership practices reach beyond the realms of law and politics. They have significant repercussions on these individuals' sense of place identity, their ability to access other human rights, and their capacity to carry out key life projects. Immobilized, or displaced in situ, these individuals discover that personhood does not suffice for them to enjoy the rights that supposedly no longer attach to citizenship in a postnational world.

PART III

Noncitizen Insiders and
the Right to Belong

CHAPTER 5

Noncitizen Insiders

Citizenship . . . is also experienced by those who lack
presence within the nation and are unintelligible
according to the master-narrative of sovereignty as they
neither belong, nor are they outsiders, vis-à-vis the state.
—Ní Mhurchú

Whereas the two previous chapters examine how the human right to a nationality is instantiated in reality through the operation of a state's laws
and practices, this chapter investigates the repercussions that being forcibly
displaced in situ has upon the stateless. Far from being a mere legal anomaly,
statelessness affects a person's ability to carry out key life projects and ham-
pers her or his ability to enjoy many other human rights. Thus, like their
stateless counterparts elsewhere in the world (see Chapter 2), stateless persons in The Bahamas and the Dominican Republic are unable to rely on their
mere personhood to access rights, freedoms, and protections. Moreover,
their peculiar form of forced displacement generates an ambiguous sense
of place identity. They do not know where they belong, even though they
remain physically rooted in the place of their birth.

Ambiguous Belonging

In their work on irregular citizenship, Peter Nyers (2011) and Aoileann Ní
Mhurchú (2015) explain how people can be culturally and legally part of a
nation as citizens, but outsiders nonetheless. These individuals, often the racialized other, are holders of "irregular citizenship." The formal citizenship

status they possess does not function adequately "or is irregularized due to the negation of rights, duties, and obligations through informal and unofficial means" (160). These people, while having an officially recognized citizen identity,[1] often bear the image of the migrant outsider on their bodies. They exist in a world of "cultural limbo" where they belong neither to "the world of migration or the world of citizenship" (167).

The noncitizen insiders (Belton 2011) of whom I write are in a similar position to the holders of "irregular citizenship" in Nyers and Ní Mhurchú's accounts. They exist in an ambiguous space of neither "here nor there"—the realm of liminality. What distinguishes the noncitizen insiders in this book from the irregular citizenship of which Nyers and Ní Mhurchú write, however, is that they do not formally belong to any state in practice. They are stateless. Furthermore, whereas the holders of irregular citizenship are made so via "informal and unofficial means," as I illustrate in the two previous chapters, Bahamian- and Dominican-born persons of Haitian descent are displaced in situ by a confluence of formal and official means (as well as informal and unofficial ones).

The ambiguous position of noncitizen insiders is perhaps even more pronounced than that of irregular citizens. As I illustrate in the Bahamian case, their ambiguity is heightened in that they are officially denied citizenship for the first eighteen years of their life and then provided the possibility (but not the guarantee) of acquiring Bahamian citizenship upon reaching adulthood. During this time, their "out of place-ness" is doubly compounded if they are not recognized *in practice* as a citizen of another state (in this case, Haiti). As persons who are born of noncitizens in The Bahamas then, they bear the image of the migrant on their bodies, akin to irregular citizens. Unlike the latter, however, they are legally excluded from formal belonging in the country of their birth. As Dumercy remarks,

> The Bahamas don't want to claim you and Haiti don't either. . . . Like we always say, "Bahamas don't want us and Haiti don't want us." So we are on our own basically. We're in limbo. We are on our own because we don't really have anyone looking out for us or looking for our interests to protect us. [Haitians say], "You wasn't born here, you're a Bahamian." But then . . . it's the same thing where the Bahamians say, "Well you're born of Haitian parents, you're Haitian."[2] So that's why a lot of us [are] saying we're stateless or we're in limbo because the Haitians don't look at us as part of them. . . . Haiti don't

look at you as part of their country and, well, literally you could say The Bahamas don't want you to be part of their country until you're 18, until you're an adult.

In the Dominican case, individuals who were forcibly displaced into liminality (or "forced to be Haitian") via Sentence TC/0168/13 were, as I explain in the previous chapter, once Dominican citizens and grew up thinking they were Dominican. Some of them clearly identify with being Dominican, but admit they no longer know where they belong. Unlike irregular citizens, then, they, too, are rendered liminals by formal and official means. Like their Bahamian counterparts, and perhaps even more so given the racialized nature of anti-immigrant discourse in the Dominican Republic, they bear the imprint of the migrant on their body, but are excluded from the country of their birth. In both the Bahamian and the Dominican cases then, the stateless suffer an ambiguous place identity akin to irregular citizens, but their situation is all the more problematic because they lack citizenship and often the means to challenge their exclusion through the formal and official channels by which they are rendered stateless.

Using Victor Turner's (1984) work on liminality as a basis, I thus demonstrate how the realm of statelessness is more than one where the law ceases to operate. It is one in which an individual's place in the world becomes ambiguous, or even outright negated. We have not, therefore, come very far from Arendt's conclusion that "the loss of citizenship deprived people not only of protection, but also of all clearly established, officially recognized identity" (Arendt [1948] 2004, 364).

Liminality

Liminality is a term that has been used to describe the experience of stateless people (Thomassen 2009, 19). It refers to the condition of being between statuses (Riggan 2011), "be these fixed cultural classifications or more formalised legal statuses" (Hynes 2011, 2). One arrives at this liminal space through separation from one's former identity and only leaves it via a rite of passage, taking on another identity in the process (Beech 2011, 287). Sometimes the transition from one identity to the next does not go as expected, however, and people become stranded in the liminal stage (Higgot and Nossal 1997, 170). They remain in limbo, as "entities that are neither here nor there; they are betwixt and between the positions assigned and arranged by law, custom, convention, and ceremonials. . . . They elude or slip through the network of classifications that normally locates states and positions in cultural space" (Turner [1969]1995, cited in Rumelili 2003, 220).

As I explain in the next chapter, the stateless fall outside the framework of international law and practice wherein each person is supposed to belong to some state as its national. They are "noncitizen insiders" (Belton 2011). They are insiders because they have not migrated from elsewhere. They remain, for the most part, in the states where they were born. Yet they are noncitizens because the state either rejects them as members or does not fully provide the means by which they can be prevented from falling into statelessness. The stateless have thus undergone the first stage of the initiation rite, separation. They are separated from formal citizenship through citizenship denial or deprivation in the countries of their birth. Yet, unable to take on formal citizenship, they remain "betwixt and between," in a space of invisibility, impurity, rightlessness, and reflection (Turner [1984] in Beech 2011, 287).

Invisibility

As Nic Beech, interpreting Turner (1984), explains, "the liminar[3] is socially if not physically invisible. Their ambiguity means that they are outside definition" (2011, 287). Statelessness scholarship is replete with terms expressing the invisibility of stateless populations. In Arendt's time stateless people were referred to as "'displaced persons' . . . for the express purpose of liquidating statelessness once and for all by ignoring its existence" (Arendt [1948] 2004). Today adjectives such as "ghosts" and "voiceless," and the use of euphemisms such as "without status" and "erased persons," are used to describe them.[4] Not only are the stateless described as invisible, but they are often numerically invisible as well. Most countries do not collect data on their stateless populations and neither The Bahamas nor the Dominican Republic does so.[5] It is thus often hard to gauge the extent of statelessness, which, in turn, affects policy responses toward them.

While the previously stateless or at risk participants interviewed for this study do not describe themselves as invisible, those who were not stateless, but citizens of the Dominican Republic, Haiti, or some other third country, do use the term to describe them. The Dominican UNDP officer explains how without a national ID card (cédula), people are "invisible. . . . They are not subjects of the law. They don't exist as citizens."[6] While admitting that "Yes, as human beings [they exist] because they are present," the officer emphasizes that they "do not exist in the civil sense of the word." Leonardo agrees, observing that if an individual in the Dominican Republic does not possess a birth certificate or a national ID, "civilly you do not exist." This premise stands in direct contrast to the postnational claim that personhood is what counts in the contemporary era.[7]

In those instances when they are given formal citizenship, many formerly stateless persons are still "invisible" as they are denied social recognition as a Bahamian or a Dominican citizen. As Hanauer, discussing the different types of relationships migrants can have to their host communities observes, "Legal citizenship does not mean acceptance within the nation-state" (2011, 202).[8] Several interviewees express this concern. Dolce observes how Bahamians "still see me as Haitian" even though he now has Bahamian citizenship. "For example when I go to work, if a Haitian comes into the office to make a complaint they say, 'You ga deal with your people.' They don't see me as Bahamian." Dumercy similarly states that even after obtaining Bahamian citizenship, "people are calling me 'this Haitian girl in the back of there.' Is there any change? No. So it's like the quality of life is still the same. I still have to battle. And the thing is, if anything, I have to now carry my passport everywhere—to maybe say, 'Yeah, okay, I'm a Bahamian.'" Dumercy and others like her are thus invisible as citizens or "true" Bahamians despite citizenship acquisition.

Julian Lockhart, a Bahamian of non-Haitian descent who wrote on Haitian Bahamian events as a journalist for the *Tribune*, observes how many individuals of Haitian descent born in The Bahamas are not considered fully "Bahamian" even when citizenship is acquired. Discussing the "negative connotation" that adheres to Bahamians' usage of "Bahaitian," "Bahamian Haitian," and "Haitian Bahamian," he says that "What it is, is Bahamians are letting you know, 'Hey, you may be Bahamian by status, but you're not a Bahamian. We might accept you [legally], but don't get yourself fooled [into] actually thinking you are a Bahamian.'"[9] Dolce concurs, adding that "the real issue is being recognized as a Bahamian if you're born here or if you've spent all your life here."

The societal rejection of the naturalized "Other" is part of a "shift towards xenophobic restrictionism," which, according to Gaim Kibreab, "is increasingly a universal pattern" (1999, 400). Describing the rejection faced by refugees in host countries, Kibreab explains how states, communities and individuals within geographically bounded spaces have become more territorial than ever before. Because of this, territorially-based identity has become a scarce resource which is jealously guarded and protected by those who perceive themselves as standing to lose by an influx of refugees or immigrants from other countries. (1999, 400)

In the Bahamian case at least, the guarding of a territorially defined identity is displayed when people are judged to be a "true true" Bahamian or not. "True, true" Bahamians are those who are able to trace their ancestry back to one of the Family Islands and who, in the words of one interviewee, "have a name that we can associate with one of those Family Islands, some settlement or community in one of those Family Islands." "True true" Bahamians are also black,[10] but not as black as their Haitian counterparts. As a prominent talk show personality points out,

the character, the tone, the construction that Bahamians have of Haitians is almost identical to so many racist constructions of them—of black people generally. . . . So they [Bahamians] did not create it, but they have embraced it. And they see themselves on a hierarchy of being in which the Haitian is beneath them. And that's class prejudice as well as ethnic difference.[11]

A lawyer and former government official concurs, stating that "the so-called true Bahamian sees himself as socially superior to these immigrants [the Haitians] and wants to maintain that social separation, doesn't want equalization."[12] This interviewee went on to say that it has little to do with race, however, but is more of a "class and status" issue. He continues,

Bahamian prejudice toward Haitians is something that transcends race altogether. It has nothing to do with race. It has more to do with the stratification of society along class lines and that historically a person who is born here of Bahamian parents is accorded a higher social status than a person who has either come here from Haiti or who is the immediate child of Haitian parents.

Whether or not the rejection of the Haitian noncitizen insider is due to perceived racial, ethnic, or class differences, it affects the way in which

Bahamians, Haitians, and Bahamians of Haitian descent interact with—and view—each other. Bahamians generally consider Haitians "an undifferentiated mass" (Craton and Saunders 1998, 455), made up of "illegal immigrant[s]" (Marshall 1979, 54; Fielding et al. 2008, 44). As one interviewee observes, "That's where the problem comes, they just say illegal for everyone . . . because to most people every Haitian born in the Bahamas is an illegal."[13] A former Bahamian government official is also emphatic that children born to undocumented parents are illegal: "if you're illegal, you should not be able to produce a person who becomes legal when they are born here."[14] Jn-Simon faced this forced categorization first-hand at the College of The Bahamas forum on "21st Century Slavery in The Bahamas: A Discussion on Statelessness" in October 2012.[15] After she spoke about what it is like to be stateless in the country of her birth, an audience member approached her and "had the audacity to tell me that I was born here illegally."

The premise that children born of Haitian descent are largely "illegal" is not specific to The Bahamas. The equation of Haitians with an unwelcome and unauthorized presence—domestic labor needs and evidence of work permits notwithstanding—is apparent in the Dominican Republic, too. Human Rights Watch captures then head of the Dominican Army Manuel Polanco, likewise stating that "An illegal person cannot produce a legal person" (2002, 22). Additionally, and as in the Bahamian case, many people in Dominican society view Haitians as an undifferentiated mass or illegals.[16] As discussed in Chapter 4, the inability of many Dominicans to accept otherwise hails in part from the particularly strong and historical form of anti-Haitianism that exists in the country. This anti-Haitianism, while not rendering people of Haitian descent completely invisible, takes away their humanity.

Impurity

Even when not rendered invisible or emplaced in the space of their skin color, individuals of Haitian descent are often described in derogatory terms or associated with unclean or impure practices.[17] This is a common phenomenon "when people, things and practices are seen as 'out-of-place'" (Cresswell 2004, 103). During Arendt's time the stateless were described as "the scum of the earth" (Arendt [1948] 2004, 341), "outlaw(s)" (360, 363) and "barbarians" (384). In the Caribbean context, they are often associated with unclean animals such as pigs, hogs, or dogs. For example, Dominican anthropologist Tahira Vargas comments on how Dominicans often say that "all Haitians are dogs."[18] In their report to the UN Human Rights Council on the situation in the Dominican Republic, Doudou Diène and Gay McDougall[19] also recount how "references [were] made to blacks as being 'pig feed,' ignorant or unhygienic" (UN HRC 2008c, 13).

One of the two local politicians interviewed in Abaco, Bahamas, consistently compares the people living in Haitian settlements in Abaco to hogs. For example, when describing the living conditions of those of Haitian descent, the person says that "only hogs can live like that."[20] When discussing crime in the settlements and how locals attempt to get a "Haitian Bahamian" informant from within the communities to identify any illegal activity, the interviewee says that "the Bahamian-Haitian will say yes, but he never does [act as an informant] because *they don't squeal on their own breed. They don't squeal.*" The same participant, when asked about solutions to the issues surrounding citizenship denial and the problems confronted by people in the settlements, only offered to "bulldoze" the settlement because "as long as they're left there in that square, they'll be the same low-class pigs! Living like pigs." The other local Abaconian official also thought that the settlements should be bulldozed. The individual stated the Bahamian government ought to "hire two big tractors and we push down all those houses which have been built here illegally. Put diesel and gas on it and burn it. *Purify the place.*"[21]

Associations with impurity are also present when the Bahamian-born persons of Haitian descent are associated with criminal activity due to their "betwixt and between" status. As one Abaconian official asserts, "The Haitian Bahamians is the ones that's breaking in and stealing. They're the worst. The Haitian-Haitians aren't half as bad as the Haitian Bahamians."[22] The interviewee continues,

Haitian-Haitians are nicer people than Bahamian Haitians. The Bahamian Haitians is too biggity. They too sassy. They too stealing, into stealing. The Bahamian-Haitians are worse. A Haitian Haitian, like this man I'm talking about,[23] they're more trustworthy. They don't steal. I wouldn't say you might find one out of a hundred that steals out of the Haitian Haitians, but the whole hundred of Bahamian Haitians will steal.

The interviewee attributes the criminal nature of Bahamian-born persons of Haitian descent to the fact that "They don't know where they belong. They're not accepted. They're not accepted by the Haitians and they're not accepted by the Bahamians." The other Abaconian official, after declaring that "Bahamians are peaceful people, generally speaking," affirms that "Any time you find these fellas getting out of hand and they're doing the serious, serious cruel acts, check it close—some kind of Haitian blood mix."[24] Thus the fact that they are neither Bahamian nor Haitian, but some "impure" mixture of the two, results in their criminal inclinations in the latter interviewee's eyes.

Due to their "impure" nature, individuals of Haitian descent must therefore be contained. As Beech explains, liminals "are regarded as unclean with contact being prohibited or curtailed during liminality lest they should 'pollute' those who have not been 'inoculated' against them" (2011, 287). The settlements where many persons of Haitian descent reside within The Bahamas and the Dominican Republic are often in poor condition, separated from citizens' homes. Batey residents for example, housed in settlements adjacent to sugarcane plantations, "live in pitiable conditions with no access to running water, sanitation or electricity. . . . They live in informally constructed shelters with dirt floors" (UN HRC 2008c, 24). In its study of HIV/AIDS in the bateyes, the Center for Social and Demographic Studies (CESDEM)[25] found that nearly 40 percent of the homes of Haitian migrants lacked sanitation facilities, with only 12 percent having a fully operational toilet (2008, 21).

On my visit to the batey of El Caño in 2013, I was taken to the home of a person who had the only private latrine in the neighborhood. The only way to flush the toilet was to carry water from an outside water source and fill the tank. The home had cement floors, but no covering for the floors. It had several bedrooms, but no doors. Curtains served to separate one space from another. Inside the bedrooms, plywood, covered with a sheet, lay on top of box springs to serve as mattresses. The house was minimalist in nature, but it was not dirty.

During my visit to the settlements of The Mud and The Peas in Abaco in 2012, I noticed that the homes were haphazardly placed, many with barely a walkway between them. Due to the fact that many settlement residents in The Bahamas "still cook outside on charcoal burner stoves" (Weatherford 2011, 108) and that several homes illegally tap into one electricity source, fires often break out in these communities. Pastor Robin Weatherford, who has worked with and ministered to the Haitian community in Abaco for decades, notes that "A feeling of dread never fails to enter our mind when we look out our windows to see a plume of black smoke rising from that area, knowing that it more than likely could be disastrous" (108).[26]

Besides vulnerability to fires, the homes in The Mud and The Peas are surrounded by dirt roads that are prone to flooding whenever hurricanes or storms pass through because of the settlements' location on reclaimed swamp land. As in many bateyes in the DR, the majority of homes in The Mud and The Peas also lack access to running water, sanitation, or electricity. When I visited The Mud, however, I did not observe any open cesspits (as are often rumored to exist), and the homes appeared to be well maintained despite their close proximity and largely wooden frameworks.[27] Instead, what struck me was how clearly the settlements were delineated from the surrounding "citizens'" homes.

Whether the delineation between the spaces where the descendants of Haitian migrants live and citizens reside is purposeful in either country, the offspring of Haitian migrants are made to feel separate from, and even "dirty" to, the citizens who surround them. According to Dolce, being a "Haitian" was made to "seem like it's a bad thing. A child growing up . . . [is hearing] a Haitian is something bad" and ends up "thinking 'I don't want to be Haitian no more. Haitian is bad. Haitian is a bad thing.'" Louis agrees, stating that "the term Haitian, growing up for me, that stigma was always this concept that 'They're illiterate. They're poor' and such."

Jn-Simon believes that it is worse than that, "it almost seems as if in this country [The Bahamas] to be a Haitian, you're ostracized almost like a person who has HIV."[28] She tells the story of her younger sister who was teased at primary school because of her Haitian ethnicity and how her sister stopped speaking Krèyol; "she would even tell you that she is not a Haitian. The way how she felt when she went to school and children would tell her—like this one girl in particular would tell her that she looks like garbage or 'You need to go back on the boat with your mother.'" Akin to The Bahamas, Diène and McDougall found in the Dominican case that "'Haitian' is also used as a label for improper behavior, lack of civility, and often as an insult in Dominican society" (UN HRC 2008c, 15).

Petit-Homme insinuates that Bahamians' pejorative use of "Haitian" is more than a means to label someone unclean or uncivil, however; it has strong connotations of enslavement:

it's almost like Haitians now are like the field niggas, you know what I mean? . . . Look at the way they call Haitians. Like if you have a Haitian gardener maybe you call him "My Haitian." . . . But then they [Bahamians of non-Haitian descent] don't like the other Haitians. They want to get rid of all the other ones, but then they want to keep "theirs." And sometimes they even use citizenship-residency papers as leverage. They own these people, you know?

Just as the Atlantic slave trade engendered the deaths of millions of persons of African descent in the New World, Beech explains that during the "impurity" stage of liminality, "there is a link to death" and the liminal "may be ritually buried/lie motionless/stained black/covered in blood" (2011, 287). The "link to death" reveals itself in various ways in the two cases studied here. First, there is the practice of "kill[ing] the juridical personality" of an individual (Arendt [1948] 2004, 577) through document denial and deprivation. According to Chidi Anselm Odinkalu, this is civicide. Describing denationalization procedures in Nigeria, Odinkalu explains, "There are two ways to kill in human community: you can kill a human being or you can kill the citizen. The first is biological; the second is sociological but no less real. The former is called homicide; the latter is civicide" (2009 n. pag.). I explain in Chapters 3 and 4 how the Dominican government (and to a lesser extent the Bahamian government) engages in civicide against its Haitian migrant descended population via practices of citizenship denial and deprivation.

Second, there is the association of blood and death not with the liminals or noncitizen insiders, but with the citizens. For example, when I question the aforementioned local Abaconian official about the effects of a "bulldoze and purify" policy on Bahamian-born children who could one day become Bahamian citizens, the official responds, "That's what's killing us now."[29] Former minister of state for immigration Branville McCartney similarly stated that "We need to stop the bleeding" when it comes to giving citizenship to children born in The Bahamas of "illegal immigrant[s]" (Dames 2011 n. pag.).

In the Dominican context, the portrayal is slightly different. It is not that the Haitians and their descendants are bleeding the non-Haitian citizens dry, but that the latter are perhaps out for the Haitian-descended population's blood. As reported by the Inter-American Commission on Human Rights after its visit to the Dominican Republic in December 2013,

Ana María Belique, a leader and activist with Movimiento Recono-
cido [who had spoken up against Sentence TC/0168/13], reportedly
received threats from individuals via the social media network Twit-
ter: "We're going to have to move Belique to the same barrio where
Sonia Pierre lives" (a reference to a human rights activist and defender
who died in 2011), and "we're ready for anything; if it's blood they
want, blood they shall have." (Organization of American States 2013a
n. pag.)

Jn-Simon relates the story of a Bahamian woman (of non-Haitian descent) who
insinuates that death is the best response to, and place for, Bahamian-born
Haitians: "the best Haitians in The Bahamas are those in the cemetery." Despite sporadic episodes of violence in the Dominican Republic, however, the
stigmatization of and discrimination against Bahamian and Dominican-born
persons of Haitian descent has not engendered the type of ethnic conflict
that occurs in other parts of the world when a minority group is oppressed
or the ethnic majority feels threatened. Nonetheless, and contrary to postnational assertions of the severance of human rights from citizenship, it has
generated a group of people whose access to human rights is seriously curtailed because of their liminal status.

Rightlessness

Beech writes that "during liminality, the liminar has no rights" (2011, 287).
As I illustrate in Chapter 2, statelessness is a condition wherein the fulfillment of rights is contingent at best or nonexistent at worst. This is because
citizenship is an intrinsic human right—important to hold in and of itself—
but also because it is an instrumental human right. Its nonfulfillment leaves
almost every other right in the UDHR susceptible to violation (Belton 2015).
As the IACtHR states in *Yean and Bosico,*

nationality is a prerequisite for recognition of juridical personality . . .
the failure to recognize juridical personality harms human dignity,
because it denies absolutely an individual's condition of being a subject of rights and renders him vulnerable to non-observance of his
rights by the State or other individuals. (2005, 67)[30]

As individuals who occupy a liminal space, the stateless encounter difficulties in accessing many of the rights, freedoms, and protections that citizens take for granted. Specifically, those who are stateless, or at risk of statelessness, in The Bahamas and the Dominican Republic face limits in the areas of education, employment, access to health care and justice, as well as restrictions upon their movement.

As parties to the Convention on the Rights of the Child (UN 1989), both The Bahamas and the Dominican Republic should provide free public elementary education to those children resident in their territories. This does not always occur in practice, however. One participant, who ministers in the Haitian community in The Bahamas, notes that when Haitian migrants go to register their children for school they are sometimes turned away and told that registration is not taking place for a few more weeks yet when, in fact, registration is underway. When the Haitian parent returns, registration is closed. This interviewee also says that some Haitians have set up a school of their own to get around this type of discrimination, noting that children coming from Haiti are even less likely to be able to attend public school than their Bahamian-born counterparts: "children who [are] born in Haiti, who come here, you have a 90% chance they will never take them in [public] school. . . . They will have to go to private school."[31]

While an elementary school administrator in Abaco asserts that all children are provided elementary school education, the interviewee also states that "we will not register a child without any documents" because "we risk exposing the children to danger in terms of health if we do that. . . . That's why we say that the immunization card must be up to date." This school official was unable to provide information on how many children have been turned away from this particular Abaco school because of lack of documentation or an up-to-date immunization card, but the participant's comments lead one to question how many children of Haitian descent are being prevented from attending school due to their parent's irregular status/lack of documentation.

Even when these students manage to enroll in school, a few of the Bahamian case study interviewees remark that this education is not free from exposure to discriminatory teachers or classmates. Dumercy, for example, relates how confrontations between Bahamians of non-Haitian descent and "Haitians" would become violent when she attended school. "They would go to war. It became physical. It's not like you [just] feel it mentally, socially, or whatever—it

became physical to some extent. It affects every aspect of your life as a child."
She narrates how children of Haitian descent do not feel the hostility until
"they get to school" because their parents "are very protective" of them.

> So when they get to the schools, a lot of kids, they don't know how to
> handle it. So they react to how they're being treated. You'd be sur-
> prised at how young these little Bahamian kids would come to school
> and they already feel hostile toward Haitians. Why? Because that's
> what they're hearing from their parents. So they already have that
> hostile feeling towards us. So they start picking on these kids or start
> picking fights—and trust me, you fight, they'll fight hard. . . . So then
> they'll always have war.

The aforementioned elementary school administrator in Abaco admits that
sometimes "quarrels" occur between the two groups where one accuses the
other of being "Haitian," "Bahamian," or "black," but that the confrontations
do not get "to the point where it's something that we have to deal with or it
becomes a school problem where we have to look into it."[32]

As concerns the Dominican case, until 2012, the country limited children's
access to post-elementary school education if they lacked a birth certificate
(Féliz 2012).[33] This is one of the reasons why UNDP-DR placed so much em-
phasis on registering school children in its strengthening the civil registry sys-
tem program, discussed in Chapter 4. However, a fact-finding mission to the
Dominican Republic, conducted by Georgetown University Law School's
Human Rights Institute (GULSHRI), found that primary school students of
Haitian descent continue to encounter problems accessing education:

> problems of arbitrary denial of education in primary school still ex-
> ist. Although the Ministry of Education has stated that children are
> allowed to attend primary school while pursuing documentation,
> not all schools seem to understand this policy. Of those interviewed,
> fourteen school officials and families reported that some primary
> schools turn away children without birth certificates, and some offi-
> cials have publicly stated that they are opposed to letting "Haitians"
> attend school. (GULSHRI 2014, 28)

Moreover, high school students allegedly still need to possess a Dominican
birth certificate in order to take the national high school exams, which are

required in order to attend university (UN HRC 2008c, 23). Francía Calis García,[34] for example, a twenty-one-year-old born in the Dominican Republic to Haitian parents had difficulties finishing high school because the local Junta Central Electoral office would not give her a certified copy of her birth certificate. After overcoming many obstacles, she finished high school, but has been unable to attend university or secure a job because the authorities will not grant her a cédula. Participants in the Georgetown study report similar stories, noting that "In contrast to the capricious implementation of state regulations regarding high school enrollment, graduation, and national testing, access to university is uniformly denied to those students over the age of eighteen who are unable to obtain a *cédula*" (GULSHRI 2014, 36).

Several of the participants from El Caño confirm that they were unable to pursue their university studies after completing high school. One notes that although she received good grades in high school and was the recipient of a scholarship for her work, the scholarship was never given to her because she was "from a batey."[35] She feels like she was discriminated against because of her Haitian heritage and adds that the denial of scholarship opportunities to Dominican-born students of Haitian descent "happens a lot."

Interviewees in Civolani Hischnjakow's work (2011) similarly observe how their inability to procure a certified birth certificate from the JCE prevented them from taking the national exam, continuing their postsecondary studies, or taking part in overseas athletic opportunities.[36] "*It prevents me from doing many things*," says Eduardo Dierdito Exilien, such as attending workshops and traveling, visiting the doctor, and continuing his studies, which "is what I most want to do" (2011, 29; italics added). Nico Paredes and Rogelio Exil de La Rosa explain how their athletic careers were cut short and that they were unable to continue their studies as well (31). In addition, the rate of illiteracy among those located in bateyes, such as El Caño, is particularly elevated. Nearly a third of those ten years and older are illiterate (CESDEM 2008, 15), and a quarter of the children aged six and older have no schooling whatsoever (13). The latter statistic is more than double the national rate of 11 percent (15).

The Bahamian-born interviewees of Haitian descent also faced limited educational prospects or roadblocks on their way to finishing high school and attending college. Several explain how they had to pass up educational opportunities overseas because they could not travel to study in the United States using the aforementioned Bahamian-government issued "travel document," or Certificate of Identity. Others note how they had to pay the

non-Bahamian school tuition or "foreigner's fee" at their tertiary institutions in The Bahamas, while most lament their inability to apply for scholar-
ships or take part in extracurricular activities. The immobilization they feel
as a result of their forced displacement in situ is revealed in the italicized
portion of the comments below.

Akin to the participants who were denied athletic opportunities in Civolani Hischnjakow's study, Bahamian-born Louis describes how

> growing up there are many opportunities that came my way, but
> because I didn't have a passport, it kind of like *hindered me*. I could
> just give you one [example]. In high school, I was in athletics, into
> sports pretty good. I had an opportunity to be a part of the Bahamian
> national soccer team, but that chance was crushed because, you know,
> they said that I don't have a Bahamian passport. . . . I was hurt.

Dumercy similarly notes how her younger sister was encouraged by a local
police officer in Abaco to apply to the Ministry of Youth, Sports and Culture
for a sports scholarship. This officer was so impressed with her sister's athletic ability that he personally took the application to Nassau, confidant that
she would get a scholarship. As Dumercy relates, however, the Ministry never
even sent a letter of acknowledgment about the application.

> So to this day what she's doing now actually, is she is working in my
> [other] sister's store—because she has a children's store. That's what
> she's doing now. But this girl could have gone on to run in the Olym-
> pics. This girl had the fastest time. Like, she broke all kinds of rec-
> ords. But because of her last name, *she never got anywhere*. There's a
> lot of talented kids out there who *could have been achieving so much
> more*.

Dumercy also notes that Bahamian-born students of Haitian descent are often passed over for prestigious positions in high school. "I've seen kids who
they don't give you valedictorian because you're Haitian. They'll give you
maybe salutatorian." She says that this type of discrimination happens "every
day . . . it's so regular." Jn-Simon faced this discrimination first-hand. She became Deputy Head Girl, but was actually threatened by a parent of another
(non-Haitian descended) student. This parent, whose daughter had been in
the running for Head Girl, grabbed her and "told me she was investigating

me. . . . Teachers started shifting me in my seats in class. . . . *I was so depressed.* I didn't even want to go to school anymore. It was that serious." Her grades plummeted due to the harassment.

After-school programs, such as the police and nursing cadets, were also off-limits to the Bahamian-born interviewees of Haitian descent. St. Cecile explains how in grade twelve she "wanted to join the cadet corps and I remember the police officer—she was a lady—telling me 'You can't join the cadet corps because you don't have a Bahamian passport.' Yes, I remember that. And then *it hinders you from moving forward.*" Jn-Simon similarly adds how the police cadets, which is "a very, very good program . . . once you go to school under them, they pay for your school tuition," is off-limits to Bahamian-born students of Haitian descent. She adds,

If you don't have a [Bahamian] passport, you can't join the police cadets. Then there is the nursing cadet program where they have this nursing program in high school and then when you get out of high school, they pay for your tuition to go to nursing school. However, if you don't have a passport, you don't get the nursing grant.

Desmangles says that many Bahamian-born children of Haitian descent want to be included and want to participate "in the economic well-being and the growth and the building of this nation. . . . They want opportunities, but *it gets to the point where they are stagnated* from these opportunities." Former attorney general Sears agrees, stating that

some of the highest achieving students are Haitian Bahamian students. The challenge for many of these young people is when they finish high school. They would have done well. Some would have gotten distinction and awards for their academic, athletic, and civic performance within the school, but *they cannot advance . . . they are faced with this roadblock.*

Due to the varied obstacles that immobilize them during high school, and the limited prospects they have of attending a tertiary education institution, Bahamian- and Dominican-born students of Haitian descent often end up either unemployed, underemployed, or engaged in 3D work—work that is dirty, degrading, or dangerous. Jn-Simon, for example, relates how her Bahamian-born friend was a great basketball player and had been offered a basketball scholarship to study in the United States. Once his Bahamian passport was revoked, however, this opportunity was taken away.[37] He ended up not graduating from high school, has two children—and "one on the way"—and is unemployed. She explains how another friend "who got the highest [Bahamas Government Certificate in Secondary Education exam results] in the government schools in her year . . . didn't even have an opportunity to go to [university] because . . . she wouldn't be able to get a scholarship." Jn-Simon says that after working so hard in high school, her friend now "has to work and *settle for mediocrity*. Like certain jobs that she would never see herself doing, she has to settle for them in order to get where she wants to get in life."

Jn-Simon, who is currently a College of The Bahamas student, adds that many of the young female students of Haitian descent in her neighborhood see limited opportunities post-high school because of their ethnicity. They thus decide to "jump out of school pregnant. And then they'll tell you *you're wasting your time going to school cause you still can't do anything* because you're a Haitian." The Dominican-born interviewees of Haitian descent in the Georgetown Law report relate similar experiences of frustration and "impoten[ce]" (GULSHRI 2014, 40), finding their ability to carry out key life projects severely disrupted.

Several of them dropped out of school, either fearing that they would be asked to show documents that they did not have or because they knew that even if they did well in high school, it would not matter because they would be unable to attend university afterwards. Juan, who had been denied his cédula and prevented from attending university "despite an excellent academic record," laments that "*my future has been destroyed*. . . . Very early I had a vision that at twenty I would finish high school, go to college, and earn a degree and by 25 have a family. Now I am 25 and I have not even begun" (GULSHRI 2014, 37; italics added). Lack of citizenship thus leaves many of these Bahamian- and Dominican-born persons of Haitian descent with little hope for the future.

Government jobs are out of the question without a Bahamian or a Dominican passport, as are many jobs in the private sector. Desmangles notes how many young Haitian Bahamians "take menial positions and then some of them *they get stuck in them*" because of difficulties in securing Bahamian citizenship. Dumercy adds that "The stigma of the last name" haunts those who get an education and who try to advance in a career. She says that "local employers here, they look at your name and not at your qualifications."

St. Cecile, who previously worked in the healthcare industry, explains how, "when I applied for jobs . . . they see the qualifications there" but that "just by looking at my name . . . you *won't get hired.*" Petit-Homme describes how one's last name automatically places a person in certain menial positions in the eyes of many non-Haitian Bahamians. He describes how he was at The Bahamas National Film Festival holding a conversation with an American filmmaker when

> this lady, this Caucasian Bahamian, decides to interrupt our conversation. "Oh I haven't met you two guys. Are you filmmakers?" And he said, "Yeah." He told her his name and I told her my name and she asked me where my name was from. And I told her my name was Bernard Petit, and she said, "Where's that from?" And I said, "That's from Haiti." "Oh really? Do you mow lawns and weed gardens?"

Apparently some Bahamians have difficulties envisioning individuals of Haitian descent in any profession other than manual labor. Dumercy argues that it is not in their interests to do so. She says that while it is common to find persons of Haitian descent in "risky and life-threatening" jobs, you will not find them "in tourism or some of the other key areas that might be useful to have international, multicultural knowledge" because "The stigma of the last name" is so great.

These Bahamian-born interviewees' Dominican counterparts encounter similar obstacles in employment. Calis García explains how although she took courses in accounting, computing, and basic English, without a cédula she cannot find employment as a teacher. Once, when she found employment as a teacher's aide, she was paid very little money and told that she could not continue because she did not have a cédula. She has faced many such career limitations and it has left her despondent. *"Many times I don't feel like going on,"* she says. Exilien likewise expresses dejection: *"They killed me morally* because when you are in a society and you cannot have a career, you cannot be in a job unless you are doing things that a person who has no worth does," it is like being "an immigrant, an unknown, an undocumented person" (Civolani Hischnjakow 2011, 35; italics added). He says that he has had to take on jobs that he would not have chosen if he had been given his cédula and been able to pursue the opportunities that had been presented to him (42). Other interviewees agree and lament their inability to advance economically as a result.[38]

Although part of the lowest economic classes, poverty affects Haitian descendants in The Bahamas and the Dominican Republic differently when it comes to healthcare. Like their citizen counterparts, noncitizens are readily able to access healthcare in The Bahamas. In fact, one of the biggest complaints from Bahamian society is that undocumented or "illegal" persons are using the nation's hospitals and clinics without paying for the services. Dr. George Charité, who runs his own medical clinic in Abaco and who is a Bahamian of Haitian descent, "[does not] know if it is true or false that they are overcrowding the public system because once it's affordable, they pay" for private care. He states that not only are persons of Haitian descent "paying for their services," but "there's a preference, even the ones who go to the public system, they go to the public doctor's private residence and they pay to see him at his house."

Moreover, those who have to use the public clinic end up paying a higher fee, according to Dumercy. "We're paying two to three times what you're paying," she says, "and then you're criticizing me for going to see the doctor when I need it." In contrast, in the Dominican Republic, health care services for people who are undocumented are limited, whether due to lack of proximity to such services or because of discrimination. NGOs, like Batey Relief Alliance-Dominicana, end up providing vaccines, gynecological and dental care, and a range of other health services to those who live in the bateyes, irrespective of their status in the country.[39]

Although the health care situation is different for the noncitizen insiders in The Bahamas and the Dominican Republic, similarities exist when it comes to lack of freedom of movement and access to judicial remedies. Beside the aforementioned inability of some interviewees to travel overseas for athletic and educational activities, participants in both countries explain that when authorities perform roundups to deport individuals, many individuals of Haitian descent, both legal and illegal, feel trepidation and are reluctant to leave their communities. As described earlier in the Dominican case, being black—whether of Haitian descent or not—can get one forcibly removed to Haiti. As Human Rights Watch reports, "The threat of deportation causes Haitians and Dominicans of Haitian descent to restrict their travel, avoiding cities and remaining within the bateyes, which migration officials rarely enter" (2002, 12).

That many of these people lack Dominican identity documents due to the various practices described in Chapter 4, and "that Dominicans are legally required to carry the national identity card (cédula), the lack of official documentation also imperils individuals' right of free transit within the country" (Martínez 2011, 61). One of the participants in Civolani Hischnjakow's study, Feliciana Pelsien Yan, reveals for example that she leaves for work very early and returns late because she is afraid of being rounded up and deported to Haiti for lack of a cédula. "I feel very insecure," she admits (2011, 28).[40] Organization of American States representatives heard a story from a woman who, "out of fear of being deported to Haiti, 'where I don't have anyone,' . . . does not travel to see her grandchildren, who live in a city less than an hour away from where she lives" (OAS 2013a n. pag.).[41]

These comments reveal how "deportability" (De Genova 2002) affects the everyday lives of persons of Haitian descent by causing them to restrict their activities—a form of self-immobilization that results from fear due to their liminal status.[42] Children may be especially vulnerable in these situations. Diène and McDougall report, for instance, that "Deportations occur so rapidly that family members are not informed. Parents are deported leaving children unaccompanied" (UN HRC 2008c, 5). Several years later, Charpantier affirms that this activity is still occurring. "And they leave the children behind," he says, "and we are also denouncing that they are leaving children abandoned."

In the Bahamian case, Bahamian-born and educated students sometimes spend weeks or months in detention because of their parents' undocumented status, while an untold number are uprooted via deportation: "sometimes you find more children who born in The Bahamas than Haitians themselves" in the detention center, notes one interviewee.[43] Even those who hold Bahamian government issued travel documents are deported, according to this participant, who adds that this happens "All the time. All the time." Jn-Simon concurs, "I know a lot of Haitian children whose parents are deported and they have to live with, you know, Haitians. They have all sorts of family. Everybody is their cousin—and then they have to live with a cousin's cousin. The things that happened to them, it's depressing. And my mother takes in a lot of people. So I could tell you, these people go through a lot."

Dr. Charité sees the problem of deportation of Bahamian-born children as particularly pressing when it comes to their identity. He explains how the Department of Immigration rounds up irregular migrants and deports their Bahamian-born children along with them.

When the child reaches Haiti that child knows nothing about Haitian culture. Most of them can't even speak Krèyol. So what's going to happen? That child has to now try to learn the culture, which he or she might not be able to fit in. When that child reaches Haiti, that child is going to be also a misfit because the people in Haiti don't understand the child either. Whenever the child reaches 18 . . . that child is going to pine to come back to The Bahamas. That child now comes back to The Bahamas, knows nothing about Bahamian culture, knows not how to read English or write in English. So what [do] you do with that child now? *You put that child in an environment where he or she can't function.*

Dumercy explains how in The Bahamas some Haitian migrant parents are trying to counteract this situation by enlisting a service wherein they "sign these papers to say if something happened to you [e.g., deportation], this person can be a legal guardian for your child. So now a lot of persons in Nassau are filling out these documents in advance. So if something happened to them, their kids would still be able to go to school and have a life here [in The Bahamas] because they don't know anything about Haiti." Others find themselves in a situation of family separation, unable to accompany their sick children to overseas hospitals or unable to join their partners in another country.[44] The right of a family "to protection by society and the State" (UN 1948, Article 16) is therefore jeopardized when one is stateless.

As pertains to legal remedies and access to justice, one of the main problems that stateless people face is that they lack a juridical personality. As I note earlier, the IACtHR asserts that "The right to the recognition of juridical personality implies the capacity to be the holder of rights (capacity and exercise) and obligations; the violation of this recognition presumes an absolute disavowal of the possibility of being a holder of such rights and obligations" (2005, 66). A stateless individual, the court continues, "ex definitione, does not have recognized juridical personality, because he has not established a juridical and political connection with any State" (66–67). Lacking this connection, stateless people are unable to lawfully acquire property, obtain loans, credit, enter into contracts, or sue. Thus, as Leonardo points out, the stateless

really have nothing to lose. The only thing [those who were denationalized] had was their juridical personality. They are poor people, extremely poor. The only thing they have is their juridical personality, which allows them to develop in society; to get married, purchase, sell, open a bank account—all of these possibilities were taken from them arbitrarily by the State. They have nothing to lose. They don't have anything.

On their recent trip to the Dominican Republic, OAS representatives "spoke with many people who stated that without a cédula they are unable to file a claim or follow through with a judicial proceeding. One mother informed the delegation that, since neither she nor her son have documents certifying that they were born in the country, she cannot sue her son's father for child support" (OAS 2013a n. pag.). Not only is it nearly impossible to press a case in the courts, but those who are stateless also encounter difficulties registering the births of their children. As I noted previously, three of the five participants from El Caño were mothers and related how they were unable to register their Dominican-born children because of their own lack of a birth certificate or a cédula. "I feel terrible," confesses one, knowing that her child's ability to carry out key life projects has diminished as a result. Not only do the stateless "live in a state of extreme vulnerability" (OAS 2013a n. pag.) because of these various challenges, but the rejection they feel from society poses an additional hurdle on their quest to carry out key life projects and to establish their place identity (who they are and where they belong).

Reflection

Lack of citizenship from the countries of their birth not only immobilizes the stateless in terms of life opportunities and rights enjoyment, but it also leaves them without a psychological home, even though the majority remain physically rooted in the countries of their birth. As persons stuck in a state of liminality, stateless interviewees, or those who had been at risk of statelessness, readily reflect[45] upon what their "betwixt and between" status means to them in terms of their place identity.

It was commonplace for the Dominican interviewees who were stateless or who had been at risk of statelessness to evince a strong sense of Dominican identity. The five persons interviewed in El Caño felt Dominican, even though they were facing problems in obtaining their cédula or in registering their children as Dominican.[46] Tejeda contends that "They feel like Dominicans because they were born here. They learned our cultural system and our history and they talk Spanish and they don't practice voodoo. They're

Dominicans in the whole sense of the word." Paraison agrees, "They are culturally much more Dominican than Haitian. . . . They all know the Dominican national anthem, but not the Haitian national anthem. They play baseball; they don't play football."

The participants in Civolani Hischnjakow's study also "All felt very Dominican despite the discrimination they had received" (2011, 45). Yan, for example, states that "I am Dominican even if they keep my document: I am Dominican . . . it is an identity that is mine, not theirs" (24). She adds that "I am simply of Haitian descent, but I carry Dominican culture in my blood. . . . I have no knowledge of Haiti" (25). Gamboa contends, however, that the strength of one's sense of Dominican identity depends on whether a person feels entitled to Dominican citizenship or not:

> there's people who will say, "No I am Dominican and I feel Dominican. I have documents that say I am Dominican. They are just now trying to discriminate against me." . . . There's other people who say, "Well we've always been discriminated [against]. The government has not wanted us and they are making us stateless." . . . And then there's the other people who do not necessarily feel entitled to Dominican nationality because it's been so hard for them to actually even get it or to have their children obtain it. . . . Not sure if stateless would be the word they would use. But [they are] definitely unwanted here and [are] not able to access Haitian nationality either.

While a stronger sense of "being Dominican" exists among many of those who have been rendered stateless in the Dominican Republic, a strong sense of "being Bahamian" does not as readily exist among the study participants from The Bahamas. Arguably what accounts for this difference is the sense of entitlement that Gamboa spoke of. As noted earlier, those born in The Bahamas of Haitian descent, or of noncitizens generally, have no right to Bahamian citizenship. Most of them know that they can apply for Bahamian citizenship at eighteen,[47] but few of them grow up thinking they are Bahamian. As Desmangles states, the possession of a Bahamian government issued Certificate of Identity, which demonstrates where and to whom a noncitizen child is born so that they may apply for Bahamian citizenship at eighteen, only leads a person to being "treated as though you are a foreigner." Anyone born in the Dominican Republic prior to the 2010 constitutional amendment, however, had the right to Dominican citizenship. Thus, as explained in Chapter 4, many of the persons who are being rendered stateless now once held Dominican citizenship documents and this affects the strength of their sense of belonging to the Dominican state.

Although the Bahamian-born interviewees of Haitian descent were under no illusion that they were Bahamian citizens, they did not consider themselves Haitian either. Dumercy explains how there were two soccer teams in her neighborhood when she was growing up. One "was a 'real' Haitian team" while the other was made up of "Haitian Bahamians." "I'd side with the Haitian Bahamians as a spectator compared to the real Haitians," she says, "because I'm Haitian Bahamian" and she feels that "unless you're part of the family," the "real Haitians" reject those of Haitian descent. "The real Haitians look at us, they're like, 'Oh yeah, you born here, you little Bahamian,'" she remarks in a pejorative tone.

Despite her self-identification as a "Haitian Bahamian," Dumercy then states something that reveals how ambivalent she is about the "Bahamian" side of her identity. Describing how she would "pick who I like" if two Haitian soccer teams played against each other, she adds that she would "side with the Haitian team"—whether or not they were good players—if they "went up against Bahamians." Yet when asked by the Haitian ambassador during her Haitian "renunciation" procedure for Bahamian citizenship if she was "sure you want to give up" Haitian citizenship, Dumercy did not hesitate to renounce Haitian citizenship and become a Bahamian. "So when I finally got to see him, he asked the question [of whether she knew what she was giving up]. I was like, 'Yes! Where do I sign?'" Dumercy admits that she feels "conflicted" over where she belongs, but this is because of the rejection she—and others—feel from the Haitian and Bahamian communities. "I don't feel like, you know, if they had to pick between me and them, they'd pick me. They would always pick themselves." So she identifies with the "Haitian Bahamian" even though she is now a Bahamian citizen.

Discussing the use of "Haitian Bahamian" to refer to children born of Haitian descent in The Bahamas, Jn-Simon asserts that she feels "neither" Bahamian nor Haitian. She admits, however, that "I feel more comfortable saying that I am Haitian." When asked why she is uncomfortable calling herself a Bahamian, Jn-Simon relates, "Okay, let's say I am in class and I am asked 'What are you?' And you say, 'Bahamian.' You get that look. You know? And let's say, you're filling out an application; you put Bahamian and they look at your last name. You get the look" of disapproval. A person of Haitian descent cannot be a "true true" Bahamian. When questioned whether her answer could change once she naturalizes, Jn-Simon says she will still call herself Haitian.

> Yes. Most definitely. Because, I mean, them giving [citizenship] to us when we're 18 it's like, "Oh, I've been holding it from her long enough. Let me just give her it for giving's sake." It's not like it was ever mine and they gave it to me. It's not like that. It's just, I guess, so other nations would see that they're not that cruel. I think that's why they do the [allowing you to apply at age] 18. Otherwise they would not have given [citizenship] at all in my opinion.

Additionally, when I asked the study participants about any Haitian nationality or identity documents they possessed growing up, they were perplexed. They did not have any. While a few were unaware of the possibility of going to the Haitian Embassy in Nassau to try to obtain a Haitian birth certificate or passport, Dumercy openly admits, "frankly, I didn't even want one. I'm like why should I have to get a Haitian passport when I was born here?" Others comment on the strangeness of renouncing a nationality (Haitian) they never felt they had as part of the Bahamian citizenship application process. "That was always something that I questioned," says Louis. "Why? Because I am denouncing a nationality that genetically I have. However, according to [the] State, I am not a Haitian." When I asked why he thought he was not considered a Haitian by Haiti, he responded, "I did not have a Haitian passport. I was not born in Haiti."

Jn-Simon, who is in the Bahamian citizenship application process, calls her alleged Haitian nationality her "quote unquote citizenship," while Dumercy, who never had a Haitian passport, comments that "we don't know what we're giving up" when they go to the embassy and renounce Haitian citizenship. "We're just going through the motion. You don't understand it. But okay, this is what I need to get my [Bahamian] passport. I'm gonna do it." Participants thus renounce a nationality they either never knew they had or never felt like belonged to them. As Petit-Homme remarks, "I felt like I wasn't really a Haitian citizen because I never saw the place and I didn't really feel a direct connection to Haiti other than through my parents and speaking some of the language and some of my associations."

Despite the Haitian identity that is firmly attributed to these Bahamian-born interviewees by non-Haitian Bahamians, Haitians from Haiti do not necessarily consider these persons "Haitian" either. Dolce observes how, "You have one group of people saying, 'You are this' and the other person saying that you are not. It's like *you are stuck in between*. . . . You're saying I am Haitian, but if I go to Haiti they say that I am not Haitian. I am Bahamian." Desmangles concurs, explaining how when he visited Haiti at age fifteen people told him,

> "Oh, no, no. You're not Haitian, you know." They look at me. . . . I say, "Ah my parents are Haitian. I understand that once you're Haitian, you're Haitian." "No, no, no! That's not the case. You have to be born here." . . . And the thing is, with Haiti, they don't really want individuals who born in The Bahamas to be Haitians. That's not something that they want to practice.

Although Jn-Simon, as noted earlier, says she will continue to call herself "Haitian" even if she naturalizes, she admits that when her mother took her on a trip to Haiti, "how I was treated, I can't ever say that I'm, okay, a Haitian." When I ask her whether the Haitians on that trip considered her to be a Haitian, she declares, "No. Not at all." Disturbingly, in a revelatory comment made during his 2012 Bahamas country visit, former Haitian president Michel Martelly said that "until they're 18 [persons born in The Bahamas of Haitian descent] *don't belong to anywhere*, and yet they were born here, meaning do I have to tell anyone if you send them back to Haiti they probably don't know anybody or won't recognize the place where they land?" (K. Rolle 2012b; italics added). That the president of the country whose laws *in theory* are supposed to cover these individuals as nationals did not recognize them as Haitian only compounds the forced displacement they already suffer via formal rejection from their state of birth and residence. They are thus truly "betwixt and between" national classification statuses, unrecognized by either Haiti or The Bahamas as belonging.

St. Cecile, discussing the personal and societal rejection that many of them feel from both The Bahamas and Haiti, remarks that "to be stateless means you have no identity. You have no say in what's going on. . . . It feels like you're nonexistent. . . . *You feel like you're trapped; you're held a prisoner*. . . . Yeah, you feel like you're trapped and there's no way out for you. You have no identity."[48] Louis had a similar definition of statelessness: "to be stateless is to not have a nationality that is publicly known or I can say that falls under a country's group of identity."

The relationship that St. Cecile and Louis observe between identity and nationality is revealing in that the Convention on the Rights of the Child is explicit that nationality is a fundamental part of one's identity. Article 8 of the convention asserts that "States Parties undertake to respect the right of the child to preserve his or her identity, *including nationality*, name and family relations as recognized by law without unlawful interference"[49] (UN 1989; italics added).

Dr. Charité believes that lack of (place) identity is one of the greatest problems facing the Bahamian-born population of Haitian descent. "They don't have an identity, even though they've been in The Bahamas for all the days of their lives."[50] He adds that this is why "they're stateless according to them. Cause they don't know Haiti and they'll never go to Haiti. They'll never go to Haiti. The only place they know is The Bahamas."

Gustavius Smith, writing for the *Haitian Times*, explains how "lack of citizenship certainty provides *an inability to plan for a prosperous future* and is one of the primary reasons that Generation Y Haitian-Bahamians mentally check out of the Bahamas at an early age" (G. Smith 2012 n. pag.; italics added). Citing a "lack of identity" and feeling as if they would not "ha[ve] a future in the Bahamas," yet "ha[ving] no history or roots in Haiti," Smith describes how some Bahamian-born persons of Haitian descent seek to live in the United States. Dumercy, describing how frustrating the citizenship application process was for her, admits that she "was actually at the point where I was ready to give up. That's how bad it was. Just move and leave the country."

Their limbo-like status weighs heavily on their sense of worth and many of the Bahamian-born persons of Haitian descent question where they belong. "They don't make us feel like we belong here [in The Bahamas]," says Dumercy. "So it's a sense of belonging. . . . You shouldn't be stateless in the place [where] you were born and where you feel like you're not included or not wanted." Like some of the youth in the Smith article, Dumercy describes how the sense of rejection is so strong that some persons, born in the country of Haitian descent, feel the need to embark on dangerous sea journeys to try and find a more welcoming community. "And it's so sad you know, where *you feel you have to leave your country to get better treatment.*"

Reflecting on the death of the young woman who had embarked on such a journey (discussed at the beginning of this book), Dumercy asks, "If the Bahamas is so great, why [do] you think they'd rather die than stay here? If people would rather risk their lives and die that means something is wrong, drastically wrong." Lack of citizenship, compounded by societal rejection, thus drives some of these individuals to the extreme. Their peculiar form of forced displacement can thus, at times, lead to treacherous border crossings.

The participants in Civolani Hischnjakow's study also evidence uncertainty as to where they belong. Although more youth of Haitian descent born and raised in the DR feel Dominican, in comparison to the "Bahamianness" felt by those born in The Bahamas, the former also become "confused about what their nationality is and where they belong" (2011, 24). The participants in her study readily admit that it affects them to the point where "your personality changes. If you're not from here or there, where are you from?" (24). Ramona Petión declares, *"We don't know where we belong. It's like when you have an animal and you let it loose without its brand. . . . We're not even in that position. We're not even branded animals because without those documents, nobody recognizes us"* (25; italics added).

De la Rosa adds that without any Dominican documentation it is as if "I were a stranger, but in my own country or in my own nation . . . *it's like I am physically here, but when it comes to the laws it's as if I don't exist"* (Civolani Hischnjakow 2011, 26; italics added). Tejeda explains that although these individuals "feel like Dominicans" and "want to be Dominicans and integrate in the nation," denationalization is very hard upon them. "They're Dominicans in the whole sense of the word and it's very difficult for a child when in an instant they say, 'No, you're not Dominican anymore.' It's very, very hard from a human rights perspective to accept this situation." As a result, these Dominican-born individuals of Haitian descent feel "anguish, anxiety and insecurity," humiliation, confusion, and frustration (36; see also 27 and 34)—sentiments shared with their Bahamian-born counterparts to the north.

Conclusion

The chapter illustrates that noncitizen insiders of Haitian descent exist in limbo in Caribbean democracies such as The Bahamas and the Dominican Republic. They are neither citizen, nor migrant, but displaced in situ within the countries of their birth. They are largely immobilized through various exclusionary membership practices and unable to carry out key life projects. They exhibit many of the features associated with persons caught in liminality—invisibility or nonrecognition of belonging; treatment or association with impure practices or death (civicide); limited access to rights and protections; and, in the reflective stage, a pronounced realization of their ambiguous place identity. They do not fully belong to the countries of their birth as they are legally (and typically socioeconomically) excluded.

Yet when these individuals are removed from their enforced liminality, it is only to be forcibly emplaced within the classification of Haitian national although most have never been and never will go to Haiti (and even though it is questionable whether Haiti considers them nationals).

Their noncitizen insider status, combined with a lack of effective citizenship—or proof of such citizenship—from Haiti, highlights how difficult it is to enjoy the rights, freedoms, and protections that supposedly adhere to personhood in the contemporary era. It also brings to the fore not only the ambiguity and precarity of belonging (even within democratic states), but it illustrates the need to move beyond an understanding of statelessness as an either/or legal phenomenon: either one is a citizen or one is not. The issues surrounding statelessness surpass the legal realm, touching upon the very core of what it means when "belonging to the community into which one is born is no longer a matter of course and not belonging no longer a matter of choice" (Arendt [1948] 2004, 376). The nature of the stateless' forced displacement thus reveals the need to address the fulfillment of the human right to a nationality and the resolution of global statelessness from an alternative framework.

CHAPTER 6

Sharing the World with Others:
A Right to Belong

Statelessness [is] nothing less than the categorical
unwillingness to share the world with others.
—Patrick Hayden

Postnational assertions of the severance of human rights from citizenship
and the weakening of citizenship in the state do not apply everywhere and
do not hold for those who are citizens of nowhere. As I have illustrated in
this book, the descendants of migrants who are unable to obtain or retain
citizenship in the countries of their birth are more than "symbolically returned to their [alleged] native lands" (Hanauer 2011, 203). They are forcibly
displaced in situ as liminals or made to take on a nationality with which they
do not identify when the state can no longer tolerate their ambiguous status.

As Bahar Rumelili explains, "social structures of international politics
respond to liminality mainly by attempting to 'domesticate' it, either by constructing new social categories, or by repositioning the liminal in one of the
existing categories" (2012, 498). When The Bahamas and the Dominican
Republic place Bahamian- and Dominican-born persons of Haitian descent
into the existing category of Haitian national (often without proof that they
have said nationality in practice), they are, in effect, "domesticat[ing]" the
liminality within their borders. They are regulating the "exceptions" within
(Schmitt [1922] 1985).

As I make clear in this book, stateless people are made. They do not exist
outside exclusionary state citizenship practices: "statelessness is not an aber-
rant or accidental phenomenon occurring despite the best efforts of states to

prevent it, but a 'normalized' systemic condition produced by an international order predicated upon the power to exclude as the essence of statist politics" (Hayden 2008, 250). Through the comparative case study of the membership practices of The Bahamas and the Dominican Republic, I have demonstrated that statelessness as forced displacement is not a phenomenon generated only within illiberal states or states undergoing crisis or conflict situations. Disturbingly, democracies can—and do—forcibly displace people into statelessness, often under the cover of seemingly banal bureaucratic procedures or neutral laws.

As Chapters 3 and 4 amply illustrate, exclusionary state practices of citizenship denial and deprivation occur through protection gaps in nationality law, the reinterpretation of legal doctrine (the "in-transit" clause in the case of the DR), the retroactive application of law (Ley 285-04 of the DR), the incorporation of gender discriminatory provisions in law (the Bahamian Constitution) or the poor application of the law (consider the myriad bureaucratic failures in the nationality acquisition or retention process in both case studies). Moreover, as in Arendt's time, the stateless are often labeled or treated as "illegal" residents or made to fall outside the framework by which states categorize populations, thereby becoming "an outlaw by definition" (Arendt [1948] 2004, 360).

Bearing in mind "Arendt's insight . . . that the crisis of the 20th century has taught us the fallacy and naiveté of believing that human rights can be defended by legal means alone; human rights need something in addition to merely legal or formal structure" (Parekh 2008, 50),[1] I argue that the fulfillment of the human right to a nationality, and the resolution of statelessness in particular, must be approached from the framework of global distributive justice (GDJ). That is, it is not merely a matter of law whether an individual enjoys his or her human right to a nationality. It is a matter of global justice.

In order to make this case, the chapter begins with an overview of the contemporary literature on global justice, illustrating its largely socioeconomic focus, and the arguments that have been put forth as to why principles of justice apply at the global level. The second part outlines some of the core works that address "just membership" within the global justice framework, highlighting how the stateless have been largely ignored within this scholarship. The next section uses the theories put forth in the preceding sections to explain why the fulfillment of a human right to a nationality is an issue of global distributive justice. The chapter ends with an argument for a right to belong, which entails stateless people's right to formally belong to the *specific* states of their birth and residence as a means of removing them from their forced displacement in situ.

Global Justice

Although questions of global justice have a long pedigree in cosmopolitan thought (G. Brown and Held 2010, 9), there is no readily agreed upon definition of global justice and not all commentators of global justice consider themselves cosmopolitans.[2] Sometimes global justice is defined as "a duty to provide all human beings, as far as possible, with the opportunity to lead a self-fulfilling life" (Beardsworth 2011, 113). At others it is expressed as the "moral matters that concern how global and international institutions should be structured so as to ensure that persons' justified claims are met" (Pogge and Moellendorf 2008, xxv). In still other instances, global justice is understood as the application of "the conventional scope of distributive justice, formerly restricted to the nation-state," to the transnational sphere (Cordourier-Real 2010, 5).

Despite differences in definition, similarities exist among the diverse global justice accounts. The first commonality is an emphasis on people, whether as individuals or as groups, as the proper subject of justice. The second is on the equality of all human beings regardless of gender, ethnicity, nationality, or other ascriptive criteria. The third similarity is a concern with creating, or modifying existing institutions, so that they can better provide basic goods to, or fulfill the basic needs of, all people on an equal basis. What these basic goods are differ depending on the theorist, but scholars of global justice have generally centered upon the provision of socioeconomic goods, such as food, foreign aid, income, and housing.[3] They are concerned about the fair distribution of such goods, or "'who has what,' not 'who does what,'" so that people are able "to live decent lives" (Nardin 2006, 456). The fair provision of such goods to all persons based on their equal moral worth is known as global distributive justice.

A very lively debate has ensued as to whether principles of distributive justice apply globally or are only applicable within the confines of the state. Some of the supporters of GDJ take a Rawlsian basic structure approach to make the case that principles of justice apply to the global level. The basic structure refers to "the way in which the major social institutions fit together into one system, and how they assign fundamental rights and duties and shape the division of advantages that arises through social cooperation" (Rawls 1977, 159). Theorists who take the Rawlsian basic structure approach argue that such a structure exists at the global level. While Rawls focused on social cooperation as the means of identifying where a basic structure holds, other political theorists have argued from a pervasive impact or coercion perspective. As Arash Abizadeh explains,

> The pervasive impact theory defines the basic structure as those major social and political institutions that have [a] pervasive impact on persons' life chances; justifies the claim that such institutions are the primary site of justice by referring to their pervasive impact; and equates the scope of justice with the scope of that impact. Finally, the coercion theory defines the basic structure as those institutions subjecting persons to ongoing state coercion; justifies the claim that such institutions are the primary site of justice by reference to the autonomy principle's demand that coercion be justified; and equates the scope of justice with the range of persons subjected to ongoing state coercion. (2007, 357)

Theorists who apply the Rawlsian framework beyond the domestic sphere have generally focused on the contemporary global economic order and argued that it is a basic structure to which principles of justice apply. For instance, Charles Beitz's *Political Theory and International Relations* (1979) is often cited as an example of an argument for GDJ based on cooperation or interdependence (C. Brown 2005, 378). Beitz argues that social cooperation surpasses state boundaries, distributing advantages and disadvantages. Since "boundaries are not coextensive with the scope of social cooperation, they do not mark the limits of social obligation" (1979, 151). Consequently, an international resource distribution principle applies to the international sphere. In Beitz's understanding, this distributive principle consists of allocating scarce resources from resource-rich to resource-poor countries.[4] Thomas Pogge (1994) and Darrel Moellendorf (1996), among others, make similar claims and postulate their own global resource dividend and international resource distribution principle regarding the allocation of particular socioeconomic goods at the global level.

Existence of a global basic structure is not the only case that global justice scholars make for the application of principles of justice beyond the state. In *Frontiers of Justice* Martha Nussbaum incorporates Rawls's ideas on political liberalism and overlapping consensus, but discards his basic structure argument. In contrast to theorists like Pogge, she asserts that "there is no coercive structure over the whole that would enforce on any given part a definite set of tasks" at the global level (2006, 315). She also disputes the idea that "principles of justice have to secure mutual advantage" as stipulated by the cooperation theory perspective (89). Instead, Nussbaum argues that benevolence and shared human dignity are the bases for ensuring that basic capabilities[5]—the goals of any just institution (75)—are provided to all people so that they may flourish. In her conception then, "the good of others is an important part of one's own scheme of goals and ends" (91) no matter where one is positioned on the globe. Principles of justice therefore apply wherever human capabilities are lacking.

Writing from a distinct perspective in *Cosmopolitan Regard* (2010), Richard Vernon argues that we share a "risk society" in the form of the state. The state both poses and reduces risks to its citizens. We have special obligations toward cocitizens because they share in the same risky societal enterprise as we do and are complicit in its maintenance. Our exclusion of noncitizens from the good of membership is permissible based on the assumption that they, too, have their own parallel risk societies where they may enjoy membership. When people are members of failed or criminal states, however, we have a duty to aid them and not to harm them. Principles of justice apply because "participants in one social project have duties to aid, and not to impede, the social projects of others" (2010, 167).

In nearly all these cases, however, whether the global justice argument rests on a global basic structure and its effects, shared human dignity, or one's membership in a shared risk society, few political theorists have engaged with the subject of citizenship itself as a question of global justice, much less of global distributive justice. As Benhabib points out, "Political membership has rarely been considered an important aspect of domestic or international justice" (Benhabib 2004b, 1). A few exceptions exist in this regard.

Just Membership

Just membership refers to the fair conditions under which people become members of a polity. In the literature, membership may be defined along a spectrum from the exclusive and legal (as in the right to a nationality) to the inclusive and informal (as in socioeconomic belonging without formal recognition of status). Scholarship on just membership has run the gamut of addressing questions about noncitizen incorporation and treatment to state refugee policies, the human rights of noncitizens, and the inequalities in life opportunities that arise due to the circumstances of birth in one state and not another, among other topics. As I explain elsewhere (Belton 2011), the stateless have rarely appeared in this scholarship.

Among the earliest accounts of just membership is Michael Walzer's *Spheres of Justice*. In this work, Walzer contends that "The primary good that we distribute to one another is membership in some human community" (1983, 31) and he sets out to establish the grounds for including and excluding people from membership in a particular state. He argues that while states have the right to control who enters the polity, once admitted, people must be provided some means of formally becoming members: "every new immigrant, every refugee taken in, every resident and worker must be offered the opportunities of citizenship" (62). Walzer is concerned that people who have gained admittance into the polity will end up living under the "tyranny" of citizens otherwise.

Beside a prohibition on the permanent alienage of those who have gained entrance into the polity, Walzer also argues for what he calls a "territorial or locational right" (1983, 43). "The state owes something to its inhabitants simply," he says, "without reference to their collective or national identity. And the first place to which the inhabitants are entitled is surely the place where they and their families have lived and made a life" (43). Walzer's account of just membership thus acknowledges the deep connections that are established between an individual and the state when the former has "made a life" in the latter through work, social relations, residence, and the like.[6]

Walzer also argues that it might be "morally imperative" to admit into the polity those "who have no other place to go"—the "destitute and hungry, persecuted and stateless" (1983, 45). He further contends that when states have had a hand in turning a particular people into refugees, then "we may well have obligations of the same sort that we have toward fellow nationals" (49). Despite these claims and the assertion that "everyone must have a place to live, and a place where a reasonably secure life is possible," Walzer recognizes that "this is not a right that can be enforced against particular host states" (50). His just membership account is thus circumscribed by the bounds of statehood and traditional statist understandings of self-determination.

Benhabib's account of just membership—a term that she may be the first to use—is more open to non-statist approaches to belonging. Thus, while Walzer solely addresses just membership in terms of citizenship in a state, Benhabib initially does so from the perspective of personhood.[7] In *The Rights of Others* Benhabib describes personhood as consisting of "the right of every person 'to have rights,' that is, to be a *legal person*, entitled to certain inalienable rights, regardless of the status of their political membership" (2004b, 3). She adds that "the human right to membership is more general than the specific citizenship legislation of this or that country" (141). Recognition of legal existence, and the rights that adhere to this status, is therefore more important for Benhabib than the possession of a particular citizenship. However, like Walzer, Benhabib is against permanent alienage. She holds that "membership ought to be open to all" who have gained first admittance (entry) into a state, whether through regular channels of immigration or not (Benhabib 2007, 453).

Akin to Walzer, Benhabib recognizes that those who are subject to a state's authority, and who have established some sort of genuine link to the state, ought to be provided the means of becoming formal members. So although she argues from a moral vantage point that people ought to be able to enjoy human rights without having the citizenship of a particular state, she recognizes that citizenship is still an important status to hold. Benhabib consequently claims that "the right to naturalization" is "a universal human right" (2004b, 50).[8] Pending the fulfillment of certain conditions on the part of the immigrant, the individual ought to be given an opportunity to become a citizen. Her theory of just membership thus includes a "right to know" how to go about the naturalization process (139) and "the right to withdraw consent to exist within certain state boundaries" (137). It consists of

> recognizing the moral claim of refugees and asylees to *first admittance*; a regime of *porous* borders for immigrants; an injunction against denationalization and the loss of citizenship rights, and the vindication of the right of every human being "to have rights," that is, to belong to some human community. (2004a, 1787; italics in original; see also 2004b, 3)

Like Benhabib, William Barbieri argues for a human right to membership. In *Ethics of Citizenship* Barbieri asserts that "political membership is a matter first and foremost of human right" (1998, 115). Through an investigation of the treatment of guest workers in Germany, Barbieri illustrates how countries might go about distributing their citizenship in an ethical manner. Just as Walzer eschews the tyranny of citizens over noncitizens, Barbieri argues that the primary human right is not to be dominated. While domination may take many forms, it is "the essence of tyranny" (1998, 131). "It is the experience, directly or mediated through social structures, of harm or deprivation or subordination at the hands of others occupying a position of power" (131).

According to Barbieri, those who lack membership in the polity are dominated by citizens; "they are subjected to policies that affect nearly every aspect of their lives, yet are set by a collectivity of which they are not part and which need not consider their well-being" (1998, 137). As a result, Barbieri designs a just membership theory made up of the following components: 1) the distribution of citizenship such that it meets human rights norms, 2) the consideration of relations of domination so that individuals and certain groups may be self-determining, 3) the recognition of "a provisional right of the political community to exclusion, and a categorical right of all settled residents to political membership" (115), and, finally, 4) the presumption of citizenship for all those resident in the polity "at a certain point" unless they specifically ask not to be citizens (116).

Up until now, the just membership theorists discussed here have generally focused on how states should respond to noncitizens who are either already present on their territories or who wish to gain entrance. They all posit a theory of either what just membership should look like or what it should address, and they all see citizenship as either a good, a right, or both. Walzer and Barbieri, for example, both contend that citizenship is the primary distributive good, although Barbieri also asserts that it is a human right. Benhabib, too, claims that membership in a political community is a human right and laments how global justice theorists, with their focus on the distribution of socioeconomic goods, have failed to address "one of the first principles of distribution, namely the distribution of human beings as members of diverse communities" (2004b, 22). Two scholars who have gone against the grain in this regard are Ran Hirschl and, especially, Ayelet Shachar.

In their article, "Citizenship as Inherited Property" (2007), Shachar and Hirschl make the case that the typical acquisition of citizenship via birth on the territory or through parentage is akin to the feudal systems of old wherein property was passed down through generations to maintain wealth in a given family.[9] They explain how this system of citizenship acquisition leads to unequal starting points in life globally and deserves special attention because of the arbitrary nature by which citizenship is obtained; that is, no one consents to citizenship in a particular state when he or she obtains it through jus soli or jus sanguinis measures.

Shachar and Hirschl thus want to find a solution to what they deem to be the unequal and arbitrary nature of birthright citizenship.[10] Whereas Beitz, Pogge, and Moellendorf argue for international redistribution principles of different kinds, Shachar and Hirschl argue for the creation of a birthright privilege levy. The birthright privilege levy is a tax that wealthy states would be obligated to pay for their citizens' inherited citizenship privileges. The revenues earned through the levy would be placed in a fund, the money of which would be "devoted to specific projects designed to improve the life circumstances of children who are most adversely affected by the legal connection drawn between circumstances of birth and citizenship" (2007, 279).[11]

As I note earlier, however, none of these aforementioned just membership works focuses explicitly on statelessness as a matter of GDJ. In Shachar's case, while she admits that "there is little doubt that securing membership status in a given state or region . . . is a crucial factor in the determination of life chances" (2009, 21), she chooses to center on the inequalities of life opportunities that exist between those who have birthright citizenship from a prosperous state and those who do not. The fact that the stateless do not possess citizenship from any state, and that they are susceptible to severely circumscribed life opportunities precisely because they lack citizenship in any state, is not a concern that she takes up. Additionally, the works of Walzer, Benhabib, and Barbieri "fail to engage statelessness comprehensively . . . Walzer brackets the question of statelessness . . . the stateless are eased out of Benhabib's analysis . . . [and they] fail to show up other than in passing in Barbieri's account" (Belton 2011, 65). As I argue in the next section, however, the fulfillment of the human right to a nationality is a matter of global distributive justice and we need to treat it as such if we are to end global statelessness.

Making the Case

First, from both the pervasive impact and the coercion theories, the Rawlsian basic structure argument can be used to illustrate that statelessness is a matter of global distributive justice. To reiterate, the pervasive impact theory holds that the basic structure consists of those socioeconomic and political institutions that have an inescapable impact upon people's life chances. Principles of justice apply to those who are pervasively influenced by such institutions. The coercion theory, on the other hand, holds that the basic structure is composed of those institutions that subject people to the coercive power of the state. Principles of justice apply to those who undergo such coercion in their lives. Citizenship in the state is both a pervasive and a coercive institution.

A Pervasive Institution

Although the modern understanding of citizenship as status originated in the West, it spread across the globe with the rise of the international system of states and the spread of colonialism. Consequently, all states today have laws on the acquisition and loss of citizenship, even if these laws are not always uniformly applied in practice. As Arendt observed, "Treaties of reciprocity and international agreements have woven a web around the earth that makes it possible for the citizen of every country to take his legal status with him no matter where he goes. . . . Yet, whoever is no longer caught in it finds himself out of legality altogether" (Arendt [1948] 2004, 373). More recently, Shachar points out how "reliance upon the accident of birth is inscribed in the laws of all modern states and applied everywhere" (2009, 4). Citizenship as formal, legal membership in the state, therefore, is a pervasive institution in the sense that it is found all around the globe.

But it is pervasive in a different sense also. As Abizadeh notes, Rawls argued "that the basic structure of the society to which a person belongs has a 'profound and pervasive' impact on his or her life chances and, indeed, on his or her 'aims, aspirations, and character'" (2007, 341). Citizenship is one such institution that has a "profound and pervasive" impact upon people's life chances. As Shachar and others illustrate, the citizenship one holds largely conditions the opportunities one will be able to enjoy or the rights and protections one will be able to access. On the other hand, as I show in Chapters 2 and 5, noncitizenship everywhere (statelessness) also has a "profound and pervasive" impact upon people's abilities to be self-determining agents, capable of carrying out key life projects. Citizenship as an institution and formal legal status is thus a pervasive basic structure around the world from both perspectives. Principles of justice therefore apply to citizenship as a pervasive institution of international order.

A Coercive Institution

On the coercion account, citizenship as status is a coercive institution. Abizadeh, for example, argues that individuals in "the contemporary Westphalian interstate system . . . are subject to a vast network of ongoing coercion by foreign states that restrict their movement across state borders" (2007, 348). Such movement is typically the prerequisite to establish a legal presence that can consequently allow one to naturalize or at least attempt to gain formal entry into a different polity. Shachar similarly explains how "On both the literal and metaphorical planes, membership-defining principles represent a category of laws that simply cannot be characterized as having effects borne only, or even primarily, by their beneficiaries; their coercive authority is also felt with major force by those whom they exclude" (2009, 138). As I have shown in this book, typically through a confluence of legal, political, and bureaucratic factors, the stateless are forcibly displaced and are everywhere excludable as a result. They are either coerced into liminality or, without their consent, made to take on the nationality of a country with which they do not identify when their presence becomes intolerable.

Coercion also exists in a different sense, however; each person *must* be a citizen of some state. Questions of citizenship—who gets it and how, and who loses it and on what basis—have typically been considered a sovereign right of the state or a "fundamental legitimating principle of the national-sovereign system" (Hall 1999, 72; see also Kostakopoulou 2008, 26). As Kay Hailbronner notes, "Nationality under public international law is an integral element of national sovereignty. That is, there is no statehood without a state's authority over its nationals, internally or externally" (2006, 86). Moreover, of the four characteristics that qualify a polity as a state, a permanent and stable population is one of them (International Conference of American States 1933). Control over citizenship matters thus becomes one of the main venues through which states maintain permanent and stable populations.

Citizenship is not only "a fundamental instrument both of the government of populations within states and of the regulation of movement between them," but "the emerging global order in fact relies upon the capacities of territorial states to govern their own populations" (Hindess 2005, 256). Citizenship is of such import in the international sphere, that no international norm or recognition of the right to be voluntarily stateless exists. Thus while some people have voluntarily renounced their citizenship and not acquired another, international law and practice do not readily accept such an anomalous status. Instead, as noted earlier in the book, there is an international norm against statelessness. As Hailbronner points out, "The avoidance of statelessness is probably the oldest and most commonly recognised principle of nationality law" and its avoidance "has become part of customary international law" (2006, 64,65).

One of the earliest prohibitions against statelessness is found in the Convention on Certain Questions Relating to the Conflict of Nationality Law, where it states that loss of citizenship is not permitted unless a person "possesses another nationality or unless and until he acquires another nationality" (League of Nations 1930, Article 7). Just over thirty years later, the 1961 Convention on the Reduction of Statelessness similarly claims that a person should not lose citizenship from one state until acquiring the citizenship of another state first (UN 1961, Articles 5–7).

The idea that each person must be a citizen of somewhere (League of Nations 1930, Preamble) became entrenched as a human right in the Universal Declaration of Human Rights, which, as we saw in Chapter 1, states that "Everyone has the right to a nationality" and "No one shall be arbitrarily deprived of his nationality nor denied the right to change his nationality" (UN 1948, Article 15). Later UN conventions would reiterate this right to a nationality.[12]

Thus, international order is premised on the presupposition that everyone must belong to some state through the legal bond of citizenship. The fact that all states have nationality laws that adhere to jus soli, jus sanguinis, or some combination thereof, and that, outside the ten million or so stateless people, the majority of individuals around the planet are born and acquire citizenship through these means, illustrates the coercive and systemic nature of the institution of citizenship. Moreover, its coercive nature is patently clear when one considers that the attribution of citizenship at birth via jus soli and jus sanguinis does not require consent. People are automatically forced to hold a particular citizenship from a given state through the operation of existing nationality laws. Principles of justice therefore once again apply to the institution of citizenship as a coercive institution of international order.

Human Capabilities

Beside the Rawlsian-type basic structure arguments, the fulfillment of the human right to a nationality is arguably a matter of global distributive justice on other grounds. According to Nussbaum's capabilities perspective, political control over one's environment is central to justice: "Being able to participate effectively in political choices that govern one's life; having the right of political participation, protections of free speech and association" (2006, 77) are all part of what a person needs to be a functioning and flourishing individual.

While the stateless today are a diverse lot and by no means devoid of agency as in Arendt's postwar account, the majority of them do lack the basic human capability of control over their political environment. Without citizenship from anywhere, they are not only subject to indefinite detention and deportation, which greatly affect their autonomy and dignity as human beings, but they are often unable to partake in the political decisions that affect their lives because of their noncitizen everywhere status. They are unable to vote, hold political office or even certain jobs without citizenship. Nussbaum argues that "a society that does not guarantee these [capabilities] to its citizens, at some appropriate threshold level, falls short of being a fully just society" (2006, 75).

Although Nussbaum uses the term "citizens," one may assume that her ten "Central *Human* Capabilities" (2006, 76; italics added) do not apply only to those who have formal, legal membership in the polity. She states that these capabilities are "universal" in scope and that "each person is to be treated as an end" (76). As such, stateless people should also have access to Nussbaum's capabilities or entitlements. Since stateless people often lack the specific capability of political control over their environment, as well as other capabilities like bodily health and affiliation, it would appear, using Nussbaum's logic, that the states in which they reside fall short of being "fully just" in these arenas. Moreover, as I note in Chapter 2, since no region of the globe is unaffected by statelessness, and since Nussbaum argues that her ten capabilities are applicable as goals of justice everywhere these capabilities are violated or not provided for, principles of justice once again apply.

Shared Risk Society

Beside a basic structure or a human capabilities rationale, we can also use Vernon's notion of a shared risk society to demonstrate that principles of justice hold at the global level regarding the stateless. Vernon asserts that "States . . . derive their justification from the reduction in vulnerability that they bring to their members" (2010, 51); they are shared risk societies. We have special obligations toward co-citizens because we all share in the same risky societal enterprise and are complicit in its maintenance.

According to Vernon, our exclusion of noncitizens from membership goods "evaporates if we simply suppose that those excluded from our in-group can form an in-group of their own, in turn excluding us from its special benefits" (2010, 106). Thus, as long as a person is a citizen of somewhere else, or belongs to a parallel "risk society," it does not matter that we exclude that person from our membership or its benefits. They have their own risk society that can provide them such goods. This logic does not hold up when it comes to the stateless, however.

Since the stateless are not an "in-group" who possess a parallel risk society of their own—one of the main issues is that they do not formally belong to any so-called "risk society" in the form of a state—then the problems that their exclusion from membership generates do not simply "evaporate." Principles of justice therefore apply.[13] Furthermore, when Vernon claims that we have duties "to aid and not to impede" the social projects of others, it must surely apply to the stateless whose forced displacement results in their inability to be self-determining agents, able to carry out key life projects.

These are but some possible arguments for why principles of justice apply to the stateless as a global matter and why we should consider the fulfillment of the human right to nationality a matter of global distributive justice, specifically. It is not a matter of citizenship being redistributed from those who hold this status in a wealthy democracy to a person residing in a poor or illiberal one. It is not even a matter of taxing those born into wealthy democracies and redistributing the tax to those born in less well-off states so that they may be compensated for their unequal starting point in life. Instead, statelessness is a matter of global distributive justice because it is an issue of citizenship not being distributed at all.

If, as Walzer and others posit, citizenship is the primary good which allows access to other goods, if it is a human right as the UDHR and other conventions proclaim, and if each person is supposed to be a citizen of some state as international doctrine holds, then it is a grave injustice that millions of people are stateless globally. In order to remedy this injustice, we must go beyond Arendt's declaration that the great "calamity" to befall the stateless is that they lack the "right to belong to *some kind* of organized community" (Arendt [1948] 2004, 377; italics added) and recognize, instead, their right to belong to the *specific* community within which they have made their lives.

A Right to Belong

To avoid the "tyranny" of the citizens over the noncitizens (Walzer), or the domination of the former over the latter (Barbieri), a right to belong within a just membership framework must address two distinct stateless groups when it comes to the fulfillment of a human right to a nationality. The first are those who are born and continue to reside on a state's territory (noncitizen insiders) and the second are the minority who have come from elsewhere, but who have made their life in a given state. In both cases, their right to belong needs to be developed.

Although Walzer's "right of place . . . is not a right to a 'particular place' " (Belton 2011, 65), when he discusses the situation of refugees, he contends that a community that has had a hand in their forced displacement "may well have obligations" toward them of the same kind that it has toward its citizens. Since, as I demonstrate in this book, states are directly involved in the generation of statelessness, they should, by extension, have an obligation to grant citizenship to those individuals born on their territories who would otherwise be stateless. This is not a novel proposition, but it would be radical if implemented.

As Yaffa Zilbershats points out, Hersch Lauterpacht argued that Article 15 of the UDHR should include a stipulation that "Every person shall be entitled to the nationality of the state where he is born" (Lauterpacht cited in Zilbershats 2002, 16). Additionally, Article 1 of the 1961 statelessness convention asks that states party to the convention grant nationality to someone born on their territory who would otherwise be stateless. Admittedly, the convention is limited in that it allows states to place restrictions on a person's ability to acquire citizenship in the country of their birth pursuant to various conditions. These conditions include, among others, habitual residence (which is often difficult to achieve for children who are deported to their parent's "home" state) and the situation of always having been stateless (not everyone is born into statelessness, as the Dominican case makes clear).

Furthermore, the 1961 convention—like any international treaty—is only binding upon those states that have ratified it. This is problematic from the perspective of global justice since it allows for noncontracting states to continue perpetuating statelessness. As I argue earlier, because citizenship is an institution of international order to which principles of justice apply, a globally just approach to the resolution of statelessness must pertain to all states, regardless of whether they are party to the 1961 convention or not. Hence a right to belong for the stateless must entail the right to citizenship of a particular place *from the moment a person is born, irrespective of the circumstances of their birth.*[14] This "place" is the country of their birth and residence for the first group of stateless persons.[15] This is a markedly distinct position from that of the 1961 Convention on the Reduction of Statelessness.

The 1961 convention asserts that a state party to the treaty "shall grant its nationality to a person born in its territory who would otherwise be stateless" either "(a) At birth, by operation of law, or (b) Upon an application being lodged with the appropriate authority, by or on behalf of the person concerned, in the manner prescribed by the national law." The convention then stipulates that "A Contracting State which provides for the grant of its nationality in accordance with subparagraph (b) of this paragraph may also provide for the grant of its nationality by operation of law at such age and subject to such conditions as may be prescribed by the national law."

It is this latter subparagraph (b) that is problematic. States parties to the 1961 convention do not have to provide citizenship to children born on their territory who would otherwise be stateless *at birth.* The convention is clear that a second option exists—national law can prescribe the age and manner by which a person born on the territory applies for citizenship. We have seen in the case of The Bahamas, for example, that children born to noncitizens on the territory are only able to apply ("register") for citizenship at age eighteen and within a one-year time frame. Some persons, therefore, are susceptible to statelessness at least through to adulthood if we allow subparagraph (b) to condition when a person can formally belong.

Furthermore, Spiro contends that UNHCR's position regarding citizenship acquisition for the stateless is "that individuals should have *some state* to turn to protect them against mistreatment by other states" (Spiro 2011, 733; italics added).[16] Spiro's statement is corroborated by a UNHCR official in the Dominican Republic who asserts that "to get to the point of UNHCR's perspective on these nationality issues in the Dominican Republic . . . our main concern is that people have, that everyone has a link with a State. *It doesn't really matter what the State is—Haiti, the Dominican Republic, wherever.*"[17] Such a position, however, ignores the agency of stateless people and limits their ability to be self-determining persons and fulfill key life projects in the place they consider home. It is thus not enough from a just membership perspective that a person should have just any citizenship. A globally just and less statist response to the fulfillment of the human right to a nationality, and to the resolution of statelessness, must include a thorough examination of where it is these people want to belong (their sense of place identity).[18]

To take the analogy of statelessness and liminality a step further then, "the essence of liminality is to be found in its release from normal constraints, making possible the deconstruction of the 'uninteresting' constructions of common sense" (Turner 1985, 160). The sovereign prerogative of states to determine membership matters is one of these "constructions of common sense" that permeates our understanding of the world. We take it for granted that we should automatically be assigned formal belonging to a particular state at birth. But what if we were "release[d] from normal constraints" and envisioned the fulfillment of the human right to a nationality from the perspective of individual self-determination, as opposed to exclusionary statist politics? That is, what if we allowed the noncitizen insider to emerge from liminality and "return to society in a new identity with new responsibilities and powers" taking into consideration where it is she or he wants to belong (Beech 2011, 287)?

Self-Determination

In the Hobbesian world of the social contract, we do not arrive at the drawing table an equal partner to the state. As Thomas Nagel remarks, the institution of sovereign states, and our membership within it, is not a "voluntary association or contract among independent parties" (2005, 140). I showed earlier that this imbalance is generated by the coercive nature of citizenship as an institution of international order. The state creates the membership contract and decides who, and on what basis, may be party to it. We do not get to decide which state we will formally be assigned to via citizenship.

The majority of us are born on a given state's territory or to parents from a particular state and acquire citizenship without consent at birth through jus soli or jus sanguinis. For the minority who are able to naturalize elsewhere, we do not do so on our own terms. The state establishes the process we must follow, the tests we must pass, and then gets to decide whether to grant us formal membership or not on this basis. For those who fall outside the formal state boundaries of politico-legal inclusion altogether, the stateless, the situation is even more imbalanced.

To remedy this imbalance and to provide a globally just response to statelessness, recognition of a right to individual self-determination is necessary. In international law, self-determination is the right of peoples to decide how, and under what authority, they will govern themselves.[19] It is a principle that came to the fore during decolonization (UN 1960) and is an important collective right of indigenous peoples.[20] But it is a right of "peoples" and not individuals. Notwithstanding the group nature of this right, Walzer and other political theorists have cogently argued that those who live within a state, and who are consequently subject to its laws and policies, should have a say in these very laws and policies. As Nussbaum makes clear, a basic human capability is "Being able to participate effectively in political choices that govern one's life" (2006, 77). If people are denied the opportunity to take part in the political processes that affect their lives, then it is akin to tyranny (Walzer 1983) or domination (Barbieri 1998, 137).

An important element of stateless individuals' self-determination would be a right to choose to belong to their states of habitual residence.[21] For the first category of stateless persons, this component of the right to belong would come to the fore when they reach maturity. At this time they can choose whether they wish to retain the citizenship of their state of birth or, if they want and are able to do so, choose a different nationality and present proof of said nationality. Thus in the case of The Bahamas, for example, children born of noncitizens on its territory should be provided Bahamian citizenship at birth if they would otherwise be stateless. At the age of maturity, instead of choosing to apply for Bahamian citizenship via registration, they can choose to remain Bahamian—potentially pending the fulfillment of certain qualifications[22]—or acquire (and provide proof of having) another nationality.[23]

As pertains to the second group—the minority of stateless persons who have crossed an international border, but who have made their life in another state—their ability to choose where they belong could be established through naturalization procedures. Barbieri's suggestion that a just naturalization policy would presumptively offer citizenship "to all established residents," who would then have the choice to refuse such citizenship, should be taken into consideration. Such an approach would "take the problem of the nature of choice into account" and, Barbieri argues, "constitutes a stronger expression of consent than when one simply declines to apply for naturalization" (1998, 142).

Given the nontransparent and arbitrary manner in which some states perform their immigration and citizenship functions, however (as illustrated in Chapters 3 and 4), just membership for the stateless—whether of the first or second group—should also take into consideration residence as a foundation for a right to belong formally to the state. Peter Spiro (2011), for example, envisions the rise of a norm wherein people access citizenship via residence in the future and Vicki Jackson argues that "Perhaps international human rights law needs to move in the direction of recognizing 'rights' to become citizens of countries in which one lives after some extended but reasonable period of time and subject to reasonable conditions" (2009, 448). Zilbershats likewise contends that "the time is ripe to create a rule of international law obliging States to grant nationality to persons living within their territory" (2002, 112). She continues,

> Taking into consideration residence as a central basis for conferring nationality is needed in order to do political justice and in order to preserve global justice. From the point of view of political justice, a person who takes part in the economic, social and cultural life of the State, is a person who is entitled to take an active part in its political life . . . a person resident in a State for a significant portion of his life is entitled to become a citizen of that State. . . . the duty to confer nationality by virtue of residence is the basis and the justification for the existence of immigration laws. In its absence, the immigration laws may lead to global injustice. (2002, 112)

Thus for noncitizen insiders who are unable to prove birth on a state's territory, or for those stateless persons who have migrated from elsewhere, Barbieri's suggestion that "Already established residents . . . not only have a right to political membership, but should be granted full . . . membership status unless they make a point of refusing it" (1998, 143) is pertinent for this second group.

Other scholars have made a similar argument for citizenship through residence based on the fact of social membership. In *Immigrants and the Right to Stay*, for example, Joseph Carens posits that irregular migrants who have developed "social membership" via several years' residence in a state should be granted a right to remain. This is because the longer the residence in a state, the deeper the attachments, interests, and impact upon one's identity. To not recognize someone's social membership would thus be "cruel and unjust" (2010, 11). A right to remain, according to Carens, must thus include permanent residence "and all the rights that go with that, including eventual access to citizenship" (18). Carens reiterates this argument in *The Ethics of Immigration* (2013),[24] and scholars such as Ernst Hirsch Ballin (2014) and Barbieri (1998) also contend everyone should have citizenship in the society where they make their life.

These scholars' position echo the declaration of Manley Hudson, the Special Rapporteur on Nationality, Including Statelessness, in his report to the fourth session of the International Law Commission over a half century ago. Therein Hudson stated that "Any attempt to eliminate statelessness can only be considered as fruitful if it results not only in the attribution of a nationality to individuals, but also in an improvement of their status. *As a rule, such an improvement will be achieved only if the nationality of the individual is the nationality of that State with which he is, in fact, most closely connected, his 'effective nationality'"* (Hudson 1952, 20; italics added).

Hudson's reflection found legal support just a few years later when the International Court of Justice (ICJ) declared in the *Nottebohm* case[25] that "the habitual residence of the individual concerned is an important factor" in determining the actual nationality of an individual (ICJ 1955, 22). In this same case, the ICJ also declared that "there are other factors such as *the centre of his interests, his family ties*, his participation in public life, *attachment shown by him* for a given country and inculcated in his children, etc." (22; italics added) that must also be considered when determining where a person has a "genuine and effective" link to a state for nationality purposes.

Although the ICJ was addressing the issue of dual nationality in the *Nottebohm* case, as opposed to those who have no nationality whatsoever, Mirna Adjami and Julia Harrington contend that "the principle of a 'genuine, effective link' is slowly emerging as a principle to guide State practice in granting citizenship" generally (2008, 106). They further posit that "A genuine and effective link suggests that citizenship should correlate with where individuals *need* citizenship in order to exercise the qualities of citizens and enjoy the state protection provided by citizenship" (106; italics added). Arguably, in the cases I analyze in this book, the Bahamian- and Dominican-born persons of Haitian descent need citizenship in the countries of their birth, which also happen to be their place of residence, employment, and family ties. As Jn-Simon, discussing the option of obtaining a Haitian passport, asks,

> What use is that to you in The Bahamas? What could you do with it? Regardless of the fact that it proves you have an identity, you still have to consider that I have to go look for a job. I have to go apply to school. With that Haitian passport I would be charged non-Bahamian fees. With that Haitian passport I have to go and apply for a work permit in order to work in The Bahamas, which I have been here all of my life, and that's just silly.[26]

Outside of need, however, an important element of individual self-determination takes into account where it is a stateless person wants to be a citizen of, or in the words of the *Nottebohm* decision, where his or her attachment and center of interests lie. It is for this reason that I argue that just membership for the stateless must include a process for citizenship acquisition (or retention) that fully takes into account where it is these noncitizen insiders want to belong (versus where the state of their birth thinks they should belong). As Goris remarks,

> At some point in some cases, it should become immaterial whether another State will claim them as a citizen or not. Because if they have no effective ties to that country, *if they do not want to be nationals of that country. . . .* Does it matter that this other—their "country of origin" however many generations back—could give them citizenship *if that's not where they're going to make their life?*

As I discuss in Chapter 5, many Bahamian-born persons of Haitian descent think that it is strange that they have to go to the Haitian Embassy and renounce a nationality they either never knew they had or felt like did not belong to them as part of the Bahamian citizenship application process. Similarly, those who have been denationalized or denied citizenship in the DR nonetheless feel Dominican. Not only do these Bahamian- and Dominican-born persons of Haitian descent often consider their birthplace to be home, but numerous interviewees—and even former President Martelly[27]—acknowledge that these individuals "have no effective links to Haiti as a country. Haiti is not their country of origin."[28] As Dumercy emphatically asserts, "You're not of there."

Whether called social or sociological membership or an "effective nationality," the majority of stateless persons, whether globally or those who were interviewed for this work, demonstrate a genuine and effective link with their states of residence. The majority have lived in one place (the country of their birth) all their lives and they could likely articulate where it is that they hold attachments and interests. Furthermore, even though they evince an ambiguous sense of place identity—due to rejection by the country of their birth and their alleged state of nationality—if given the opportunity, many could probably articulate where it is they want to formally belong for the purposes of carrying out key life projects. Just membership for the stateless must therefore move beyond statist practices of membership inclusion and exclusion. It must allow the stateless the right to belong to the country of their birth and residence, if they so choose.

Having the opportunity to acquire citizenship at birth if stateless (whether de jure or de facto) and then the choice to retain said citizenship upon reaching maturity (or acquire and provide proof of another) would assuage many of the deleterious effects that the stateless face from their peculiar form of forced displacement in situ. It would provide for a better balance between the two parties of individual and state when it comes to the so-called social contract and it would, as Desmangles remarks, give the stateless the "opportunity to partake in the fabrication of a country they call home."[29]

Other Considerations

Regardless whether individuals fall into the first or the second group of stateless persons, it is also important that the right to belong not be made contingent upon "rightful" presence. While Walzer contends that "every immigrant and every resident is a citizen too or at least a potential citizen" (Walzer 1983, 52), he problematically assumes that "these 'potential' citizens are 'rightfully where they are'" (Belton 2011, 65). As I note in this book, however, the stateless are not necessarily considered lawful or "rightful" residents of the state in which they reside even though it is the very states that label these people unlawful or "illegal" that make them unlawful or "illegal" in the first place through their practices of citizenship denial or deprivation. It is thus unjust, in many cases, to predicate the stateless' human right to a nationality, and the subsequent rights that attach to citizenship, on their "lawful" presence within a state.[30]

Just membership for the stateless must not only include the aforementioned right to citizenship from their state of birth *at birth* and the right to choose to continue to belong—regardless of circumstances of birth—at maturity, but it should also include the essential human right norm of nondiscriminatory treatment, as well as judicial review of state citizenship decisions, and the provision of documentation in order for the right to be effective in practice. That is, just membership for the stateless entails that they not be treated in an arbitrary or discriminatory manner in the citizenship application/acquisition (or retention) process because they are the racial or ethnic "Other." As I demonstrate in the book, discrimination often occurs under the cover of what appears to be banal bureaucratic procedures or neutral laws. In the case of The Bahamas, for example, the denial of citizenship to persons born of foreigners on its soil applies to all noncitizens, not just Haitian nationals. In the case of the Dominican Republic, the 2010 nationality amendment to the Dominican Constitution (and other applicable migration directives) applies to all persons who are present on Dominican soil without authorization, regardless of ethnicity or race. Yet the reality is, individuals of Haitian descent are the ones who are most significantly affected by these laws and the obscure and politicized processes that surround their implementation.

Fulfilling the human right to belong in an equitable manner thus entails the establishment of transparent rules and procedures for citizenship acquisition (or retention). The relevant citizenship-granting body must provide regular status updates at predetermined intervals so that individuals are not left in limbo as they await a response. This is Benhabib's "right to know" that I mentioned earlier (2004b, 139). Discussing "the right to naturalization" (50) of all persons who have already been admitted into the polity, Benhabib argues that such persons have "the right to know" how to go about the naturalization process (139). In the Bahamian and Dominican cases, where poor communication, requests for extraneous documentation, and nontransparent rules and procedures for citizenship claims are serious impediments to the fulfillment of many Haitian-descended persons' human right to a nationality, "the right to know," from the outset of the process, *all* the documents, deadlines, and procedures for claiming citizenship is vital to fulfilling the human right to belong.[31]

Additionally, it is important that those states that do not allow dual nationality, such as The Bahamas, eradicate the waiting period between the renunciation of one's "original" nationality and the acquisition of another nationality. As I explain in Chapter 3, people may become de jure stateless during this time. Applicants have to renounce their "original" nationality as part of the Bahamian citizenship application process and do not become Bahamian citizens until they are officially sworn in, which can take several months to occur. Leaving someone stateless for months, in a condition of "infinite danger" (Walzer 1983, 32), is far too long. Just membership for the stateless thus requires the immediate provision of citizenship to those whose application has been approved. Each person should be able to go to a justice of the peace or an immigration officer with the citizenship approval letter and immediately be sworn in and registered as a Bahamian citizen. If said person would like to wait for the next official group swearing-in ceremony, he or she may choose to do so; but the option for an individual, rapid swearing-in must also exist.[32]

Another means of avoiding discrimination or arbitrary treatment in the processing of citizenship claims is to ensure that judicial review exists. Although international law does not recognize nationality "as a prohibited ground for differentiation" among people when it comes to the provision of human rights (Lillich 1984, 41; Tiburcio 2001, 56), some scholars contend that "the recognition of the human rights aspects of nationality implies procedural fairness and independent review" (Hailbronner 2003, 79). Since states can—and do—engage in discriminatory membership practices under the cover of seemingly neutral laws or procedures, it is imperative that just membership for the stateless entails the right to judicial review of their citizenship application (e.g., The Bahamas) or citizenship status investigation (e.g., the Dominican Republic) by an independent third party.

As I note in Chapter 3, the Bahamian Constitution provides broad leeway for the minister in charge of naturalization and immigration to make membership decisions without heeding the advice of any other body; while the cabinet, which in practice makes the majority of citizenship decisions, does so in an overtly politicized and nontransparent environment. Individuals consequently have no recourse to contest any rejection of their citizenship application. As the Bahamas Constitutional Commission asserts,

> such preclusive provisions can be misused by the executive for political or other reasons to deny registration to persons who are entitled to be registered as citizens. The Commission is therefore firmly of the opinion that the Minister's decision should be subject to review for breach for natural justice . . . the Commission is of the opinion that the current system under which the grant or refusal of citizenship is a purely executive power exercised directly by the political director-

ate, specifically the Cabinet, is *inherently unfair and arbitrary.* (Government of The Bahamas 2013b, 99–100; italics added)

Likewise, and as I explain in the Dominican case, the Junta Central Electoral is the body that grants citizenship and investigates "irregular" citizenship cases, yet it is composed of some officials who arbitrarily deny or deprive people of their citizenship identity documents. As Gamboa states, the JCE is "judge and jury" of its own actions. Because of the suspect nature in which matters dealing with citizenship acquisition and denial are handled in The Bahamas and the Dominican Republic, both countries' governments need to establish independent judicial bodies that can transparently and fairly review citizenship claims if they are to effectively address the problem of statelessness within their borders.[33]

Finally, since "the global era is increasingly legalistic, [and] invisibility to the law is a profound assignation indeed" (Dauvergne 2008, 174), just membership for the stateless must include the provision of citizenship documents, whether in the form of a birth certificate, a passport, or some other proof that serves to illustrate formal belonging. As I show in this book, it is not enough to be covered in theory under the operation of a state's law. An individual must have proof of it. Personhood alone does not yet suffice for membership and the enjoyment of the rights, freedoms, and protections that are associated with formal belonging in the state.

None of these suggestions for a right to belong should be viewed as particularly radical, especially if we consider that each person is supposed to belong somewhere as a citizen from the perspective of international doctrine and practice. Moreover, prior work (both from political theory and international judicial opinion) elaborates the necessity of belonging to the place where one has made a life and has attachments. What makes the present formulation of a right to belong distinct is its challenge to the position that states alone should determine their membership. In this configuration of citizenship acquisition and retention, people have a pronounced say in where it is they want to belong.

Conclusion

We seem far removed from the realms of international law, human rights practice, and forced displacement as we sit on the beach, the sun beating warmly on our faces and the waves gently lapping at our feet. Yet even as the landscape accepts our presence, our placement within it, the laws, policies, and practices of the state that we call home reminds us of the precariousness of our belonging. Dumercy is the child of migrants. Born in a country that denied her citizenship for the first eighteen years of her life, and without proof of any other nationality during that time, she was effectively stateless into adulthood. I, on the other hand, come from a long line of Bahamians on my mother's side. But as the child of a Bahamian mother born overseas, I was constitutionally unable to obtain Bahamian citizenship at birth. If it were not for the ability to acquire the citizenship of my father's country, I could have been stateless.

Dumercy and I are fortunate to hold the citizenship of the place we call home, even though formal recognition of our belonging came later in life. Others are less so. Whether rooted through birth on the territory or through having made a life within it via long-term residence, others remain forcibly displaced via practices of citizenship deprivation and denial. Stuck in the realm of the "betwixt and between," they are not captured in practice within any legal framework by which people become formal members of a state. Unable to carry out key life projects and be self-determining agents, their access to human rights, freedoms, and protections is tenuous at best and nonexistent at worst.

While I have argued that the stateless' plight is similar to that suffered by other types of forced migrants, the stateless have not garnered similar attention from human rights, humanitarian, academic, or policy-making circles. Part of this may be because their peculiar form of forced displacement takes place "in place." The stateless, as I have explained, are not generally border crossers. The majority are born in, and remain within, the states of their residence. Their nonmovement across state borders, and the fact that their displacement typically takes place under noncrisis and nonconflict conditions, makes their situation all the more disturbing because they often lack the visible hardship associated with other types of forced displacement and they do not necessarily live within undemocratic or failing states. They are thus left to languish in the netherworld of liminality.

This netherworld, as I explain, is often generated under the guise of allegedly neutral laws or banal bureaucratic procedures. These laws and procedures are often highly discriminatory in practice, however, and democratic states are not immune from generating stateless people via such means. Since "the law" is often misused, misapplied, or misinterpreted to exclude the stateless (typically the ethnic, racial, or religious "Other") from formal belonging, I argue that we must seek an alternative approach to fulfilling each person's human right to a nationality and the resolution of global stateless-ness. This alternate framework is global distributive justice and it is composed of two key tenets: first, it is unjust not to share the world with others and to exclude millions from citizenship; second, every stateless person has the right to belong. That is, each stateless person has the right to the good of citizenship in the state of his or her birth from the moment he or she is born or to the right of citizenship in the state where he or she has made a life via residence.

In a world of increasing population growth and heightened human mobility, where so many rights, freedoms, and protections continue to attach to citizenship, "shar[ing] the world with others" (Hayden 2008, 266) through the fulfillment of a human right to a nationality from a just membership perspective is crucially important. It will not only remove the stateless from the "tyranny" of the citizens (Walzer 1983, 62), but it will provide them the space—and place—to carry out key life projects and be self-determining agents in the place they consider home. This, after all, is what is fundamentally "at stake when belonging to the community into which one is born is no longer a matter of course and not belonging no longer a matter of choice" (Arendt [1948] 2004, 376).

APPENDIX 1

This section includes IRB-approved documents from the first stage of the author's Caribbean fieldwork (2009).

IRB PROTOCOL H09-130 DOCUMENTS

Consent Form for Participation in a Research Study

University of Connecticut

Principal Investigator: Shareen Hertel, PhD.
Student Researcher: Kristy A. Belton
Study Title: People Without Citizenship: Phase I – The Commonwealth of the Bahamas

INTRODUCTION

You are invited to participate in a research study that examines statelessness (the condition of having no citizenship) among people in the Bahamas. You are being asked to participate in this study because of your knowledge about, or experience with, this or a similar issue.

WHY IS THIS STUDY BEING DONE?

The purpose of this research study is two-fold: 1) to understand the situation of statelessness in the Bahamas and identify the number of stateless people, 2) to gather information so that a research framework for investigating this subject elsewhere in the Caribbean and Latin America can be created. The main objective of the first part of the research study is to determine the extent of statelessness in the Bahamas and possible gaps in protection of stateless people; the principal objective of the second part is to develop a method for carrying out research on statelessness elsewhere in the region.

WHAT ARE THE STUDY PROCEDURES? WHAT WILL I BE ASKED TO DO?

If you agree to take part in this study, you will be asked to answer questions about people without citizenship. These questions are asked by the student researcher in an interview. This interview will take place in a location that is of mutual benefit to the participant and the student researcher and will be audio-taped with your permission. The length of the interview depends on the available time that you have. It can last from half an hour to an hour, although shorter interview periods will be considered for participants who are pressed for time. The interview consists of questions regarding statelessness in general (for example, what it is, the effects of statelessness, etc.) and statelessness in the Bahamas (for example, the nature and extent of the situation, government policies and laws regarding statelessness, etc.).

If time does not permit an interview and you would still like to take part in the research, you may answer a questionnaire that includes questions similar to those asked in the full-length interview. This questionnaire may take up to an hour to complete and needs to be submitted to the student researcher prior to her departure from the Bahamas. Once you have completed the questionnaire, contact the student researcher at kbelton05@gmail.com or 242-393-2036 to arrange a method of delivery.

WHAT ARE THE RISKS OR INCONVENIENCES OF THE STUDY?

We believe there are no known risks associated with this research study; however, a possible inconvenience may be the time it takes to complete the study.

WHAT ARE THE BENEFITS OF THE STUDY?

You may not directly benefit from this research; however, we hope that your participation in the study may lead to a better understanding of the situation of stateless people in the Bahamas, and elsewhere in the Caribbean and Latin America. A more comprehensive understanding of statelessness may lead to improved government policies in the long-term which may, in turn, lead to better assistance for stateless people.

WILL I RECEIVE PAYMENT FOR PARTICIPATION?
ARE THERE COSTS TO PARTICIPATE?

There are no costs and you will not be paid to be in this study.

HOW WILL MY PERSONAL INFORMATION BE PROTECTED?

The following procedures will be used to protect the confidentiality of your data. The researchers will keep all study records (including any codes to your data) locked in a separate and secure location. Research records will be labeled with a minimum seven (7) digit numerical and alphabetical code. For example, NB-09S-J1 refers to the location of the interview (Nassau, Bahamas), the year (2009), the season (S = Summer) the profession of the person (journalist) and the identity of the person (1 = NAME). The student researcher will transcribe the interviews from any audiotapes and only the assigned code will be present on the transcription.

All electronic files (e.g., database, spreadsheet, etc.) containing identifiable information will be password protected. Any computer hosting such files will also have password protection to prevent access by unauthorized users. Only the Principal Investigator and the Student Researcher will have access to the passwords. Data that will be shared with others will be coded as described above to help protect your identity. At the conclusion of this study, the researchers may publish their findings. Information will be presented in summary format and you will not be identified in any publications or presentations unless you have signed the waiver of confidentiality.

You should also know that the UConn Institutional Review Board (IRB) and the Office of Research Compliance may inspect study records as part of its auditing program, but these reviews will only focus on the researchers and not on your responses or involvement. The IRB is a group of people who review research studies to protect the rights and welfare of research participants.

CAN I STOP BEING IN THE STUDY AND WHAT ARE MY RIGHTS?

You do not have to be in this study if you do not want to be. If you agree to be in the study, but later change your mind, you may drop out at any time. There are no penalties or consequences of any kind if you decide that you do not want to participate. Also, you do not have to answer any question that you do not want to answer.

WHO DO I CONTACT IF I HAVE QUESTIONS ABOUT THE STUDY?

Take as long as you like before you make a decision. We will be happy to answer any question you have about this study. If you have further questions about this study or if you have a research-related problem, you may contact the principal investigator, (Shareen Hertel at [number removed]) or the student researcher (Kristy Belton at [number removed]). If you have any questions concerning your rights as a research participant, you may contact the University of Connecticut Institutional Review Board (IRB) at 1-860-486-8802 or irb@gris .grad.uconn.edu.

DOCUMENTATION OF CONSENT:

I have read this form and decided that I will participate in the project described above. Its general purposes, the particulars of involvement and possible risks and inconveniences have been explained to my satisfaction. I understand that I can withdraw at any time. My signature also indicates that I have received a copy of this consent form.

_____   _____   _____

Participant Signature: Print Name: Date:

_____   _____   _____

Signature of Person   Print Name: Date:
Obtaining Consent

Waiver of Confidentiality

🌿 University of Connecticut

Principal Investigator: Shareen Hertel, PhD.
Student Researcher: Kristy A. Belton
Study Title: People Without Citizenship: Phase I – The Commonwealth
of the Bahamas

I, the undersigned, have read the Consent Form for Participation in a Research Study on the "People Without Citizenship: Phase I – The Commonwealth of the Bahamas" project. I understand the purpose of the study and the way in which information obtained from this study may be used in future research or publication. I would like to waive my right of confidentiality and understand that the student researcher may attribute my responses in the interview or questionnaire to me, if needed, in any such future research or publication.

_____   _____   _____

Participant Signature: Print Name: Date:

_____   _____   _____

Signature of Person   Print Name: Date:
Obtaining Waiver

This section contains IRB-approved documents relating to the author's second phase of fieldwork in the Caribbean (2012–2013).

IRB PROTOCOL H11-261 DOCUMENTS

Consent Form for Participation in a Research Study

🌿 University of Connecticut

Principal Investigator: Shareen Hertel, PhD.
Student Researcher: Kristy A. Belton
Study Title: Westphalian (Dis)Order: Postnational Theses and Developing World Realities
Sponsor: N/A

INTRODUCTION

You are invited to participate in this research study that examines people with insecure or undocumented citizenship status in their country of residence. You are being asked to participate in this study because of your knowledge about, or experience with, this or a similar issue.

WHY IS THIS STUDY BEING DONE?

This study is part of my dissertation research. The data obtained during the interview process will be used to either support or refute two claims: a) states are no longer in control of membership matters and b) citizenship is no longer needed for rights fulfillment or protections due to the ascendancy of human rights.

WHAT ARE THE STUDY PROCEDURES? WHAT WILL I BE ASKED TO DO?

If you agree to take part in this study, you will be asked to answer questions about people without formal citizenship status. These questions will be asked by the student researcher in an interview.

This interview will take place in a location that is of convenience for you. With your permission the interview will be audiotaped. The length of the interview depends on the available time that you have. It can last from half an hour to an hour, although shorter interview periods can be arranged for participants who are pressed for time. The student researcher will ask questions about your knowledge of, or experience with, persons without citizenship. She will ask specific questions regarding their living conditions and societal inclusion or exclusion. She will also ask what you think may be done to improve the lives of those without citizenship status and/or what policies should be undertaken to prevent people from obtaining this insecure status. You do not have to answer any question that you do not want to answer, and should any publication result from the data obtained during this study, the student researcher will inform you and/or send you a link to the text.

WHAT ARE THE RISKS OR INCONVENIENCES OF THE STUDY?

We believe there are no known risks associated with this study for you, although a possible inconvenience may result from the time it takes to complete the interview.

WHAT ARE THE BENEFITS OF THE STUDY?

You may not directly benefit from this research. However, we hope that your participation in the study may lead to a better understanding of the situation of people without secure citizenship status in the Caribbean. A more comprehensive understanding of the situation of people without citizenship in the region may lead to improved government policies that a) reduce the number of people without secure citizenship status and/or b) better integrate people without secure citizenship status into the host societies.

WILL I RECEIVE PAYMENT FOR PARTICIPATION?
ARE THERE COSTS TO PARTICIPATE?

There are no costs and you will not be paid to participate in this study.

HOW WILL MY PERSONAL INFORMATION BE PROTECTED?

The following procedures will be used to protect the confidentiality of your data. The student researcher will keep all study data (e.g., tape recording and/or transcript) locked in a separate and secure location. A minimum seven (7) digit numerical and alphabetical code will be assigned to your interview transcript by the student researcher for identification purposes only (should you not want your answers attributed to you in any potential publication). For example, NB-12Sp-J1 refers to the location of the interview (Nassau, Bahamas), the year (2012), the season (Sp – Spring), the profession of the person (journalist) and a numerical identifier for the person (1 = NAME). The master key to your name (e.g., 1 = Tony Smith or 8 = Louisa Brown) will be kept in a separate safety box on location while the student researcher is in the field and will then be transferred to a safety box in the United States upon her departure.

Data will be kept on the student researcher's personal laptop and will be encrypted and password protected. Only the Principal Investigator (PI) and the student researcher will have access to the data. Data that is sent to the PI by the student researcher will be sent through a secure server. At the conclusion of this study, the student researcher may publish her findings, but you will not be identified in any publications or presentations unless you agree to be directly identified in any publication. Please initial your response to the following statement:

I allow information obtained from this interview to be directly attributed to me in the published results. ____ YES ____NO.

You should also know that the UConn Institutional Review Board (IRB) and the Office of Research Compliance may inspect study records as part of its auditing program, but these reviews will only focus on the researchers and not on your responses or involvement. The IRB is a group of people who review research studies to protect the rights and welfare of research participants.

CAN I STOP BEING IN THE STUDY AND WHAT ARE MY RIGHTS?

You do not have to take part in this study. If you agree to be in the study, but later change your mind, you may drop out at any time. There are no penalties or consequences of any kind if you decide that you do not want to participate. Additionally, you will be notified of all significant new findings during the course of the study that may affect your willingness to continue.

WHOM DO I CONTACT IF I HAVE QUESTIONS ABOUT THE STUDY?

We will be happy to answer any question you have about this study. If you have further questions, or if you have a research-related issue, you may contact the PI (Dr. Shareen Hertel at [number removed]) or the student researcher (Kristy Belton at [number and email removed]). If you have any questions concerning your rights as a research participant, you may contact the University of Connecticut Institutional Review Board (IRB) at 1-860-486-8802 or irb@gris.grad.uconn.edu.

DOCUMENTATION OF CONSENT:

I have read this form and decided that I will participate in the project described above. Its general purposes, the particulars of involvement and possible hazards and inconveniences

have been explained to my satisfaction. I understand that I can withdraw at any time. My
signature also indicates that I have received a copy of this consent form.

Participant Signature:	Print Name:	Date:

Signature of Person Obtaining Consent	Print Name:	Date:

CONSENT SCRIPT – STATELESS

PURPOSE

I am inviting you to participate in this research study that examines people with insecure or undocumented citizenship status in the [Bahamas] [Dominican Republic]. I am asking you to participate in this study because you either have an insecure citizenship status in this country or know of someone who has one.

WHY IS THIS STUDY BEING DONE?

I am a doctoral student at the University of Connecticut and this study is part of my dissertation. I want to write about the living conditions and implications of having an insecure citizenship status upon people's well-being. I want to show that citizenship is still an important status to hold in today's world, even though human rights exist.

WHAT WILL I BE ASKED TO DO?

If you agree to take part in this study through oral consent, I will ask you to answer questions about people without formal citizenship status. I will ask you questions about what it is like to live without citizenship, how you would like to be treated differently (by government or society), and what you think can be done to reduce the number of people without citizenship and treat them better. You do not have to answer any question that you do not want to answer. I will ask these questions of you in a location that is of mutual benefit to you and to me and, if I have your permission, I will record the interview on audiotape. No one but my advisor (Dr. Shareen Hertel, the principal investigator) and me will have access to your interview transcript or the audiotape. Your identity will be kept confidential and nothing will link your participation in this study to any work that results from the study.

WHAT ARE THE COSTS AND BENEFITS?

In order to reduce any potential risk, only my advisor and me (*sic*) will have direct access to the audiotape and transcript of the interview, although my university's Institutional Review Board and Office of Research Compliance may inspect study records as part of its auditing program. These reviews will only focus on the researchers and not on your responses or involvement.

All interview-related information will be encrypted and password protected on my personal laptop and the audiotape will be kept in a secure location. No one will know your identity and you will not have to sign any papers that link you to this study. Also, you will not receive any payment (monetary or otherwise) for participation in the study, but we believe there is little cost to you for participating other than the giving of your time. You do not have to take part in this study and, even if you agree to take part, you may stop participating at any time without consequence.

While you may directly benefit from telling your story, no other immediate benefits are expected. In the long-term, however, we hope that your participation in the study will result in an understanding of the situation of people without secure citizenship status in the Caribbean and in better policies toward them.

WHOM DO I CONTACT IF I HAVE QUESTIONS ABOUT THE STUDY?

We will be happy to answer any questions. Please contact either the principal investigator (Dr. Shareen Hertel at [number removed]) or the student researcher (Kristy Belton at [number and email removed]). You may also contact the University of Connecticut Institutional Review Board (at 1-860-486-8802 or irb@gris.grad.uconn.edu) if you have any questions concerning your rights as a research participant.

CONSENT SCRIPT – GUARDIAN OR PARENT [STATELESS]

PURPOSE

Your child is invited to participate in a research study that examines people with insecure or undocumented citizenship status in the [Bahamas] [Dominican Republic]. I am asking your child to participate in this study because he or she has an insecure citizenship status in this country.

WHY IS THIS STUDY BEING DONE?

I am a doctoral student at the University of Connecticut and this study is part of my dissertation research. I want to write about the living conditions and implications of having an insecure citizenship status upon people's well-being. I want to show that citizenship is still an important status to hold in today's world, despite arguments to the contrary.

WHAT WILL MY CHILD BE ASKED TO DO?

If you allow your child to take part in this study, and he or she agrees to participate through oral consent, I will ask him or her to answer questions about what it's like to live without formal citizenship and what he or she thinks people can do to make their lives better. I will ask your child these questions in a location that is of mutual benefit to you, the child, and to me. Your child does not have to answer any question that he or she does not want to, or that you do not want him/her to answer. If you give me permission, I will record the interview with your child on a tape recorder. No one but my advisor (Dr. Shareen Hertel, the principal investigator) and I will have access to your child's tape recording or the interview transcript. Your identity and your child's identity will be confidential and nothing will link either of you to this study.

WHAT ARE THE COSTS AND BENEFITS?

In order to reduce any potential risk, only my advisor and I will have direct access to the tape recording and transcript of the interview, although my university's Institutional Review Board and Office of Research Compliance may inspect study records as part of its auditing program. These reviews will only focus on the researchers and not on your responses or involvement.

All interview-related information will be encrypted and password protected on my personal laptop and the tape recording will be kept in a secure location. No one will know your identity or the identity of your child and neither of you will have to sign any papers that link you to this study.

You should also know that the UConn Institutional Review Board (IRB) and the Office of Research Compliance may inspect study records as part of its auditing program, but these reviews will only focus on the researchers and not on your child's responses or involvement.

The IRB is a group of people who review research studies to protect the rights and welfare of research participants.

There are no costs to you and your child for participating in this study and your child will not be paid to participate in this study. Your child does not have to be in this study if you do not want him/her to participate. If you give permission for your child to be in the study, but later change your mind, you may withdraw your child at any time. There are no penalties or consequences of any kind if you decide that you do not want your child to participate.

Finally, while your child may directly benefit from telling his or her story, no other immediate benefits are expected from the interview. In the long-term, however, we hope your child's participation in the study will result in an understanding of the situation of people without secure citizenship status in the Caribbean and in better policies toward them.

WHOM DO I CONTACT IF I HAVE QUESTIONS ABOUT THE STUDY?

Take as long as you like before you make a decision. We will be happy to answer any question you have about this study. If you have further questions about this study or if you have a research-related problem, you may contact the principal investigator (Dr. Shareen Hertel at [number removed]) or the student researcher (Kristy Belton at [number and email removed]). You may also contact the University of Connecticut Institutional Review Board (at 1-860-486-8802 or irb@gris.grad.uconn.edu) if you have any questions concerning your rights as a research participant.

Formulario de consentimiento para participación en un estudio de investigación

🌣 University of Connecticut

Investigadora principal: Dra. Shareen Hertel
Estudiante investigadora: Kristy A. Belton
Título del estudio: (Des)orden del sistema de Westfalia:
teses posnacionales y la realidad del mundo en desarrollo
Sponsor: N/A

INTRODUCCIÓN

Se le está invitando a participar en este estudio de investigación que examina la situación de personas con ciudadanía insegura o indocumentada en su país de residencia. Se le está invitando a participar en este estudio porque tiene conocimiento de, o experiencia con, este sujeto o un sujeto similar.

¿POR QUÉ SE HACE ESTE ESTUDIO?

Este estudio forma parte de las investigaciones que la estudiante investigadora (yo) hace por su tesis. Usaré la información que obtengo durante la entrevista para defender o negar dos declaraciones: 1) que los estados del mundo no tiene control sobre quién pertenzca a la membresía política y 2) que no se necesita ciudadanía hoy en día para disfrutarse de derechos o protecciones porque los derechos humanos son suficientes.

¿CUÁLES SON LOS PROCEDIMIENTOS DEL ESTUDIO? ¿QUÉ TENGO QUE HACER?

Si ud. da su consentimiento para tomar parte en este estudio, la estudiante investigadora le a va preguntar sobre persons sin ciudadanía. La entrevista se llevará a cabo en un lugar de beneficio para ud. Con su permiso, la estudiante investigadora grabará la entrevista con grabadora. El tiempo que toma para completer la entrevista depende del tiempo disponible que ud. tenga. La entrevista puede durar media hora hasta una hora, aunque entrevistas de menos duración serán posibles para estos participantes que les falten tiempo para una entrevista completa. La estudiante investigadora le preguntará sobre su conocimiento de, o experiencia con, personas sin ciudadanía o inmigrantes con estado inseguro. Ella le preguntará específicamente sobre las condiciones en que ellos viven y la discriminación que sufren. También le preguntará su opinión de qué podemos hacer para mejorar la situación de personas sin ciudadanía y/o qué tipo de políticas podemos llevar a cabo para reducir, o prevenir, el número de personas que viven en este estado inseguro. Ud. no tiene que contestar ninguna pregunta que no quiere contestar, y si una publicación resulta de este estudio, la estudiante investigadora le informará y/o le enviará el enlace para la publicación.

¿CUÁLES SON LOS RIESGOS O INCONVENIENCIAS DE ESTE ESTUDIO?

No sabemos de ningun riesgo associado con este estudio, aunque sea posible que la duración de la entrevista sea una inconveniencia para ud.

¿CUÁLES SON LOS BENEFICIOS DEL ESTUDIO?

Es possible que ud. no se beneficie directamente de este estudio de investigación. Sin embargo, esperamos que su participación en este estudio resulte en un mejor conocimiento de la situación de personas sin ciudadanía segura en el Caribe. Un conocimiento más profundo del estado de este grupo de personas en la región puede resultar en mejores políticas que a) reduzcan el número de personas sin ciudadanía segura y/o b) se integren mejor a tales personas en los países de residencia.

¿ME VA A PAGAR AL PARTICIPAR? ¿HAY COSTOS PARA PARTICIPAR?

No hay costos y no se va a pagar por participar en este estudio.

¿CÓMO SE VA A PROTEGER A MIS DATOS PERSONALES?

Se van a usar los procedimientos siguientes para proteger a la confidencialidad de sus datos. La estudiante investigadora mantendrá toda la información que pertenezca al estudio (la grabación y/o la transcripción) cerrado con llave en un lugar seguro. La estudiante investigadora le asignará un código de numerous y letras a la grabación y la transcripción de su entrevista (si ud. no quiere que sus respuestas se le vinculen directamente a cualquier publicación futura). Por ejemplo, NB-12-Pr-P1 se refiere al lugar de la entrevista (Nassau, las Bahamas), el año (2012), la estación (la primavera), la profesión (periodista) y un número que representa su identidad (1 = el nombre). El código que pertence a su nombre (por ejemplo, 1 = Juan Gonzalez, 8 = Maria Rojas) se mantendrá en una caja fuerte en un sitio seguro mientras que la estudiante investigadora hace entrevistas y la llevará consigo a su partida.

La estudiante investigadora mantendrá los datos de la entrevista en su portátil personal. Estos datos serán protegidos por un código y se las enviará a la investigadora principal por correo cifrado. Sólo la investigadora principal y la estudiante investigadora tendrá acceso a los datos y cualquier información que la estudiante investigadora le enviará a la investigadora principal, lo hará por un servidor seguro. Al terminar este estudio, es posible que la estudiante investigadora publique sus conclusions, pero no se le relevará su identidad a menos que ud. este de acuerdo de que ella pueda identificarse directamente en cualquier publicación. Por favor, escriba sus iniciales al lado de la respuesta que prefiera:

Doy permiso para que la estudiante investigadora pueda identificarme directamente en una publicación. _____ SÍ _____NO.

También, ud. debería saber que la Junta de Revisión Institucional (JRI) y la Oficina para La Protección de Seres Humanos en Estudios de Investigación puedan inspeccionar los registros del estudio cuando haga una auditoría, pero ellos solo revisen a los procedimientos del estudio de investigación y no a sus respuestas o a su participación. La JRI es un grupo de personas que hace repaso sobre estudios de investigación para proteger a los derechos y al bienestar de los participantes.

¿PUEDO YO RETIRARME DE ESTE ESTUDIO Y CUÁLES SON MIS DERECHOS?

Ud. no tiene que participar en este estudio. Si está de acuerdo en participar, pero cambia de mente más tarde, puede retirarse a cualquier tiempo. No hay penas ni consequencias por retirarse del estudio. Asimismo, se le informará sobre cualquier información nueva que pueda afectar a su deseo de permanecer en este estudio.

¿A QUIÉN ME COMUNICO SI TENGO PREGUNTAS SOBRE ESTE ESTUDIO?

Nos gustaría contestar cualquier pregunta que tiene sobre este estudio. Si tiene más preguntas, puede ponerse en contact con la IP (la Dra. Shareen Hertel al número de teléfono [number removed]) o con la estudiante investigadora (Kristy Belton al número de teléfono [number and email removed]). Si tiene preguntas con respecto a sus derechos como un participante en un estudio de investigación, puede comunicarse con la Junta de Revisión Institucional (JRI) al número de teléfono 1-860-486-8802 o irb@gris.grad.uconn.edu.

DECLARACIÓN DE CONSENTIMIENTO:

Leí este formulario y me decidí a participar en este proyecto tal como escrito arriba. Entiendo el propósito del estudio, el tipo de participación que require, y los posibles peligros e inconveniencias que puedan resultar. Entiendo que puedo dejar de ser participante a cualquier momento. Mi firma también demuestra que recibí una copia de este formulario de consentimiento.

Firma del participante:	Escriba su nombre en letras de molde:	Fecha:

Firma de la persona que obtiene el consentimiento:	Escriba su nombre en letras de molde:	Fecha:

CONSENT SCRIPT – STATELESS

PROPÓSITO

Le invito a participar en este estudio de investigación que examina el estado de personas con ciudadanía insegura o indocumentada en [las Bahamas/la República Dominicana]. Le pido que participe en este estudio porque tiene ciudadanía insegura o porque conoce a una persona que la tiene.

¿POR QUÉ SE HACE ESTE ESTUDIO?

Soy estudiante al nivel graduado en un programa de ciencia política en la Universidad de Connecticut en los Estados Unidos. Este estudio de investigación forma parte de mi tesis. Quiero escribir sobre la situación de personas sin ciudadanía segura y las implicaciones de este estado sobre su bienestar. Quiero demostrar que la ciudadanía todvía es un estado importante poseer hoy en día, aunque hay quienes que lo disputan.

¿QUÉ TENGO QUE HACER?

Si quiere participar en este estudio y me da su consentimiento oral, le pregunataré sobre personas que faltan la ciudadanía formal. Le pregunataré qué tal está vivir sin ciudadanía, cómo quiere que el gobierno o la sociedad le trate mejor, y qué piensa se puede hacer para reducir o prevenir el número de personas sin ciudadanía. Ud. no tiene que contestar ninguna pregunta que no quiere contestar. Haremos la entrevista en un lugar de beneficio mutuo para ud. y para mí y, si tengo su permiso, grabaré la entrevista con grabadora.

¿CUÁLES SON LOS COSTOS Y BENEFICIOS?

Para reducir cualquier riesgo que podrá resultar de este estudio, sólo mi consejera (la investigadora principal, la Dra. Shareen Hertel) y yo (la estudiante investigadora) tendremos acceso a la grabación y la transcripción de su entrevista. Su identidad será confidencial y nada le identificará a ud. a este estudio. Ud. debería saber que la Junta de Revisión Institucional (JRI) y la Oficina para La Protección de Seres Humanos en Estudios de Investigación puedan inspeccionar los registros de este estudio cuando haga una auditoría, pero ellos sólo revisan a los procedimientos del estudio y no a las respuestas de ud. o a su participación. La JRI es un grupo de personas que hace repaso sobre estudios de investigación para proteger a los derechos y al bienestar de los participantes.

Cualquier datos que resulten de su entrevista serán protegidos por un código en mi portátil personal y cuando se los envío a la investigadora principal, será por correo cifrado a través de un servidor seguro. Guardaré la grabación de la entrevista en una caja fuerte. Nadie conocerá su identidad y no va a tener que firmar ninguna declaración que le identifique con este estudio.

No va a recibir ningún forma de pago por su participación en este estudio, pero creemos que que le va a costar poco participar, salvo el tiempo que tome para completar la entrevista.

No tiene que participar en este estudio y aún si me ha dado su consentimiento a participar, puede decidirse a dejar de participar a cualquier momento sin pena ni consequencia.

Aunque ud. pueda beneficiarse al relatar su historia durante la entrevista, no esperamos que vaya a haber otros beneficios inmediatos para ud. Sin embargo, al plazo largo, esperamos que su participación en este estudio se resulturá en un mejor conocimiento del estado de personas que viven sin ciudadanía segura en el Caribe, y esperamos que el estudio se resulten en mejores políticas hacia ellas.

¿A QUIÉN ME COMUNICO SI TENGO PREGUNTAS SOBRE ESTE ESTUDIO?

Tómase el tiempo para decidir si su hijo/a va a participar en este estudio. Nos gustaría contestar cualquier pregunta que tiene sobre este estudio. Si tiene más preguntas, puede ponerse en contact con la IP (la Dra. Shareen Hertel al número de teléfono [number removed]) o con la estudiante investigadora (Kristy Belton al número de teléfono [number and email removed]). Si tiene preguntas con respecto a sus derechos como un participante en un estudio de investigación, puede comunicarse con la Junta de Revisión Institucional (JRI) al número de teléfono 1-860-486-8802 o irb@gris.grad.uconn.edu.

CONSENT SCRIPT – GUARDIAN OR PARENT [STATELESS]

PROPÓSITO

Le invito a su hijo/a a participar en este estudio de investigación que examina el estado de personas con ciudadanía insegura o indocumentada en [las Bahamas/la República Dominicana]. Me gustaría que su hijo/a participe en este estudio porque tiene ciudadanía insegura en este país.

¿POR QUÉ SE HACE ESTE ESTUDIO?

Soy estudiante al nivel graduado en un programa de ciencia política en la Universidad de Connecticut en los Estados Unidos. Este estudio de investigación forma parte de mi tesis. Quiero escribir sobre la situación de personas sin ciudadanía segura y las implicaciones de este estado sobre su bienestar. Quiero demostrar que la ciudadanía todvía es un estado importante poseer hoy en día, aunque hay quienes que lo disputan.

¿QUÉ VA A PEDIR DE MI HIJO/A?

Si ud. está de acuerdo de que su hijo/a pueda participar en este estudio, y él o ella da su consentimiento oral, le pediré que él or ella conteste preguntas sobre cómo es vivir sin ciudadanía formal y lo que piensa que la gente puede hacer para mejorar a sus vidas. Su hijo/a no tiene que contestar ninguna pregunta que no quiere contestar, o que ud. no quiere que conteste. Le pediré a su hijo/a estas preguntas en un lugar que es de beneficio mutuo para mí, ud., y su hijo/a. Si me da su permiso, grabaré esta entrevista con grabadora.

¿CUÁLES SON LOS COSTOS Y BENEFICIOS?

Para reducir cualquier riesgo que podrá resultar de este estudio, sólo mi consejera (la investigadora principal, la Dra. Shareen Hertel) y yo (la estudiante investigadora) tendremos acceso a la grabación y la transcripción de la entrevista de su hijo/a. La identidad de su hijo/a y de ud. serán confidenciales y nada les identificará con este estudio. Ud. debería saber que la Junta de Revisión Institucional (JRI) y la Oficina para La Protección de Seres Humanos en Estudios de Investigación puedan inspeccionar los registros de este estudio cuando haga una auditoría, pero ellos sólo revisan a los procedimientos del estudio y no a las respuestas de su hijo/a o de su participación. La JRI es un grupo de personas que hace repaso sobre estudios de investigación para proteger a los derechos y al bienestar de los participantes.

Cualquier datos que resulten de la entrevista de su hijo/a serán protegidos por un código en mi portátil personal y cuando se los envío a la investigadora principal, será por correo cifrado a través de un servidor seguro. Guardaré la grabación de la entrevista en una caja fuerte. Nadie conocerá la identidad de su hijo/a y él o ella no va a tener que firmar ninguna declaración que le identifique con este estudio.

Su hijo/a no va a recibir ningún forma de pago por su participación en este estudio, pero creemos que que le va a costar poco participar, salvo el tiempo que tome para completar la entrevista. Su hijo/a no tiene que participar en este estudio y aún si me ha dado su consentimiento para que su hijo/a particiéper, él o ella puede decidirse a dejar de participar en este estudio a cualquier momento sin pena ni consecuencia.

Aunque su hijo/a pueda beneficiarse al relatar su historia durante la entrevista, no esperamos que vaya a haber otros beneficios inmediatos para él o ella. Sin embargo, al plazo largo, esperamos que su participación en este estudio se resultará en un mejor conocimiento del estado de personas que viven sin ciudadanía segura en el Caribe, y esperamos que el estudio se resulten en mejores políticas hacia ellas.

¿A QUIÉN ME COMUNICO SI TENGO PREGUNTAS SOBRE ESTE ESTUDIO?

Tómase el tiempo para decidir si su hijo/a va a participar en este estudio. Nos gustaría contestar cualquier pregunta que tiene sobre este estudio. Si tiene más preguntas, puede ponerse en contact con la IP (la Dra. Shareen Hertel al número de teléfono [number removed]) o con la estudiante investigadora (Kristy Belton al número de teléfono [number and email removed]). Si tiene preguntas con respecto a sus derechos como un participante en un estudio de investigación, puede comunicarse con la Junta de Revisión Institucional (JRI) al número de teléfono 1-860-486-8802 o irb@gris.grad.uconn.edu.

APPENDIX 3

Figure 8 and Table 3 provide a geographical and a typological depiction of statelessness. Figure 8 graphically illustrates officially acknowledged stateless populations globally, while Table 3 provides criteria by which to distinguish different eras in the historical evolution of contemporary statelessness.

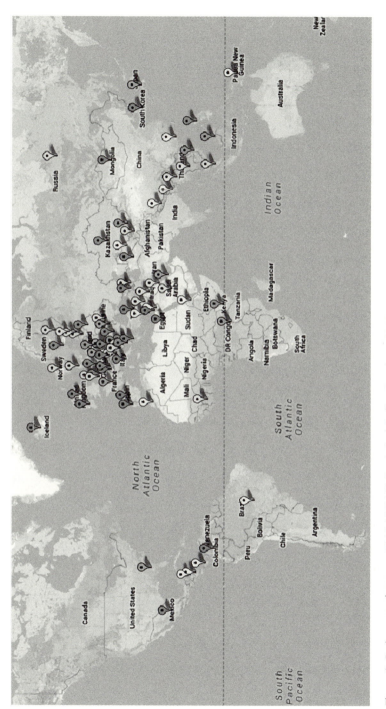

Figure 8. De jure statelessness, 2015. UNHCR Statistical Online Database 2015.

Table 3: A Typology of Statelessness over Time

	Pre-World War I era	*World War II era*	*Contemporary era*
Geographical area	Europe	Europe	Global
Regime type	Variable (although primarily authoritarian regimes)	Totalitarian/ authoritarian	All types (liberal and illiberal)
Reason(s)/context	Punishment for a crime or deemed a threat to social order; dissolution of empires	Geopolitical upheaval; context of war and genocide	Variable (discrimination a key factor)
Process	Citizenship deprivation	Citizenship deprivation	Citizenship deprivation and denial
Potential effect(s)	Exile; loss of political community; death	Forced displacement across borders, loss of all rights; lack of agency and voice; death; loss of community	Variable; forced displacement across borders not a defining feature; degree of political "voice" and agency dependent on state of residence; place identity ambiguous
Affected	Individuals found guilty of crimes	Minorities (ethnic, political, persons with disabilities, etc.)	Variable (although women, children, and minorities of distinct types are particularly vulnerable)
Means of escaping statelessness		Commit a crime, demonstrate genius, become famous (per Arendt)	Nationality acquisition processes, depending on state
Nationality as international ordering principle	Not yet present	Developing	Established
International human rights law	Nascent (slavery abolished; minorities treaties in operation; International Labour Organization established covering labor rights)	Developing (promulgation of UDHR/soft law)	Established ("core" HR treaties applicable to all human beings)

APPENDIX 4

Tables 4 and 5 provide data on whether The Bahamas and the Dominican Republic are state parties to specific treaties that incorporate the human right to a nationality.

Table 4: Status of The Bahamas Treaty Ratifications Regarding the HR to a Nationality

Treaty	Signature/ ratification date	Applicable reservation (R) or declaration (D)
Convention relating to the Status of Stateless Persons (1954)	Not ratified	
Convention on the Reduction of Statelessness (1961)	Not ratified	
International Convention on the Elimination of All Forms of Racial Discrimination (1966) ICERD	August 5, 1975	(No mention of Article 5)
International Covenant on Civil and Political Rights (1966) ICCPR	December 23, 2008	(No mention of Article 24)

(continued)

Table 4: (*continued*)

Treaty	Signature/ ratification date	Applicable reservation (R) or declaration (D)
International Covenant on Economic, Social and Cultural Rights (1966) ICESCR	December 23, 2008	"The Government of the Bahamas interprets non-discrimination as to national origin as not necessarily implying an obligation on States automatically to guarantee to foreigners the same rights as to their nationals. The term should be understood to refer to the elimination of any arbitrary behavior but not of differences in treatment based on objective and reasonable considerations, in conformity with principles prevailing in democratic societies" (D)
Convention on the Elimination of All Forms of Discrimination against Women (1979) CEDAW	October 6, 1993	"The Government of the Commonwealth of the Bahamas does not consider itself bound by the provisions of article 2(a), . . . article 9, paragraph 2, . . . article 16(h), . . . [and] article 29, paragraph 1, of the Convention" (R)
Convention on the Rights of the Child (1989) CRC	October 30, 1990	"The Government of the Commonwealth of The Bahamas upon signing the Convention reserves the right not to apply the provisions of article 2 of the said Convention insofar as those provisions relate to the conferment of citizenship upon a child having regard to the Provisions of the Constitution of the Commonwealth of The Bahamas" (R)
International Convention on the Protection of the Rights of All Migrant Workers and Members of Their Families (1990) CMW	Not ratified	
Convention on the Rights of Persons with Disabilities (2006)	September 28, 2015	(No mention of Article 18)

Table 5: Status of the Dominican Republic's Treaty Ratifications Regarding the HR to a Nationality

Treaty	Signature/ ratification date	Applicable reservation (R) or declaration (D)
Convention relating to the Status of Stateless Persons (1954)	Not ratified	
Convention on the Reduction of Statelessness (1961)	Signed December 5, 1961	
International Convention on the Elimination of All Forms of Racial Discrimination (1966) ICERD	May 25, 1983	(No mention of Article 5)
International Covenant on Civil and Political Rights (1966) ICCPR	January 4, 1979	(No mention of Article 24)
Convention on the Elimination of All Forms of Discrimination against Women (1979) CEDAW	September 2, 1982	(No mention of Article 9)
Convention on the Rights of the Child (1989) CRC	June 11, 1991	(No mention of Article 7)
International Convention on the Protection of the Rights of All Migrant Workers and Members of Their Families (1990) CMW	Not ratified	
Convention on the Rights of Persons with Disabilities (2006)	August 18, 2009	(No mention of Article 18)

NOTES

Chapter 1. Displaced in Place

Epigraph: Arendt (2004), 376.

1. Personal interview, Marsh Harbour, Abaco, November 12, 2012. All the quotations I attribute to Luzena Dumercy in the rest of the book took place in Marsh Harbour on the aforementioned date. With the exception of "Marie St. Cecile," no pseudonyms are used.

2. See CNN (2012) and Fox News (2012) for a brief overview of the tragedy.

3. Citizenship typically refers to the legal bond between a person and the state at the domestic level and nationality refers to this bond at the international level. Although I prefer the term "citizenship" (since even boats have a "nationality" under international law), "citizenship" and "nationality" are used interchangeably in the book as is common practice in the literature on citizenship and statelessness (see, for example, Sokoloff 2005; UN High Commissioner for Refugees and the Inter-Parliamentary Union 2005; Batchelor 2006; Perks and de Chickera 2009).

4. The Institute on Statelessness and Inclusion estimates the number to be higher than fifteen million (ISI 2014).

5. The Rohingya, a Muslim minority from Myanmar, are a notable exception in this regard.

6. For Arendt, the stateless were arrivals from elsewhere ([1948] 2004, 341, 352, 356): "Nonrecognition of statelessness always means repatriation, i.e., deportation to a country of origin" (355).

7. See Kesby (2012) for a thorough analysis of the different ways the right to have rights has been interpreted and how each interpretation results in the exclusion of some group of people.

8. See *Perez v. Brownell* (U.S. Supreme Court 1958); Gibney (2009); Weissbrodt and Collins (2006, 248).

9. The Declaration on the Rights of Indigenous Peoples (DRIP) specifies that "Indigenous peoples and individuals have the right to belong to an indigenous community or nation, in accordance with the traditions and customs of the community or nation concerned" (UN 2007b, Article 9). It is, however, particular to indigenous peoples' right to belong and not to human beings' right to belong to a given community generally.

10. Article 5 of the International Convention on the Elimination of All Forms of Racial Discrimination, for instance, states that citizenship is a civil right (UN 1965). Article 24 of

the International Covenant on Civil and Political Rights asserts the right of every child to acquire a citizenship (UN 1966a)—a right repeated in Article 7 of the Convention on the Rights
of the Child (UN 1989). In a related vein, Article 29 of the International Convention on the
Protection of the Rights of All Migrant Workers and Members of Their Families (UN 1990)
states that the children of migrant workers have the right to a nationality. Finally, Article 9 of the
Convention on the Elimination of All Forms of Discrimination against Women affirms that a
woman has the right to acquire, change, and retain her nationality (UN 1979), and Article 18
of the Convention on the Rights of Persons with Disabilities states that persons with disabilities have the right to obtain a nationality and change this nationality regardless of their disability (UN 2007a).

11. See also Chan (1991, 3); Donner (1994, 245).

12. In "The Legal Status of Statelessness: An Overview" (Belton 2015) I explain how the
violation of a right to a nationality affects the enjoyment of other human rights.

13. See Chapter 5 for an explanation.

14. Alice Sironi explains, for example, that only "prohibitions" exist in the international
sphere when it comes to nationality. She outlines the following propositions as corresponding
to international customary law: "the prohibition of impinging on the rules on nationality of
other states, the prohibition of forced conferral of nationality upon individuals who have another nationality, the prohibition of discrimination in the granting or withdrawal of nationality, the right to change nationality or to renounce to a nationality [sic], and the obligation to
prevent statelessness at birth and in the context [of state] succession" (2004, 55). Note, however,
that Weis contends that "Statelessness is not inadmissible under international law" (1956, 128).

15. Arendt remarked, "The Rights of Man, supposedly inalienable, proved to be unen-
forceable . . . whenever people appeared who were no longer citizens of any sovereign state"
([1948] 2004, 372).

16. See also Jacobson (1996, 2); Basok, Ilcan, and Noonan (2006).

17. See also Falk (2000); Jacobson (1996); Muller (2004).

18. Christian Joppke (1999) and Randall Hansen (1999) also make this case, albeit from a
different perspective from mine.

19. In *Contested Citizenship*, Ruud Koopmans et al. observe that the postnational "perspective cannot explain why such extensions of rights to migrants can only be observed in
Western democracies, whereas other countries, such as the Persian Gulf states, extend very
few rights to their labor migrants" (2005, 76). See also Joppke (1999, 273).

20. Manby (2009) is a notable exception in the African context, although her work is not
postnational in orientation.

21. See also Brubaker (1989, 146, 155).

22. See also Aidoo (1993); Donnelly (1999).

23. In fact, some groups of stateless people belong to communities that have lived for generations as stateless people within a state's territory.

24. UNHCR recently articulated its position regarding a stateless person's "own country."
In its Handbook on Protection of Stateless Persons, it recognizes that "certain stateless persons" could be considered in their "own country," even if not citizens, if they are long-term

residents and have a "profound connection with the State in question" (2014g, 57). UNHCR then recommends that the state of habitual residence provide such persons citizenship.

25. Note that the OAS, as well as the Organization of African Unity (OAU), formally recognize a more expansive definition of refugeehood. In the case of the OAS, its Cartagena Declaration allows people to be classified as refugees if they "have fled their country" due to "generalized violence, foreign aggression, internal conflicts, massive violation of human rights, or other circumstances which have seriously disturbed public order" (OAS 1984). The OAU Convention Governing the Specific Aspects of Refugee Problems in Africa recognizes similar grounds for refugeehood (OAU 1969).

26. To be fair, the agency's emphasis on its first mandate may be due to the fact that it was created for the purpose of refugee protection and operated for nearly twenty years before it was given its second mandate of the protection of stateless persons via General Assembly Resolution 3274 (UN 1974). Also, the agency launched its ambitious #IBelong Campaign in 2014 as a means to strengthen its mandate in the areas of statelessness protection and identification and statelessness prevention and resolution (see Chapter 2 for more on this campaign; also Belton 2016; UNHCR 2014i).

27. See, for example, Batchelor (1995, 1998, 2006); Bosniak (2000); Massey (2010); van Waas (2008).

28. See, for instance, Belton (2013); Lynch (2005); Kingston et al. (2010); Office of the High Commissioner for Human Rights (2006); Perks and de Chickera (2009); Southwick and Lynch (2009); Weissbrodt and Collins (2006).

29. For example, Belton (2010a, b); Blitz (2006); Blitz and Lynch (2009); Campbell (2014); Chari et al. (2003); Ghosh (2004); Khan (2001); Lynch and Ali (2006); Singh (2010); Sokoloff (2005); van Waas (2010); Zorn (2004). Note that not all these works deal exclusively with stateless persons. Also, these approaches are common to the literature concerning noncitizens generally; see, for instance, Lillich (1984); Tiburcio (2001); Goldston (2006); Bosniak (2006); Weissbrodt (2008).

30. See, for instance, Blitz and Sawyer (2011a and b); Krause (2008); Gibney (2011); Gündoğdu (2015). Margaret Somers applies a similar framework to those who, while not living on the fringes of legality or lacking identity documents, are easily excludable from the state. Examining the treatment African Americans received during and after Hurricane Katrina in the Gulf area of the United States, Somers argues that although they were U.S. citizens, they were in practice "no longer in any meaningful sense citizens; they were now, in effect, stateless people" (2008, 114).

31. Refer to Belton (2011) and Staples (2012) for examples.

32. Staples, *Retheorising Statelessness: A Background Theory of Membership in World Politics*, discusses how the stateless can be included in the "character of citizenship" (2012, 16) without possessing this status formally. See also the scholarship on political action among noncitizens in the United States and the *sans papiers* in France (e.g., Suárez-Navaz et al. 2007; Manzano et al. 2009; McNevin 2011; Monforte and Dufour 2011; Gündoğdu 2015).

33. Redclift notes, but does not elaborate as Lubkemann (2008) does, that "displacement cannot be reduced to mobility" (2013, 4).

34. This conference took place in The Hague, September 15–17, 2014. See Tilburg University (2015) for further information.

35. It is of note, however, that the 1997 European Convention on Nationality does address statelessness in the context of state succession (Council of Europe 1997).

36. See *Forced Migration Review*'s issue on "Crisis" (2014) and Forced Migration Online (2015), especially their three-pronged understanding of forced displacement, which focuses upon these drivers of forced displacement.

37. Belize and Costa Rica also ratified the Convention, but they are not small island developing states (SIDS) and also belong to the Latin American region. They are thus not included in this figure.

38. Costa Rica ratified the Convention, but is again not included in this figure because it is not a SIDS, but classified as a state in the Latin American region. Note that the Dominican Republic signed the 1961 Convention in that same year, but never ratified it.

39. It is estimated that 30,000–60,000 Haitian migrants reside in The Bahamas (International Organization for Migration 2005, 98), and around 380,000 in the Dominican Republic (Wooding and Moseley-Williams 2004a). According to the 2010 Bahamian census, 39,144 residents are Haitian nationals; and 311,969 of the residents in the DR were born in Haiti according to their 2010 census (Government of the Dominican Republic 2010a). The number of stateless persons in each country is unknown.

40. The 2010 census did not take account of individuals' religious affiliation, but more than half the Dominican population is estimated to be Catholic (U.S. Department of State 2015, 1).

41. Interviews were carried out in conformity with Institutional Review Board (IRB) Protocol H09-130. Interviews lasted an average of fifty-one minutes. No pseudonyms are used for the interviews conducted under this protocol. When a person is quoted, I use the term "anonymous" to refer to him or her. See Appendix 1 for the associated consent forms pertinent to this protocol.

42. COB officially became the University of The Bahamas in November, 2016.

43. Interviews were carried out in conformity with IRB Protocol H11-261, which allowed me to interview "Special Populations." Interviews lasted an average of fifty-seven minutes. A few of these participants chose to be anonymous and I reference them as such if quoted. See Appendix 2 for the associated consent forms pertinent to this protocol.

44. The conference was entitled "21st Century Slavery in The Bahamas: A Discussion on Statelessness" and took place on October 24, 2012, in the Harry C. Moore library at COB.

45. An individual "registers" as a Bahamian if he or she applies during or before the eighteen-year mark. The application requirements are less stringent than if one naturalizes, which occurs if an individual applies after age nineteen.

46. A *batey* is the traditional name for a settlement where sugarcane workers resided during the heyday of the sugarcane industry in the DR, from the 1930s to the 1980s. Today, these settlements are primarily shantytowns where many Dominicans of Haitian descent, many of whom continue to work in the sugarcane industry, live.

47. I am aware that this is a contentious assertion given the tendency in some spheres of Dominican society not to use the term black to describe their ethnic/racial identity (see Chapter 4).

48. The Centro Bonó is a Jesuit organization that focuses on social justice and solidarity for persons who face poverty and social exclusion. The organization legally assists many denationalized Dominicans in trying to reacquire or retain their Dominican nationality documents.

49. Sonia Pierre was a prominent Dominican activist of Haitian descent. She was the founder of the Movement for Dominican Women of Haitian Descent (MUDHA) and fought against the discrimination of individuals of Haitian descent in Dominican society. She passed away in 2011.

50. The Sociocultural Movement for Haitian Workers (MOSCTHA) has its origin in the fight for Haitian migrant labor rights, but has since expanded to address the needs of individuals of Haitian descent on the island of Hispaniola and is actively engaged in the "No Human Being Is Illegal" campaign.

51. The symposium was entitled, "Jornada de Diálogo sobre el Derecho a la Nacionalidad y el Estado de Derecho en República Dominicana: Retos y Perspectivas" and took place on February 8, 2013, in the Hotel Dominican Fiesta, Santo Domingo.

52. See n 42 above.

53. "Statelessness and The Bahamas: A Discussion," which took place on April 10, 2014, at the Harry C. Moore library of COB.

54. For an analysis of the Brazil Plan of Action's chapter on statelessness in the Americas, see Belton (forthcoming 2017).

55. See Tables 4 and 5 in Appendix 4 for the status of The Bahamas' and the Dominican Republic's treaty ratifications.

56. The majority of formerly stateless or at-risk of statelessness persons that I interviewed were of Haitian descent. However, Bianca Zaiem, whom I quote in various places in the book, was born in The Bahamas of noncitizens who were not Haitian (she is of British-Syrian descent). It should also be noted that statelessness may affect children born to Guyanese, Jamaican, and other nationals in The Bahamas. Further research needs to be done in this area.

Chapter 2. Statelessness

Epigraph: UNHCR Goodwill Ambassador Barbara Hendricks, quoted in Sturm (2014).

1. See Hayden (2008, 254); Vishniak (1945, 15); Weis (1956, 122–23).

2. See Table 3 in Appendix 3 for a typology of statelessness over time.

3. See also Rürup (2011, 119).

4. See Chapter 5 for a discussion of statelessness and liminality.

5. While these are rights violations that stateless people continue to face no matter where they find themselves globally, it would be inaccurate to describe them as having no other relationships or any other qualities other than their humanness.

6. Arendt believed that human dignity "not only does not exist but is the last and possibly most arrogant myth we have invented in all our long history" ([1948] 2004, 631).

7. Arendt argues that "rights exist because we inhabit the earth together with other men" ([1948] 2004, 629).

8. See, for example, Inter-American Court of Human Rights (2005, 89); Kanics (2011, 131); Macklin (2007, 365); Manly (2007, 257); Southwick and Lynch (2009, 1); Weissbrodt and Collins (2006, 263).

9. See, for instance, Brouwer (2003, 4); Perks and de Chickera (2009, 44); Robinson ([1955] 1997, 7). Note, however, that Massey points out that lack of protection is "a key defining characteristic of a stateless person, be the person stateless *de jure* or stateless *de facto*" (2010, 2).

10. Refer to Manly (2007, 257); Weissbrodt and Collins (2006, 263).

11. Park also notes that de jure statelessness would arise if states do not offer diplomatic recognition to a government that loses its physical territory (2011, 18).

12. Bidoon is "an Arabic word which means 'without nationality'" (Shiblak 2009, 37). These are nomadic and seminomadic persons of the Gulf region who have been unable to acquire citizenship.

13. Rohingya are a Muslim minority group who are denied citizenship in Myanmar, the country of their birth, due to their ethnicity.

14. The Lhotshampas are ethnic Nepalis whose ancestors migrated to Bhutan for work. Although they were initially politically accepted in Bhutan, the merger of the Hindu polities of Sikkim and India led the Bhutanese government to fear that the Hindu Lhotshampas would wish to secede and join India. Consequently, restrictive citizenship laws were enacted that allegedly directly targeted the Lhotshampa (Khan 2001).

15. See Geschiere (2009); Fonchingong (2005); Manby (2009); Odinkalu (2008).

16. See also UN HRC (2008b, 16) for a similar account.

17. This behavior is not limited to Africa. Refer to Fahim (2014) for a more recent example in the case of Kuwait, where the government has increasingly been using denationalization as a tool to silence those who oppose the government. Bahrain has been engaging in a similar activity (Associated Press 2015).

18. According to Claude Cahn and Sebihana Skenderovska, "Croatia adopted a citizenship law aimed at excluding Serbs, Roma and others from access to belonging in the new state, and has reinforced this law with extremely restrictive practice in this area, including forced expulsions of Roma from Croatia," while "Macedonia implemented an extremely restrictive citizenship law after independence, giving rise to a number of categories of excluded groups, most notably ethnic Albanians and Roma" (2008, n. pag.).

19. These examples are found in the U.S. Office of Personnel Management's "Citizenship Laws of the World" report (U.S. Office of Personnel Management 2001).

20. Most developed democracies (as well as other regime types) have some stipulation that citizenship can be revoked when a naturalized citizen poses a threat to public safety/order. See USCIS (2015) for the U.S. provisions in this regard. Whereas in the United States a person cannot be denationalized if he or she was born on U.S. territory, in the UK, British-born citizens who hold another nationality can be—and have been—stripped of their British citizenship.

21. See also Sec. 35A, para. 1e(v) of the act.

22. See Nyers (2011) for a description of how other, primarily racialized, citizens are unmade or irregularized (although not rendered stateless).

23. According to Equal Nationality Rights, more than fifty states discriminate against women in other aspects of nationality law outside of passing it on to their children (Global Campaign for Equal Nationality Rights 2016).

24. Many "Lost Canadians"—persons who either lost Canadian citizenship upon reaching a certain age or unknowingly never acquired Canadian citizenship despite having been born in the country—were denied or deprived of citizenship due to gender discriminatory nationality clauses. See Chapman (2008). There are, of course, historical examples of gender discrimination among "developed" democracies, too, and the UN Convention on the Nationality of Married Women (UN 1957) attempted to address some of these issues for women married to noncitizens.

25. See Mutharika (1989), specifically 106–29a, and chap. 4 of van Waas (2008) for further examples of how conflicts in nationality laws can render a person stateless.

26. As Chapter 4 illustrates, birth registration is not the same as obtaining a Dominican birth certificate that paves the way for Dominican citizenship acquisition.

27. Sub-Saharan Africa and West and Central Africa are close behind with an estimated 56 percent and 53 percent of the child population under age five unregistered, according to UNICEF (2013, 43). Manby (2015) states that a third of West African states have a birth registration rate less than 50 percent (see pp. 2, 32 of her report).

28. Sudan is now denying citizenship to those considered "Southerners." "Southerners" is a label used to identify those who are black Sudanese of non-Arab descent.

29. See Korir Sing'oei (2009, 43); van Selm (2009, 46).

30. Refer to Ahmed (2004).

31. For example, Lewa (2009, 13); Aird et al. (2002, 7).

32. See Lynch and Cook (2006); Southwick and Lynch (2009).

33. See Lynch (2005); Kingston et al. (2010).

34. Refer to Belton (2013).

35. See Bhabha (2009).

36. From Lynch and Ali (2006, 8–9).

37. Refer to Aird et al. (2002, 3); Kingston (2013, 76).

38. See Equal Rights Trust (2010); Weissbrodt and Collins (2006, 267–69).

39. See Belton (2010a).

40. See Kelley (2010, 359–360); Sokoloff (2005, 22); Physicians for Human Rights (2010); Hussain (2011) for similar accounts.

41. See, for example, Kingston et al. (2010, 8 and 10); Human Rights Watch (2010, 48–49; 2011, 40); Lynch (2008, 12); Pérez (2011, 1038); UNAIDS (2011, 16).

42. See European Roma Rights Center (2005); Feller (2009) for examples.

43. Refer to Aird et al. (2002); Farzana (2008); Feingold (2006, 5); Lynch (2008, 6; 2009); Southwick and Lynch (2009, 3); Pérez (2011, 1039); Sokoloff (2005, 23) on the trafficking of stateless persons.

44. See also Lynch and Cook (2004).

45. See Jirawattanapisal et al. (2010, 8); Modikwa (2012); Slip (2006) for examples.

46. See Kingston et al. (2010, 9); Physicians for Human Rights (2012); UNHCR and Plan International (2012, 15). Refer to Lynch (2008); Bhabha (2011); UNHCR (2015a) for more on the specific effects of statelessness upon children.

47. See also UN HRC (2008b, 18).

48. Refer to Human Rights Watch (2010, 54); Lynch and Ali (2006, 6); Sokoloff (2005, 20).

49. See Belton (2015) for an elaboration of the ways in which statelessness affects the fulfilment of each right in the UDHR, and Lynch (2005) for a global overview of the problems that stateless people face.

50. Note, however, that through the legal analysis of two recent UN Human Rights Committee (HRC) decisions regarding Article 12.4 of the ICCPR, Ryan Liss shows how the HRC "drew from a line of reasoning strongly advocated in prior dissenting opinions to conclude that a non-national's state of residence could qualify as his or her 'own country' depending on the breadth of his or her sociological ties with the state" (2014, 1130). Although this is not the same as a right to citizenship, and Liss recognizes this, it at least provides (albeit tentative) grounding for a stateless person's right not to be denied reentry into the country where she or he has made a life.

51. Personal interview, Santo Domingo, DR, July 14, 2012; interview conducted in English. All the quotations I attribute to Rodríguez throughout the rest of the book took place in Santo Domingo on the aforementioned date.

52. See also Marshall (1979, 207); Sears (1994, 15).

53. Personal interview, Nassau, Bahamas, July 29, 2009.

54. Personal interview, Nassau, Bahamas, August 6, 2009. Jacqueline Bhabha similarly reflects, "What sort of juror or voter with a contribution to make to his or her peers is one who has been forced to live outside the community during the pre-majority period? How is such a person to engage with the concerns of the polity in a meaningful and contributory, rather than hostile or resentful way?" (2014, 93).

55. See Amnesty International (2013); IRIN (2013).

56. Refer to Seet (2016) for an alternative explanation of when UNHCR finally took on its statelessness mandate.

57. The International Convention on the Protection of the Rights of All Migrant Workers and Members of Their Families (UN 1990) has the fewest states parties.

58. The first expert meeting was held in Prato, Italy, May 27–28, 2010; the second in Geneva, Switzerland, December 6–7, 2010; the third in Dakar, Senegal, May 23–24, 2011; the fourth in Tunis, Tunisia, October 31 to November 1, 2013.

59. For further information on UCB's position and involvement, refer to UNHCR (2014j).

60. Specifically, the GAP's ten Action items include: resolving current major situations of statelessness (Action 1); preventing children from being born into statelessness and ensuring birth registration (Actions 2 and 7); preventing the denial, loss, or deprivation of nationality on discriminatory grounds (Actions 3 and 4) and in cases of state succession (Action 5); granting protection status to stateless migrants and facilitating their naturalization (Action 6); issuing nationality documentation to those who are entitled to it (Action 8); increasing accession to the two UN statelessness conventions (Action 9); and, finally, improving data—both quantitative and qualitative—on statelessness (Action 10) (UNHCR 2014e).

61. I only focus on activity in the Latin American/Caribbean region for the purposes of this book, but there have been initiatives elsewhere. The Asia-Pacific region, for example, has declared that it will establish civil registration for all, including stateless persons, by 2024

(UNHCR 2014b); and Central Asia is moving forward with discussion and action around statelessness, hosting two conferences in the past few years on the subject (UNHCR 2014a). Also of note, the Economic Community of West African States (ECOWAS) issued the Abidjan Declaration on the Eradication of Statelessness last year (ECOWAS 2015), which asks the African Union to adopt a protocol to the African Charter on Human and Peoples' Rights on the right to a nationality, among several other measures.

62. It is of note that the Dominican Republic sent representatives to this meeting.

63. Since 2005, CLARCIEV, an organization composed of regional civil registry offices, provides tools and a space for countries to share their practices and information on various forms of identity documentation and registration. See their website for further information (CLARCIEV 2015).

64. I was one of the civil society participants during the Caribbean subregional meeting of the Cartagena +30 process. At the invitation of the Norwegian Refugee Council, I took part in the preparatory meeting in Grand Cayman in September 2014 and also attended the Ministerial Meeting in Brasilia in December 2014, when the new Brazil Declaration and Plan of Action were issued. Other subregional meetings included the March 18–19 MERCOSUR meeting held in Buenos Aires, Argentina; the Andean meeting held in Quito, Ecuador, June 9–10; and the MESOAMERICA meeting, which took place in Managua, Nicaragua, July 10–11 (all subregional meetings took place in 2014; for more information see UNHCR 2016).

Chapter 3. The Bahamas: Neither Fish Nor Fowl

Epigraph: former governmental official; personal interview, Nassau, August 4, 2009.

1. One can go even farther back to the years immediately after Haitian Independence for examples of political instability. As Philippe Girard explains, "The first half-century of Haitian independent rule was far from peaceful. By the time it was over, twenty-nine of the thirty-four men who had signed the declaration of independence had met a violent end. . . . Haitians could only find solace in the fact that their dictators were able to fend off most of the many coup attempts" (2010, 76).

2. The Bahamas ranks 49 of 182 states listed in the Human Development Index. It is a "high human development" country, less than a point away from being classified as a "very high human development" country (UNDP 2013b, 144). Haiti, by comparison, is classified as a "low human development" country, ranking 161 out of 182 states (154).

3. The Dominican Republic and British Overseas Territory of Turks and Caicos are the other two.

4. Specifically, 39,144 persons of the total population of 351,461 are Haitian nationals.

5. A Haitian Embassy official says that his "estimate is 40,000" when it comes to the number of children born of Haitian parents in The Bahamas and "between 20 to 25,000" as regards the number of Haitians born in Haiti living in the country (personal interview, Nassau, July 28, 2009).

6. Freedom House (2011 n. pag.) estimates that between "30,000 and 40,000 recent Haitian immigrants reside illegally in the Bahamas."

7. Personal interview, Nassau, July 27, 2009. The Free National Movement is one of the two major political parties in The Bahamas.

8. Personal communication (email), April 15, 2013.

9. Personal interview, Nassau, July 27, 2009.

10. Personal interview, Nassau, November 8, 2012. Sears therefore recommends that there "should be a committee of cabinet" that considers each application instead. All the quotations I attribute to Sears throughout the rest of the book took place in Nassau on the aforementioned date.

11. Personal interview, Nassau, August 7, 2009.

12. The now defunct Nationality Support Unit (NSU), established in 2012, was a legal clinic housed at the Eugene Dupuch Law School in Nassau. It provided legal support to "persons who were born in the Bahamas to Haitian parentage" (quote from Brice-Adderley, personal interview, Nassau, July 11, 2012) so that they could apply for Bahamian citizenship.

13. Personal interview, Nassau, Bahamas, July 11, 2012. All the quotations that I attribute to Brice-Adderley throughout the rest of the book took place in Nassau on the aforementioned date.

14. Personal interview, Nassau, October 29, 2012. All the quotations I attribute to Dolce throughout the rest of the book took place in Nassau on the aforementioned date.

15. Personal interview, Marsh Harbour, Abaco, November 13, 2012. All quotations I attribute to Charité throughout the rest of the book took place in Marsh Harbour on the aforementioned date.

16. The Bahamas Constitutional Commission is a body instituted by Prime Minister Perry Christie to examine the existing Independence-era Constitution and make recommendations for change in diverse areas, one of which is nationality. In its final report, the Constitutional Commission made recommendations regarding nationality, but decided not to opine on the situation of children born to noncitizens in the country. The commissioners state instead that this should "be the subject of further study" and that another commission should be appointed "to consider further questions relating to nationality and the basis on which nationality should be acquired by children born in The Bahamas to non-Bahamian parents" (Government of The Bahamas 2013, 35).

17. See Evans (2012) and Dames (2012a).

18. The same *Nassau Guardian* article lists figures that illustrate the greater number of approved citizenship applications (2,038)—in addition to grants of permanent residency and the like—during the previous PLP administration.

19. According to another *Nassau Guardian* article, of the forty-four persons granted Bahamian citizenship two weeks prior to the 2012 general election, none, were able to vote in the election "as voter registration had come to an end by the time they became Bahamians" (Dames 2012b).

20. Personal interview, Nassau, Bahamas, October 31, 2012. All quotations I attribute to Ambassador Rodrigue throughout the rest of the book took place in Nassau on the aforementioned date.

21. Personal interview, Nassau, Bahamas, November 5, 2012. All quotations I attribute to Petit-Homme throughout the rest of the book took place in Nassau on the aforementioned date.

22. Personal interview, Nassau, October 30, 2012. All quotations I attribute to Desmangles throughout the rest of the book took place in Nassau on the aforementioned date.

23. Personal interview, Nassau, November 11, 2012. All quotations that I attribute to Zaiem throughout the rest of the book took place in Nassau on the aforementioned date.

24. Personal interview, Nassau, November 1, 2012. All quotations I attribute to Jn-Simon throughout the rest of the book took place in Nassau on the aforementioned date.

25. If a Bahamian-born person of noncitizen parents applies for citizenship between ages eighteen and nineteen, she or he "registers" as a Bahamian citizen and fewer documents are needed as part of the application process. If, however, the individual misses the one-year time frame, that person must go through the regular naturalization process.

26. The individual was born in Haiti, which may account for a longer waiting period than if the person had been born in The Bahamas of noncitizen parents. Nevertheless, the waiting period is excessive.

27. Personal interview, Nassau, November 1, 2012. All quotations I attribute to St. Cecile throughout the rest of the book took place in Nassau on the aforementioned date.

28. Personal interview, Nassau, November 5, 2012. All quotations I attribute to Louis throughout the rest of the book took place in Nassau on the aforementioned date.

29. As happened in Zaiem's case, Dumercy relates, "they tell you on the letter [of approval for citizenship that] it takes 3 to 4 weeks before you get a call for the swearing-in, but that's not true. They don't call you in 3 to 4 weeks. It could be months—some people, a year." However, the letter sent to applicants on their approval for Bahamian citizenship clearly states that "After you have submitted the required documents, please allow at least three (3) complete weeks before contacting the Naturalization Unit at telephone 502-0533 to arrange an appointment to be registered as a citizen of The Bahamas." It thus appears incumbent on the applicant, on receipt of his or her approval letter, to contact the Naturalization Unit to be registered as a Bahamian citizen.

30. Personal interview, Nassau, August 7, 2009.

31. Personal interview, Nassau, July 27, 2009.

32. Personal interview, Nassau, July 31, 2009.

33. This person also notes that "Since July 2012, the Department has increased the frequency of the swearing-in ceremonies to shorten the period between the submission of documents and the ceremony" (personal communication [email], April 13, 2013).

34. Personal interview, Nassau, August 7, 2009.

35. Personal interview, Nassau, August 7, 2009.

36. The Bahamas is only one of two states in the Western hemisphere that discriminates against women in the passing of citizenship from mother to child. The other is Barbados.

37. Only if the Bahamian mother is unmarried does the child acquire Bahamian citizenship at birth. Note also that the gendered dimension of citizenship acquisition continues in the arena of marriage since the Bahamian Constitution makes explicit reference to non-Bahamian women being "entitled" to register as Bahamian citizens, provided certain criteria are met, if they marry a Bahamian man (Article 10), but Bahamian women who marry non-Bahamian men are not provided the same right.

38. Article 15 of Chapter 191/Immigration Act (Government of The Bahamas 1967) briefly discusses how the Immigration Board "shall grant" a permanent residence certificate to children born "legitimately" to a Bahamian woman married to a non-Bahamian man outside the country.

39. Although bill 1 spoke most strongly to issues of potential statelessness, the other bills also touched upon it (bill 2 if the foreign spouse were stateless and bill 3 if the Bahamian man had a child out of wedlock with a noncitizen who could not pass on her citizenship).

40. Refer to the International Foundation for Electoral Systems "Election Guide: Bahamas" for the 2016 results (IFES 2016).

41. Personal interview, Nassau, July 28, 2009.

42. Personal interview, Nassau, November 9, 2012.

43. Personal interview, Nassau, July 27, 2009. A different MFA participant stated that "Information on these children [who are deported with their mothers] are carefully taken and kept for safekeeping to assist in their subsequent application for Bahamian citizenship at the age of 18" (email correspondence, April 15, 2013).

44. As of March 2014, the Haitian government is set to launch a program to provide documents to its overseas nationals in the DR and Turks and Caicos (Daniel 2014).

45. Personal interview, Nassau, July 28, 2009.

46. Personal interview, Nassau, July 28, 2009.

47. Chapter 5 discusses how these individuals have an ambiguous place identity.

48. Email correspondence, 2013.

49. Email correspondence, 2013.

50. Personal interview, February 7, 2012, New York.

51. Personal interview, Nassau, July 27, 2009.

52. Email correspondence, April 15, 2013. This participant also notes, however, that "There is some concern about the children born to Jamaican parent/s, as a change in the Jamaican Constitution removed automatic Jamaican citizenship to children born to Jamaican parent/s outside of Jamaica. Such children now have to apply for Jamaican citizenship, but they are almost guaranteed to be granted Jamaican citizenship. The same requirement applies to the children born outside of Guyana to Guyanese parent/s."

53. "Possède la nationalité haïtienne de naissance tout individu né d'un père haïtien ou d'une mère haïtienne qui eux-mêmes n'avaient pas répudié leur nationalité au moment de la naissance de l'énfant" (Government of Haiti 2009, Article 11).

54. The Haitian Embassy was quick to issue a clarification stating, "President Martelly's sole purpose during his stay in The Bahamas was to seek opportunities to improve the lives of Haitians, so they don't have to migrate to other countries. . . . At any moment, President Martelly did not intend to interfere in any way in the internal politics of The Bahamas" (K. Rolle 2012a).

55. Email correspondence, April 15, 2013.

56. Such "gaps" affect all children born of noncitizens, as well as children born overseas to Bahamian women married to foreigners.

57. Personal interview, Nassau, Bahamas, August 4, 2009.

58. Email correspondence, April 15, 2013.

59. See Chapter 4 of this book for a similar remark Haitian foreign minister Renauld made regarding persons born of Haitian descent in the Dominican Republic.

60. Chapter 5 details why many Bahamian-born persons of Haitian descent do not feel "Haitian."

Chapter 4. The Dominican Republic: Foreigners in Their Own Country

Epigraph: Felix Callo Marcel, cited in Kushner (2015).

1. Due to the repudiation of this sentence by political progressives and others in the Dominican Republic, as well as concern from the Haitian Government, a bill was passed in May 2014 by the Dominican Congress to allow "Those without documents . . . [to] apply for legal residency and eventually citizenship if they can prove they were born in the Dominican Republic" (Archibold 2014, n. pag.). More will be discussed on the National Regularization Plan later in the chapter.

2. "forced to be Haitian" are the words of Justice Jiménez Martínez in her dissenting opinion in Sentence TC/0168/13. She stated that the Deguis case was one of denationalization, but "not only denationalization, but being forced to be Haitian" (Government of the Dominican Republic 2013e, 140).

3. Cuba is the largest.

4. Samuel Martínez (2003, 85) citing Moya Pons, states that Haitians entered Haiti at the invitation of several Spanish Haitian political elites. Haitian rule was thus "neither an 'invasion' nor an 'occupation'" (86). Haiti considered the move a means of securing itself against European attempts to invade the newly independent country from the east.

5. Refer to Human Rights Watch (2002, 8); UN HRC (2008b, 15); Martínez (2003, 85).

6. Personal interview, Santo Domingo, DR, July 13, 2012. All quotations I attribute to Leonardo throughout the rest of the book took place in Santo Domingo on the aforementioned date.

7. As per the Human Development Index, Haiti is ranked 161 of 186 countries while the DR is ranked 96 (UNDP 2013a).

8. Oficina Nacional de Estadísticas.

9. Personal interview, New York, February 22, 2012. Goris was formerly a program officer on equality and citizenship for OSJI in New York. She is now the director of administration for OSJI. All quotations I attribute to Goris throughout the rest of the book took place in New York City on the aforementioned date.

10. Personal interview, Santo Domingo, Dominican Republic, June 26, 2012. Unless otherwise indicated, I translated all interview data from the DR fieldwork from Spanish into English. The interview with Gamboa was conducted in English and all quotations I attribute to Gamboa throughout the rest of the book took place in Santo Domingo on the aforementioned date.

11. Personal interview, Santo Domingo, DR, July 9, 2012. The Fundación Zile is a nonprofit organization established to serve as "an observatory of Dominican-Haitian relations." According to Paraison, "We permanently monitor all areas of interchange between the two countries and try to provide recommendations to both governments on potentially conflictive

areas." All quotations I attribute to Paraison throughout the rest of the book took place in Santo Domingo on the aforementioned date.

12. In English, the Central Electoral Board. It is also the body mandated with setting elections.

13. This same article stipulates that if the father is Dominican, the child can be registered at a Dominican civil registry and obtain his or her birth certificate there.

14. Personal interview, Santo Domingo, July 5, 2012.

15. This think tank was founded in 2009 and initially approached the subject of migration from a gender perspective. Today it continues its work in this field by focusing on human trafficking in the region, but has broadened its scope to examine nationality issues and other concerns pertinent to regional migration flows.

16. Personal interview, Santo Domingo, July 5, 2012. All quotations I attribute to Wooding throughout the rest of the book took place in Santo Domingo on the aforementioned date.

17. Resolution 02-2007 was passed on April 18, 2007, while resolution 12-2007 was passed on December 10, 2007.

18. Personal interview, Indira Goris, New York, February 22, 2012.

19. Author's translation of "Libro Registro del Nacimiento de Niño (a) de Madre Extranjera No Residente en la República Dominicana."

20. Leonardo states, "And we are aware of people who have been transferred to the Foreigner's Book without their consent."

21. Personal interview, Santo Domingo, July 13, 2012.

22. See also Government of the Dominican Republic (2013a, 7).

23. Personal interview, Santo Domingo, July 5, 2012. All quotations I attribute to Tejeda throughout the rest of the book took place in Santo Domingo on the aforementioned date.

24. All quotes from Sentence TC/0168/13 are my own translations.

25. Personal interview, Santo Domingo, July 3, 2012. All quotations I attribute to Charpantier throughout the rest of the book took place in Santo Domingo on the aforementioned date.

26. The new biometric IDs do not have this information. See Joseph (2015) for the new format.

27. The Inter-American Commission on Human Rights (2005) has also received complaints that Dominicans of Haitian descent have been deported to Haiti.

28. A copy of Circular 17 is found in the Annex of OSJI's submission to the UN's Commission on the Elimination of Racial Discrimination (OHCHR 2008).

29. See also Sagás (2000) for further detail.

30. See UN Committee on the Elimination of Racial Discrimination (2013) and Government of the Dominican Republic (2013e, 2014b).

31. Leonardo states, "It's that the Supreme Court, the High Courts are very politicized and this subject is a very political one."

32. This is a case that was first presented to the Inter-American Commission on Human Rights. The Commission then brought the case to the IACtHR since the Dominican state was contesting the Commission's ruling. The IACtHR found that the DR had violated, among others, the rights to a nationality, name, identity, and juridical personality of several Domini-

can families of Haitian descent that it had expelled from its territory. See IACtHR (2014a) for further information.

33. She was also denied citizenship because she allegedly has the right to Haitian nationality, too: "y también conviene destacar que la circunstancia de que la demandante señora Juliana Dequis (o Deguis) no tenga el derecho a la nacionalidad dominicana por *jus soli* no la coloca en situación de apátrida, ya que tal como se expone a continuación, ella tiene derecho a la nacionalidad haitiana" (Government of the Dominican Republic 2013e, 75). After six years, Deguis was finally reinstated as a Dominican citizen in 2014 (UNHCR 2014h).

34. Those most affected by lack of documentation tend to be poor. As the UNDP participant states, "It's not the children of the rich who don't have their birth certificates. It's the children of poor people and they are not going to be able to go to High School."

35. In Spanish: "Fortalecimiento al sistema de registro civil y de identidad."

36. The UNDP participant states, "What we wanted to do was kill two birds with one stone by first resolving the critical problem of the birth certificate and [access to] education and on the other hand validate a methodology that once finalized would allow us as agents to continue using it. The objective was to validate a methodology, validate a procedure [of registration]."

37. "Declárame y me abrirás muchas Puertas"; see UNICEF (2014b) for further information.

38. Movimiento por un Registro Civil Libre de Discriminación.

39. In *Vidas suspendidas* (Lives on Hold), Civolani Hischnjakow documents the effects of Resolution 12-2007 on fifteen Dominicans of Haitian descent. Wherever I quote a source from her study within the book, the translations are my own from the original Spanish.

40. Brad Blitz and Caroline Sawyer, examining statelessness in Europe, similarly remark, "the implementation of rules and policies which destroy lives often comes about through minor administrative or bureaucratic processes whose banality belies their catastrophic effects" (2011a, 284).

41. Personal interview, Santo Domingo, July 5, 2012.

42. Charpantier also states that if the child is older than two, the embassy will not register them as Haitian.

43. Personal interview, Santo Domingo, July 9, 2012. All quotations I attribute to Delienne throughout the rest of the book took place in Santo Domingo on the aforementioned date.

44. See also Fletcher and Miller (2004, 671–72).

45. Another survey, conducted by Centro de Estudios Sociales y Demográficos in 2007, found that 22 percent of those interviewed in the bateyes did not have a birth certificate and a third did not have a cédula (CESDEM 2008, 18).

46. Article 2 of the CRC states that "States Parties shall take all appropriate measures to ensure that the child is protected against all forms of discrimination or punishment on the basis of the status, activities, expressed opinions, or beliefs of the child's parents, legal guardians, or family members" (UN 1989).

47. The full text reads, "*siendo violatoria a la constitución y las leyes la Declaración de Nacimiento del impetrante, éste no puede aprovecharse de su propia falta y recibir la nacionalidad dominicana por tal actuación ilícita*" (italics in original).

48. As the UNHCR-DR officer says, "Remember, here it's not an open denationalization, the policy of denationalization. Not at all. The only thing is that people are not given documents and you know what it means." Note that this interview took place prior to Sentence TC/0168/13 in 2013.

49. This is also pertinent in the Bahamian case.

50. Charpantier agrees, "if the child was born before 2010, they [the Haitian Embassy] are not going to accept him either because they are Dominicans. That's what they're saying. Now, from 2010 onwards, and provided the child is less than two years old, then they will accept him because the Constitution already provides for that."

51. This position was earlier expressed in the Bahamian case when former President Martelly stated that those born in The Bahamas were not Haitian nationals (see K. Rolle 2012b).

52. Plan Nacional de Regularización de Extranjeros en situación migratoria irregular (Government of the Dominican Republic 2013b).

53. See Welsh (2015) for a similar criticism of the process.

54. The Embassy of the Dominican Republic in Washington, D.C., claims, however, that "No person born in the Dominican Republic will be expelled from our territory" (Embassy of the DR 2016, n.pag.).

55. From Justice Jiménez Martínez's dissenting opinion in Sentence TC/0168/13 (Government of the Dominican Republic 2013e, 140).

Chapter 5. Noncitizen Insiders

Epigraph: Ní Mhurchú (2015, 167).

1. Nyers states, "citizenship has not been revoked per se, but . . . it has been rendered inoperable" (2011, 185).

2. Ní Mhurchú (2015, 159) similarly observes how French citizens of Arab (Algerian) descent are only French in Algeria.

3. Beech uses the term "liminar" whereas other works use "liminal." I use "liminal" when not quoting Beech.

4. See Belton (2010a, 2011); Blitz (2006); Green and Pierce (2009, 34); Hayden (2008, 249); OSJI and CEJIL (2012, 8); UNHCR (2003); Zorn (2004).

5. Of the seventy-four states that responded to a survey on statelessness commissioned by UNHCR in 2003, 43 percent acknowledged they were unable to identify stateless persons on their territory while some denied that stateless populations existed within their territory even though the UNHCR had provided technical assistance to such states concerning their stateless populations (UNHCR 2004). The situation has not improved as UNHCR observes that while "improving baseline population data has become increasingly important . . . measuring statelessness remains complicated and progress in this area limited" (2015d, 7).

6. Personal interview, Santo Domingo, July 13, 2012.

7. Rodríguez also notes that "Most people are unaware of their [the stateless] existence" and, as noted in Chapter 4, Paraison considers "the denial of their very existence" to be the biggest problem facing the Haitian diaspora in the DR.

8. See also Staples (2012, chap. 6), "Contemporary Statelessness in Eastern Democratic Republic of Congo," for an elaboration of the way in which the formal right to a nationality rings hollow when local practices of recognition are not extended.

9. Telephone interview, August 12, 2009.

10. Although Bahamian anthropologist Nicolette Bethel points out that the Eleutheran Adventurers, white Puritans of English descent from Bermuda, settled in The Bahamas long before Loyalists from the United States brought slaves to the islands (Bethel 2003).

11. Personal interview, Nassau, August 6, 2009.

12. Personal interview, Nassau, August 4, 2009.

13. Personal interview, Nassau, July 29, 2009.

14. Personal interview, Nassau, July 31, 2009.

15. The author was in attendance as a presenter.

16. See Wooding and Moseley-Williams (2004b, 33–34); Martínez in IACtHR (2005); Aber and Small (2013, 81).

17. Julia Kristeva's work (1980) focuses on the impurity that results from abjection in the spheres of literature, psychology, and religion.

18. Vargas was one of the presenters at the "Simposio sobre Derecho a la Nacionalidad y Estado de Derecho en República Dominicana" that was held in Santo Domingo on February 8, 2013. The author was also a presenter.

19. Diène was UN Special Rapporteur on contemporary forms of racism, racial discrimination, xenophobia, and related intolerance in 2002–2008 and McDougall was UN Independent Expert on minority issues in 2005–2011 (the latter position has since been renamed to Special Rapporteur on minority issues).

20. Personal interview, Marsh Harbour, Abaco, November 12, 2012.

21. Personal interview, Marsh Harbour, Abaco, November 14, 2012.

22. Personal interview, Marsh Harbour, Abaco, November 12, 2012.

23. The interviewee was describing a Haitian national who was "as clean and well-spoken as you could find" because "he married a girl [whose] family is high-class black people. So she brought him up to her level." This supports the aforementioned assertion of another interviewee (on p. 126 of this book) that Bahamians think they are of a higher social standing than Haitians.

24. Personal interview, Marsh Harbour, Abaco, November 14, 2012.

25. Centro de Estudios Sociales y Demográficos.

26. Haitian settlements in Abaco have suffered fires in recent years in which homes have been destroyed and hundreds of people left homeless (R. Rolle 2014; Turnquest 2014).

27. Few people were present on the dirt roads that day as most had left for work outside the community and only a few adult women remained to sell their wares on the ground in front of their homes.

28. In addition to "this theory that Haitians brought AIDS to the Bahamas," Jn-Simon says that Bahamians also believe that they brought tuberculosis. Petit-Homme also explains how he was listening to a radio talk show in 2002 and "this guy called the radio station and say AIDS originated in Haiti. I was so shocked. . . . I was thinking we had already passed all these things."

29. Personal interview, Marsh Harbour, Abaco, November 14, 2012.

30. UNHCR is also clear that the possession of a nationality is "a fundamental aspect of the system for human rights protection" (UNHCR 2014g, 21).

31. Personal interview, Nassau, Bahamas, July 29, 2009.

32. Personal interview, Marsh Harbour, Abaco, November 14, 2012.

33. According to an administrator at one of Abaco's primary schools, birth certificates are needed to identify when a child is born so that he or she is placed in the appropriate grade.

34. All quotes from Calis García are from the online video "Statelessness in the Dominican Republic" (MOSCTHA 2012); the translations are my own.

35. Personal interview, El Caño, Monte Plata, Dominican Republic, February 6, 2013.

36. See the Georgetown Law School's Human Rights Institute 2014 report for similar experiences.

37. I did not speak with this individual to know why his Bahamian passport was revoked. According to Jn-Simon, "His father and his mother were not married at the time when he got the passport so [Bahamian authorities said] 'It's time for it to be revoked.'"

38. On their visit to the DR, Diène and McDougall observed how batey residents were only able to find employment "for substandard pay and without contracts" (UN HRC 2008c, 24).

39. Personal interview with Maria Virtudes Berroa, Executive Director of BRA-Dominicana, Santo Domingo, July 11, 2013.

40. Even Tejeda, a Dominican of non-Haitian descent, states that "If I don't have my ID card with me, I feel afraid you know."

41. Gonzalez and Chavez's (2012) study also reveals that these types of fears are prevalent among undocumented youth in the United States.

42. Movement into the DR from Haiti can also be restricted for Bahamian-born persons of Haitian descent who carry a Bahamian-government issued Certificate of Identity/travel document. Describing a recent trip to the DR with his church youth group, Louis explains how the Dominican border authorities prevented him from entering the country. "I could not cross the border. They would not accept my travel document. . . . They wanted the passport [which he did not possess]. . . . They claimed [the Certificate of Identity] was not legitimate enough" for him to enter the country. He ended up staying in Haiti for a few days and then returned to The Bahamas.

43. Personal interview, Nassau, July 29, 2009.

44. In the case of *Emildo Bueno Oguís v. Dominican Republic* (OSJI and CEJIL 2010), for example, Mr. Bueno had solicited a certified copy of his birth certificate from the JCE so he could join his wife in the United States. Despite his having already possessed Dominican identity documents, the JCE refused to issue him a certified copy of his birth certificate and he could not travel.

45. As explained by Beech, "Turner also sees liminality as a phase in which the liminar reflects about their society and their cosmos in order to return to society in a new identity with new responsibilities and powers" (2011, 287).

46. Interviews took place in the batey of El Caño in the province of Monte Plata on February 7, 2013.

47. Bahamian lawyer Dexter Reno Johnson writes that he knows of "a number of young persons of Haitian extraction" who were born in more rural parts of The Bahamas who "were totally unaware of the constitutional requirements" (2008, 69).

48. Personal interview, Nassau, November 1, 2012.

49. It further adds—and this is important in the case of the Dominican Republic—that "Where a child is illegally deprived of some or all of the elements of his or her identity, States Parties shall provide appropriate assistance and protection, with a view to re-establishing speedily his or her identity."

50. Personal interview, Marsh Harbour, Abaco, November 13, 2012.

Chapter 6. Sharing the World with Others: A Right to Belong

Epigraph: Patrick Hayden (2008, 266).

1. Michael Freeman states something similar in "Putting Law in Its Place": "The problem is not that law is not necessary for the protection of human rights, but that it is not sufficient. The incorporation of human rights into law does not secure their protection, and may conceal the fact that human rights are persistently violated in practice" (2006, 62).

2. For example, Blake (2001); Miller (1998); and Nagel (2005) all address questions of global justice, but do not work from a cosmopolitan framework.

3. See, for example, Armstrong (2011); Beitz (1979); Pogge (1994, 2002); Moellendorf (1996).

4. Beitz has since moved away from the position that international interdependence constitutes a system of cooperation (Cordourier-Real 2010, 25).

5. Capabilities are "minimum core social entitlements" that are "central requirements of a life with dignity" (Nussbaum 2006, 75).

6. This is a leitmotif throughout Joseph Carens's work as well.

7. I say "initially" because in my critique of Benhabib's position, I note that her argument for membership is really an argument for citizenship (see Belton 2011, 67).

8. This assertion stands in contrast to the basic argument of her book, however, which is that liberal-democratic states should grant "first admittance" rights to refugees and asylum seekers, but continue to have the right "to regulate the transition from first admission to full membership" (2004b, 221; see also 3).

9. Carens makes this observation twenty years earlier when he states that "Citizenship in Western liberal democracies is the modern equivalent of feudal privilege—an inherited status that greatly enhances one's life chances" (1987, 252).

10. Shachar and Hirschl are not the only ones to make note of the way in which citizenship conditions life chances. Andrea Giovanni, for example, recognizes that "It is, after all, to no one's credit, or choice, or effort, that they were born in the United States rather than in Mali, and yet country of birth has a much larger effect on prospects, on average, than either class of origin, gender, or race" (2011, 571). Beitz similarly states that "The balance between 'arbitrary' and 'personal' contributions to my present well-being seems decisively tipped toward the 'arbitrary' ones by the realization that, no matter what my talents, education, life goals, etc., I would

have been virtually precluded from attaining my present level of well-being if I had been born in a less developed society" (1979, 163).

11. While Shachar and Hirschl describe ways in which such a distribution scheme could work, it is Shachar's *The Birthright Lottery* (2009) that further develops the notion of citizenship as inherited property and the birthright privilege levy that could become a means of rectifying unequal life starting points.

12. See Chapter 1, n. 10 for a list of treaties that include nationality as a human right.

13. Vernon recognizes that criminal and failed states exist, which cannot adequately provide for their citizens. In such cases, a duty to aid (2010, 108), along with a "duty not to deprive others of the possibility of enjoying the political and economic conditions that rich countries standardly seek" (110), arises.

14. Children, especially, should not be penalized for the irregular migratory status of their parents and unable to enjoy their human right to a nationality as a result.

15. Zilbershats asserts that "global justice does imply that it is the duty of every State to see that citizenship, full membership in society, should be granted to each and every person, if not by that State then at least by another" (2002, 67).

16. The exception in this regard is statelessness that arises in the context of state succession (Massey 2010). People "who have the option to claim the nationality of more than one State to be able to freely decide which of these nationalities would be retained in situations of State succession" (UN HRC 2009b, 13).

17. Personal interview, Santo Domingo, Dominican Republic, July 5, 2012. Note that in the Handbook on Protection of Stateless Persons, UNHCR declares that the stateless in situ, who "are long-term, habitual residents of a State which is often their country of birth" (2014g, 57) find themselves in their "own country." It goes on to state that "The appropriate status for such individuals in their 'own country' is nationality of the State in question" (57). While this is a marked improvement on UNHCR's previous position that *any* nationality will suffice for the stateless, it is still unclear how statelessness will be avoided in those situations where domestic law only permits citizenship acquisition through application *after* birth. It is also unclear how "lawfulness" affects a stateless person's ability to acquire citizenship in this scenario. What classifies a stateless person's presence as "unlawful" such that she or he may not be considered in his or her own country? This is especially important to elucidate given that some states, as we saw in the case of the Dominican Republic, may deny or deprive people of citizenship dependent on whether a parent's presence was considered lawful at the time of a child's birth.

18. UNHCR's "right of option" in cases of state succession begins to address the issue of choice in belonging when it comes to those who technically fall under the nationality law of more than one state.

19. Both the International Covenant on Civil and Political Rights (UN 1966a) and the International Covenant on Economic, Social and Cultural Rights (UN 1966b) declare in their first articles that "All peoples have the right of self-determination" and the Charter of the United Nations (UN 1945, Article 1) also recognizes this principle.

20. The Declaration on the Rights of Indigenous Peoples (UN 2007b) asserts in Article 9 that "Indigenous peoples and individuals have the right to belong to an indigenous commu-

nity or nation, in accordance with the traditions and customs of the community or nation concerned." Article 33 similarly declares that "Indigenous peoples have the right to determine their own identity or membership in accordance with their customs and traditions. This does not impair the right of indigenous individuals to obtain citizenship of the States in which they live." See also the International Work Group for Indigenous Affairs (2014).

21. Hirsch Ballin would disagree. While he states that with respect to international law "human beings . . . have gained a place of their own, not only in their citizenship but also in their individuality" (2014, 125), he holds that "Being the citizen of a state should . . . be liberalized, but that does not make it a matter of choice" (124). I contend that an important part of self-determination, or being able to express the individuality of which he speaks, is the right to choose to belong to a political community.

22. Qualifications could include length of residence or some other similar criteria. Zilbershats (2002) argues that an individual must demonstrate loyalty to the state to acquire citizenship, while Carens (2010) makes a strong argument for why length of residence should be the only factor in determining who should belong. Ballin (2014) argues that persons must accept "the principles of a democratic constitutional state" and show "familiarity with its language and institutions" (84), while Barbieri, in addition to the residence stipulation, states that "competence" to take part in political membership could also be a reasonable restriction (1998, 137). While I need to develop this further in future work, I do not think that noncitizen insiders should be held to different criteria of belonging than those who attain citizenship at birth via the operation of jus soli or jus sanguinis provisions. Thus if residence abroad and committing a crime are not grounds for denationalizing the latter group of citizens in a state, then they should not be used as conditions for denying citizenship to noncitizen insiders.

23. Barbieri also makes this suggestion regarding the children of long-term guest workers (1998, 156).

24. Note that in the first part of *The Ethics of Immigration* Carens (2013) examines the "social membership" of distinct types of immigrants, not solely those who have entered via irregular channels.

25. In this case, the ICJ ruled that Friedrich Nottebohm, a German by birth, but a recently naturalized citizen of Liechtenstein who had resided many years in Guatemala, was not in fact a Liechtensteiner because he had no genuine or effective link to that state and had only procured Liechtenstein citizenship to become a national of a "neutral" state during World War II (ICJ 1955, 26). The court therefore judged that Liechtenstein had no standing to bring a claim on behalf of Nottebohm or offer him diplomatic protection because Nottebohm lacked a genuine and effective link with Liechtenstein.

26. Desmangles similarly observes that "at the end of the day, it's not much you could do with that [the Haitian passport]. You can't really claim many things with that particular document."

27. See Chapters 3 and 5 for Martelly's comments.

28. Personal interview with Indira Goris, New York City, February 22, 2012.

29. Desmangles' observation is in line with Hirsch Ballin's argument that people must be given the nationality "that is appropriate to everyone's life situation, where he or she is at home" (2014, 141).

30. Barbieri does not predicate the right to citizenship in his just membership account to those who are "lawfully" or "rightfully" residing within a state either. He says, "One's claim to belonging increases with residence, irrespective of the circumstances of admission" (1998, 157).

31. Along those lines, it is imperative that states have statelessness status determination procedures in place. Without an SSD procedure, it makes it very difficult for stateless persons to secure protection or many human rights.

32. Note that one of the immigration officials whom I interviewed stated that such rapid swearing-in ceremonies exist in The Bahamas in an emergency situation.

33. The Bahamian Constitutional Commission likewise recommends that "Serious consideration should be given to modifying the system to provide for the use of an independent, statutory board invested with powers to consider and recommend the grant of citizenship or asylum requests according to criteria consistently and, as far as practicable, objectively applied" (Government of The Bahamas 2013b, 100). It is also important to point out here that all countries should have statelessness status determination procedures in place, as well as clearly articulated—and effectively implemented—National Action Plans to end statelessness (see Belton [2017]).

REFERENCES

Aber, Shaina, and Mary Small. 2013. "Citizen or Subordinate: Permutations of Belonging in the United States and the Dominican Republic." *Journal on Migration and Human Security* 1, 3: 76–96.

Abizadeh, Arash. 2007. "Cooperation, Pervasive Impact, and Coercion: On the Scope (Not Site) of Distributive Justice." *Philosophy and Public Affairs* 35, 4: 318–58.

Adjami, Mirna, and Julia Harrington. 2008. "The Scope and Content of Article 15 of the Universal Declaration of Human Rights." *Refugee Survey Quarterly* 27, 3: 93–109.

Ahmed, Imtiaz. 2004. "Globalization, Low-Intensity Conflict and Protracted Statelessness/Refugeehood: The Plight of the Rohingyas." *GSC Quarterly* 13: 1–23.

Aidoo, Akwasi. 1993. "Africa: Democracy Without Human Rights?" *Human Rights Quarterly* 15, 4: 703–15.

Aird, Sarah, Helen Harnett, and Punam Shah. 2002. *Stateless Children: Youth Who Are Without Citizenship.* Washington, D.C.: Youth Advocate Program International.

Al Jazeera. 2012. "Kuwait police crackdown on stateless protestors." January 14. http://www.aljazeera.com/news/middleeast/2012/01/201211420266902157.html.

Amnesty International. 2013. "Burma: Risk of Further Violent Clashes Unless Action Is Taken." http://www.amnesty.org.uk/news_details.asp?NewsID=20691.

———. 2015. "Dominican Republic: No More Hope for Tens of Thousands Stateless and at Risk of Expulsion if Residence Deadline Expires." https://www.amnesty.org/en/latest/news/2015/02/dominican-republic-no-more-hope-tens-thousands-stateless-and-risk-expulsion-if-residence-deadli/.

Arber, Ruth. 2010. "Defining Positioning Within Politics of Difference: Negotiating Spaces 'In Between.'" *Race Ethnicity and Education* 3, 1: 45–63.

Archibold, Randal C. 2013. "Dominicans of Haitian Descent Cast into Legal Limbo by Court." *New York Times*, October 24.

———. 2014. "Dominican Republic Passes Law for Migrants' Children." *New York Times*, May 22.

Arendt, Hannah. [1948] 2004. *The Origins of Totalitarianism.* New York: Schocken.

Armstrong, Chris. 2011. "Citizenship, Egalitarianism and Global Justice." *Critical Review of International Social and Political Philosophy* 14, 5: 603–21.

Associated Press. 2015. "Bahrain: 72 People Are Stripped of Their Citizenship." *New York Times*, February 1.

Bahama Journal. 2013. "Haitian-Bahamians Want Citizenship." March 18.

Bahamas Weekly. 2012. "Hon. Dr. Hubert Minnis: PLP Across-the-Board Is Engaged in a Blatant Exhibition of Unadulterated Tribalism, Cronyism and Out Right Nepotism." September 17.

Barbieri, William A., Jr. 1998. *Ethics of Citizenship: Immigration and Group Rights in Germany.* Durham, N.C.: Duke University Press.

Basok, Tanya, Suzan Ilcan, and Jeff Noonan. 2006. "Citizenship, Human Rights, and Social Justice." *Citizenship Studies* 10, 3: 267–73.

Batchelor, Carol A. 1995. "Stateless Persons: Some Gaps in International Protection." *International Journal of Refugee Law* 7, 2: 232–59.

———. 1998. "Statelessness and the Problem of Resolving Nationality Status." *International Journal of Refugee Law* 10, 1: 56–83.

———. 2006. "Transforming International Legal Principles into National Law: The Right to a Nationality and the Avoidance of Statelessness." *Refugee Survey Quarterly* 25, 3: 8–25.

Bauböck, Rainer. 2007. "Political Boundaries in a Multilevel Democracy." In *Identities, Affiliations, and Allegiances,* ed. Seyla Benhabib, Ian Shapiro, and Danilo Petranovic, 85–109. Cambridge: Cambridge University Press.

Beardsworth, Richard. 2011. *Cosmopolitanism and International Relations Theory.* Cambridge: Polity.

Beaubrun, Saint-Pierre. 2008. "Rapport de restitution des consultations dans le cadre du Projet d'appui a la réflexion en Haïti autour du thème: 'Migration, Nationalité et Citoyenneté.'" Port-au-Prince: Groupe d'Appui aux Rapatries et Refugies (GARR).

Beech, Nic. 2011. "Liminality and the Practices of Identity Reconstruction." *Human Relations* 64, 2: 285–302.

Beitz, Charles. 1979. *Political Theory and International Relations.* Princeton, N.J.: Princeton University Press.

Belton, Kristy A. 2010a. "Arendt's Children in the Bahamian Context: The Children of Migrants Without Status." *International Journal of Bahamian Studies* 16: 35–50.

———. 2010b. "Dry Land Drowning or Rip Current Survival? Haitians Without Status in the Bahamas." *Ethnic and Racial Studies* 34, 6: 948–66.

———. 2011. "The Neglected Non-Citizen: Statelessness and Liberal Political Theory." *Journal of Global Ethics* 7, 1: 57–69.

———. 2013. "Statelessness and Economic and Social Rights." In *The State of Economic and Social Human Rights: A Global Overview,* ed. Lanse Minkler. Cambridge: Cambridge University Press.

———. 2015. "The Legal Status of Statelessness: An Overview." In *The Human Right to Citizenship: A Slippery Concept,* ed. Rhoda Howard-Hassmann and Margaret Walton-Roberts. Philadelphia: University of Pennsylvania Press.

———. 2016. "Ending Statelessness Through Belonging: A Transformative Agenda?" *Ethics & International Affairs* 30, 4: 419–427.

———. 2017. "Heeding the Clarion Call in the Americas: The Quest to End Statelessness." *Ethics & International Affairs* 31, 1: 17–29.

Benhabib, Seyla. 2001. *Transformations of Citizenship: Dilemmas of the Nation State in the Era of Globalization.* Assen: Koninklijke Van Gorcum.

———. 2004a. "*The Law of Peoples*, Distributive Justice, and Migrations." *Fordham Law Review* 72, 5: 1761–87.

———. 2004b. *The Rights of Others: Aliens, Residents and Citizens.* Cambridge: Cambridge University Press.

———. 2007. "Democratic Exclusions and Democratic Iterations: Dilemmas of 'Just Membership' and Prospects of Cosmopolitan Federalism." *European Journal of Political Theory* 6: 445–62.

Benhabib, Seyla, and Judith Resnik. 2009. *Migrations and Mobilities: Citizenship, Borders, and Gender.* New York: New York University Press.

Benhabib, Seyla, Ian Shapiro, and Danilo Petranovic. 2007. "Editors' Introduction." In *Identities, Affiliations, and Allegiances*, ed. Seyla Benhabib, Ian Shapiro, and Danilo Petranovic, 1–14. Cambridge: Cambridge University Press.

Bennhold, Katrin. 2014a. "Britain Expands Power to Strip Citizenship from Terrorism Suspects." *New York Times*, May 14.

———. 2014b. "Britain Increasingly Invokes Power to Disown Its Citizens." *New York Times*, April 9.

Bergdahl, Becky. 2012. "New Roadmap for NGOs in Haiti Aims to 'Weed Out Bad Apples.' " *Interpress Service News Agency*, September 26.

Bethel, Nicolette. 2003. "On Being Bahamian." http://nicobethel.net/nico-at-home/essays/bahamian.html.

Bhabha, Jacqueline. 2009. "Arendt's Children: Do Today's Migrant Children Have a Right to Have Rights?" *Human Rights Quarterly* 31, 2: 410–51.

———, ed. 2011. *Children Without a State: A Global Human Rights Challenge.* Cambridge, Mass.: MIT Press.

———. 2014. *Child Migration and Human Rights in a Global Age.* Princeton, N.J.: Princeton University Press.

Blake, Michael. 2001. "Distributive Justice, State Coercion, and Autonomy." *Philosophy and Public Affairs* 30, 3: 257–96.

Blank, Yishai. 2007. "Spheres of Citizenship." *Theoretical Inquiries in Law* 8: 411–52.

Blitz, Brad K. 2006. "Statelessness and the Social (De)Construction of Citizenship: Political Restructuring and Ethnic Discrimination in Slovenia." *Journal of Human Rights* 5, 4: 453–79.

Blitz, Brad K., and Maureen Lynch, eds. 2009. *Statelessness and the Benefits of Citizenship: A Comparative Study.* Geneva Academy for International and Humanitarian Law and International Observatory on Statelessness.

Blitz, Brad K., and Caroline Sawyer. 2011a. "Analysis: The Practical and Legal Realities of Statelessness in the European Union." In *Statelessness in the European Union: Displaced, Undocumented, Unwanted*, ed. Sawyer and Blitz, 281–305. Cambridge: Cambridge University Press.

———. 2011b. "Statelessness in the European Union." In *Statelessness in the European Union: Displaced, Undocumented, Unwanted*, ed. Sawyer and Blitz, 3–21. Cambridge: Cambridge University Press.

Blitzer, Jonathan. 2015. "The Front-Line Against Birthright Citizenship." *New Yorker*, September 18.

Bosniak, Linda. 2000. "Citizenship Denationalized." *Indiana Journal of Legal Studies* 7, 2: 447–509.

———. 2006. *The Citizen and the Alien: Dilemmas of Contemporary Membership.* Princeton, N.J.: Princeton University Press.

Bova, Russell. 2001. "Democracy and Liberty: The Cultural Connection." In *The Global Divergence of Democracies,* ed. Larry Diamond and Marc F. Plattner, 63–77. Baltimore: Johns Hopkins University Press.

Bradley, Megan. 2013. *Refugee Repatriation: Justice, Responsibility and Redress.* Cambridge: Cambridge University Press.

Brouwer, Andrew. 2003. "Statelessness in the Canadian Context." UN High Commissioner for Refugees. http://www.refworld.org/docid/405f07164.html.

Brown, Chris. 2005. "The House That Chuck Built: Twenty-Five Years of Reading Charles Beitz." *Review of International Studies* 31: 371–79.

Brown, Garrett Wallace, and David Held. 2010. "Introduction." In *The Cosmopolitanism Reader,* ed. Garrett Wallace Brown and David Held, 1–14. Cambridge: Polity.

Brown, Sancheska. 2013. "Christie: FNM Has No Moral Authority to Accuse PLP." *Tribune242,* May 16.

Brubaker, William Rogers. 1989. "Membership Without Citizenship: The Economic and Social Rights of Noncitizens." In *Immigration and the Politics of Citizenship in Europe and North America,* ed. William Rogers Brubaker, 145–62. Lanham, Md.: University Press of America.

Burns, Tom R. 2011. "Towards a Theory of Structural Discrimination: Cultural, Institutional and Interactional Mechanisms of the 'European Dilemma.'" In *Identity, Belonging and Migration,* ed. Gerard Delanty, Paul Jones, and Ruth Wodak, 152–72. Liverpool: Liverpool University Press.

Cabrera, Luis. 2010. *The Practice of Global Citizenship.* New York: Cambridge University Press.

Caglar, Ayse S. 2004. "'Citizenship Light': Transnational Ties, Multiple Rules of Membership, and the 'Pink Card.'" In *Worlds on the Move: Globalization, Migration and Cultural Security,* ed. Jonathan Friedman and Shalini Randeria. London: I.B. Tauris.

Cahn, Claude, and Sebihana Skenderovska. 2008. "Briefing Paper for Expert Consultation on Issues Related to Minorities and the Denial or Deprivation of Citizenship." National Roma Centrum, December 6–7.

Campbell, John R. 2014. *Nationalism, Law and Statelessness: Grand Illusions in the Horn of Africa.* London: Routledge.

Canadian Association of Refugee Lawyers. 2014. "Brief of the Canadian Association of Refugee Lawyers: Bill C-24, An Act to Amend the Citizenship Act and to Make Consequential Amendments to Other Acts." http://carl-acaadr.ca/sites/default/files/CARL%20C-24%20Brief%20to%20CIMM.pdf.

Carens, Joseph H. 1987. "Aliens and Citizens: The Case for Open Borders." *Review of Politics* 49, 2: 251–73.

———. 2010. *Immigrants and the Right to Stay.* Cambridge, Mass.: MIT Press.

———. 2013. *The Ethics of Immigration.* Oxford: Oxford University Press.

El Caribe. 2015. "Más de 350,000 personas regularizan su documentación en en [*sic*] el país." June 25.

Centro de Estudios Sociales y Demográficos (CESDEM). 2008. "Encuesta sociodemográfica y sobre VIH/SIDA en los bateyes estatales de la República Dominicana, 2007." Calverton, Md.: Macro International.

Chan, Johannes M. M. 1991. "The Right to a Nationality as a Human Right: The Current Trend Towards Recognition." *Human Rights Law Journal* 12, 1/2: 1–14.

Chapman, Don. 2008. "Who Are the Lost Canadians?" http://blog.lostcanadian.com/2008/12/who-are-lost-canadians.html.

Chari, P. R., Mallika Joseph, and Suba Chandran. 2003. *Missing Boundaries: Refugees, Migrants, Stateless and Internally Displaced Persons in South Asia*. New Delhi: Manohar.

Civolani Hischnjakow, Katerina. 2011. *Vidas suspendidas: Efectos de la Resolución 012-07 en la población dominicana de ascendencia haitiana*. Santo Domingo: Centro Bonó.

CLARCIEV (Consejo Latinoamericano y del Caribe de Registro Civil, Identidad y Estadísticas Vitales). 2015. "Quienes somos." http://www.clarciev.com/cms/?page_id=4#.VfmNRkvzmdI.

CNN. 2012. "Rescuers Search for Survivors After Haitian Migrant Boat Sinks in Bahamas." June 12.

CNN Español. 2015. "Lener Renauld: No aceptamos que quieran expulsarlos." July 24.

Cohen, Jean L. 1999. "Changing Paradigms of Citizenship and the Exclusiveness of the Demos." *International Sociology* 14: 245–68.

Cordourier-Real, Carlos R. 2010. *Transnational Social Justice*. Basingstoke: Palgrave Macmillan.

Council of Europe. 1997. European Convention on Nationality.

Craton, Michael, and Gail Saunders. 1998. *Islanders in the Stream: A History of the Bahamian People*. Vol. 2. Athens: University of Georgia Press.

Cresswell, Tim. 2004. *Place: A Short Introduction*. Malden, Mass.: Blackwell.

Cuba, Lee, and David M. Hummon. 1993. "A Place to Call Home: Identification with Dwelling, Community and Region." *Sociological Quarterly* 34, 1: 111–31.

Dahlburg, John-Thor. 1982. "Free Nationals Tackle Incumbent 'Rascals' in Bahamas Vote." *Hartford Courant*, June 10, A30.

Dames, Candia. 2011. "McCartney Wants Law Change on Citizenship." *Nassau Guardian*, July 25.

———. 2012a. "Citizenship Grants Could Shape Tone of the Election Debate." *Nassau Guardian*, February 6.

———. 2012b. "Many New Citizens Born in Bahamas, Raised Abroad." *Nassau Guardian*, May 21.

Daniel, Trenton. 2014. "Haiti to Register Migrants Abroad." *Associated Press*, February 11.

Das, Veena. 2004. "The Signature of the State: The Paradox of Illegibility." In *Anthropology in the Margins of the State*, ed. Das and Deborah Poole, 225–52. Santa Fe: School of American Research Press.

Dauvergne, Catherine. 2007. "Citizenship with a Vengeance." *Theoretical Inquiries in Law* 8, 2: 489–508.

———. 2008. *Making People Illegal: What Globalization Means for Migration and Law*. Cambridge: Cambridge University Press.

De Genova, Nicholas P. 2002. "Migrant 'Illegality' and Deportability in Everyday Life." *Annual Review of Anthropology* 31: 419–47.

Delanty, Gerard, Paul Jones, and Ruth Wodak. 2011. "Introduction: Migration, Discrimination and Belonging in Europe." In *Identity, Belonging and Migration*, ed. Delanty, Paul Jones, and Ruth Wodak, 1–18. Liverpool: Liverpool University Press.

Domínguez, Jorge I. 1993. "The Caribbean Question: Why Has Liberal Democracy (Surprisingly) Flourished?" In *Democracy in the Caribbean: Political, Economic, and Social Perspectives*, ed. Domínguez, Robert A. Pastor, and R. DeLisle Worrell, 1–25. Baltimore: Johns Hopkins University Press.

Donnelly, Jack. 1999. "Human Rights, Democracy, and Development." *Human Rights Quarterly* 21, 3: 608–32.

Donner, Ruth. 1994. *The Regulation of Nationality in International Law*. 2nd ed. Irvington-on-Hudson, N.Y.: Transnational.

Economic Community of West African States (ECOWAS). 2015. Abidjan Declaration of Ministers of ECOWAS Member States on Eradication of Statelessness. http://www.refworld.org/docid/54f588df4.html.

Edmonds, Kevin. 2013. "Dominican Republic 'Denationalization' Program Seeks to Strip Citizenship from Haitian Descendants." North American Congress on Latin America. October 3.

Ehna, Saw. 2004. "Too Scared to Access: HIV Epidemic Among Karen Refugees." Burma Library. http://www.burmalibrary.org/docs12/BI-2004-07 (Vol.14-07)-red.pdf.

Embassy of the Dominican Republic. 2016. "Dominican Republic Immigration and Documentation Policies: Key Points and FAQ." http://www.domrep.org/immigrationplan.html.

Equal Rights Trust and Amal de Chickera. 2010. *Unravelling Anomaly: Detention, Discrimination and the Protection Needs of Stateless Persons*. London.

European Roma Rights Center. 2005. "Action on Romani Women's Rights in Macedonia." http://www.errc.org/cikk.php?cikk=2132.

Evans, Kevin. 2012. "Haitians Will Punish the PLP." Letter to the editor. *Tribune242*, February 28.

Fahim, Kareem. 2014. "Kuwait, Fighting Dissent from Within, Revokes Citizenship." *New York Times*, September 30.

Falk, Richard. 2000. "The Decline of Citizenship in an Era of Globalization." *Citizenship Studies* 4, 1: 5–17.

Farzana, Kazi Fahmida. 2008. "The Neglected Stateless *Bihari* Community in Bangladesh: Victims of Political and Diplomatic Onslaught." *Journal of Humanities and Social Sciences* 2, 1: 1–19.

Feingold, David A. 2006. "UNESCO Promotes Highland Citizenship and Birth Registration to Prevent Human Trafficking." *UNESCO Bangkok Newsletter* 8.

Féliz, Yanet. 2012. "Migración recula: Educación permitirá niños indocumentados en las escuelas públicas." *El Día*, June 13.

Feller, Oded. 2009. "No Place to Go: Statelessness in Israel." *Forced Migration Review* 32: 35–36.

Ferme, Mariane C. 2004. "Deterritorialized Citizenship and the Resonances of the Sierra Leo-nean State." In *Anthropology in the Margins of the State*, ed. Veena Das and Deborah Poole, 81–115. Santa Fe: School of American Research Press.

Fielding, William, Virginia Ballance, Carol Scriven, Thaddeus McDonald, and Pandora John-son. 2008. "The Stigma of Being 'Haitian' in the Bahamas." *College of the Bahamas Research Journal* 14: 38–50.

Fletcher, Laurel, and Timothy Miller. 2004. "New Perspectives on Old Patterns: Forced Migra-tion of Haitians in the Dominican Republic." *Journal of Ethnic and Migration Studies* 30, 4: 659–79.

Fonchingong, Charles C. 2005. "Exploring the Politics of Identity and Ethnicity in State Recon-struction in Cameroon." *Social Identities* 11, 4: 363–80.

Forced Migration Online. 2015. "What Is Forced Migration?" http://www.forcedmigration.org /about/whatisfm.

Forced Migration Review. 2014. "Crisis." Issue 45.

Fox News. 2012. "Migrant Boat Sinks in Bahamas; At Least 11 Dead." June 11.

Freedland, Jonathan. 1992. "New Leader of Bahamas Vows 'Open' Government." *Washington Post*, September 5, A17.

Freedom House. 2011. "Bahamas: Overview." http://www.freedomhouse.org/report/freedom -world/2011/bahamas.

———. 2015. "Freedom in the World 2015: Discarding Democracy—Return to the Iron Fist." http://freedomhouse.org/sites/default/files/01152015_FIW_2015_final.pdf.

Freeman, Michael. 2006. "Putting Law in Its Place: An Interdisciplinary Evaluation of National Amnesty Laws." In *The Legalization of Human Rights: Multidisciplinary Perspectives on Human Rights and Human Rights Law*, ed. Saladin Meckled-García and Başak Çali, 49–64. Abingdon: Routledge.

Gamboa, Liliana. 2010. "Kafka in the Dominican Republic." Open Society Foundations, June 3. http://www.opensocietyfoundations.org/voices/kafka-dominican-republic#comments.

Georgetown University Law School Human Rights Institute (GULSHRI). 2014. "Left Behind: How Statelessness in the Dominican Republic Limits Children's Access to Education."

Georgia Straight. 2014. "If Bill C-24 Passes, Canadian Citizenship Will Be Harder to Get and Easier to Lose." May 14.

Geschiere, Peter. 2009. *The Perils of Belonging: Autochthony, Citizenship, and Exclusion in Africa and Europe*. Chicago: University of Chicago Press.

Ghosh, Partha S. 2004. *Unwanted and Uprooted: A Political Study of Migrants, Refugees, State-less and Displaced of South Asia*. New Delhi: Samskriti.

Gibney, Matthew J. 2009. "Statelessness and the Right to Citizenship." *Forced Migration Review* 32: 50–51.

———. 2011. "The Rights of Non-Citizens in Political Thought." In *Statelessness in the European Union: Displaced, Undocumented, Unwanted*, ed. Caroline Sawyer and Brad K. Blitz, 41–68. Cambridge: Cambridge University Press.

Gilbertson, Greta. 2006. "Citizenship in a Globalized World." Migration Policy Institute, January 1.

Giovanni, Andrea. 2011. "Global Justice and the Moral Arbitrariness of Birth." *Monist* 94, 4: 571–83.

Girard, Philippe. 2010. *Haiti: The Tumultuous History—From Pearl of the Caribbean to Broken Nation.* New York: Palgrave Macmillan.

Global Campaign for Equal Nationality Rights. 2016. "The Problem." http://equalnationalityrights .org/the-issue/the-problem.

Goldston, James A. 2006. "Holes in the Rights Framework: Racial Discrimination, Citizenship, and the Rights of Noncitizens." *Ethics and International Affairs* 20, 3: 321–47.

Gonçalves Margerin, Marselha, and Melanie Teff. 2008. "Dominican Republic: Time to Move Forward to Resolve Statelessness." Refugees International Bulletin, May 28.

Gonzales, Roberto G., and Leo R. Chavez. 2012. "'Awakening to a Nightmare': Abjectivity and Illegality in the Lives of Undocumented 1.5-Generation Latino Immigrants in the United States." *Current Anthropology* 53, 3: 255–81.

Goris, Indira. 2011. "Dominican Reforms Fall Short." Open Society Justice Initiative. http://www .opensocietyfoundations.org/voices/dominican-reforms-fall-short.

Government of The Bahamas. 1967. Immigration Act. http://laws.bahamas.gov.bs/cms/images /LEGISLATION/PRINCIPAL/1967/1967-0025/ImmigrationAct_1.pdf.

———. 1973a. The Constitution. http://laws.bahamas.gov.bs/cms/images/LEGISLATION/PRIN CIPAL/1973/1973-1080/TheConstitution_1.pdf.

———. 1973b. Nationality Act. http://laws.bahamas.gov.bs/cms/images/LEGISLATION/PRIN CIPAL/1973/1973-0018/BahamasNationalityAct_1.pdf.

———. 2012. *Census of Population and Housing, 2010.* Department of Statistics. http://www .soencouragement.org/forms/CENSUS2010084903300.pdf.

———. 2013. "Report of the Constitutional Commission into a Review of The Bahamas Consti- tution." Nassau. http://www.thebahamasweekly.com/uploads/13/Constitution_Commis sion_Report_2013_8JULY2013.pdf.

———. 2016. "Labour Force and Household Survey Report." Department of Statistics. http:// www.bahamas.gov.bs/wps/wcm/connect/72743405-8ab8-4746-b1e9-470312c9a205 /Labour+Force+Report+May2016_for+website.pdf?MOD=AJPERES.

Government of the Dominican Republic. 1939. "Reglamento de Migración No. 279." http://www .acnur.org/fileadmin/Documentos/BDL/2001/0241.pdf?view=1

———. 2004. "Ley General de Migración No. 285-04." https://www.oas.org/dil/Migrants /Republica%20Dominicana/1.Ley%20sobre%20migración%20N°%20285%20del%20 15%20de%20agosto%20de%202004%20(reemplaza%20la%20Ley%2095%20de%201939) .pdf.

———. 2005. "Servicio Jesuita a Refugiados y Migrantes (SJRM) and ors v. Dominican Republic, Armenteros Estrems (intervening) and ors (intervening), Direct Constitutional Complaint Procedure, BJ 1141.77, ILDC 1075." Supreme Court of Justice (SCJ). http://opil.ouplaw.com /view/10.1093/law:ildc/1075do05.case.1/law-ildc-1075do05?prd=OPIL.

———. 2007a. Resolution 02-2007. http://www.acnur.org/t3/fileadmin/Documentos/BDL/2012 /8897.pdf.

———. 2007b. Resolution 12-2007. http://www.acnur.org/t3/fileadmin/Documentos/BDL/2012 /8899.pdf?view=1.

———. 2010a. "Censo 2010." Oficina Nacional de Estadística. http://censo2010.one.gob.do.

———. 2010b. "Constitución Política de la República Dominicana." http://www.procuraduria .gov.do/Novedades/PGR-535.pdf.

———. 2011. Circular No. 32/2011. Junta Central Electoral. http://www.acnur.org/t3/fileadmin /Documentos/BDL/2012/8903.pdf?view=1.

———. 2012. Sentencia Civil No. 259-12. Poder Judicial.

———. 2013a. El Demócrata, no. 32. Junta Central Electoral. http://issuu.com/publicacionesjce /docs/el_democrata_32.

———. 2013b. Plan Nacional de Regularización de Extranjeros en situación migratoria irregular. http://www.refworld.org/docid/52fcaf984.html.

———. 2013c. "Primera Encuesta Nacional de Inmigrantes en la República Dominicana: ENI-2012, Informe General." Oficina Nacional de Estadísticas. Santo Domingo. http://country office.unfpa.org/dominicanrepublic/drive/InformeENI-2012-General.pdf.

———. 2013d. "Propuesta de proyecto de decreto relative al Plan Nacional de Regularización de Extranjeros." Presidencia de la República Dominicana. http://www.scribd.com/doc /187292945/Propuesta-de-proyecto-de-decreto-relativo-al-Plan-Nacional-de-Regular izacion-de-Extranjeros.

———. 2013e. "Sentencia TC/0168/13." Constitutional Court. http://tribunalconstitucional.gob .do/sites/default/files/documentos/Sentencia%20TC%200168-13%20-%20C.pdf.

———. 2014a. "Disposiciones Reglamentarias—Libro de Extranjería." Junta Central Electoral. http://www.jce.gob.do/Dependencias/RegistroCivil/LibrodeExtranjer%C3%ADa .aspx.

———. 2014b. "Histórico discurso del Presidente de la República, Danilo Medina, en defensa de la soberanía nacional." Junta Central Electoral. http://jce.gob.do/Noticias/historico -discurso-del-presidente-de-la-republica-danilo-medina-en-defensa-de-la-soberania -nacional.

———. 2014c. Ley No. 169-14. http://www.consultoria.gob.do/spaw2/uploads/files/Ley%20No .%20169-14.pdf.

———. 2014d. Sentencia TC/0256/14. Constitutional Court. http://www.tribunalconstitucional .gob.do/sites/default/files/documentos/Sentencia%20TC%200256-14%20%20%20 %20C.pdf.

Government of Haiti. 2009. http://www.haiti.org/wp-content/uploads/2012/09/rsolution_amen dement.pdf.

———. 2011. http://www.haiti-reference.com/histoire/constitutions/const_1987_amendee.php.

Green, Nicole, and Todd Pierce. 2009. "Combatting Statelessness: A Government Perspective." Forced Migration Review 32: 34–35.

Gündoğdu, Ayten. 2015. Rightlessness in an Age of Rights. Oxford: Oxford University Press.

Hailbronner, Kay. 2003. "Nationality." In Migration and International Legal Norms, ed. T. Alexander Aleinikoff and Vincent Chetail, 75–85. The Hague: T.M.C. Asser.

———. 2006. "Nationality in Public International Law and European Law." In Acquisition and Loss of Nationality. Vol. 1, Comparative Analyses: Policies and Trends in 15 European Countries, ed. Rainer Bauböck, Eva Ersbøll, Kees Groenendijk, and Harald Waldrauch, 35–104. Amsterdam: Amsterdam University Press.

Hall, Rodney Bruce. 1999. *National Collective Identity: Social Constructs and International Systems*. New York: Columbia University Press.

Hanauer, David Ian. 2011. "Non-Place Identity: Britain's Response to Migration in the Age of Supermodernity." In *Identity, Belonging and Migration*, ed. Gerard Delanty, Paul Jones, and Ruth Wodak, 198–217. Liverpool: Liverpool University Press.

Hansen, Randall. 1999. "Migration, Citizenship and Race in Europe: Between Incorporation and Exclusion." *European Journal of Political Research* 35: 415–44.

Hayden, Patrick. 2008. "From Exclusion to Containment: Arendt, Sovereign Power, and Statelessness." *Societies Without Borders* 3: 248–69.

Hennessy-Fiske, Molly. 2015. "Judge: Texas Can Deny Birth Certificates for U.S.-Born Children of Some Immigrants." *Los Angeles Times*, October 16.

———. 2016. "Texas, Facing a Lawsuit, Makes It Easier for U.S.-Born Children of Immigrants to Get Birth Certificates." *Los Angeles Times*, July 25.

Higgot, Richard A., and Kim Richard Nossal. 1997. "The International Politics of Liminality: Relocating Australia in the Asia Pacific." *Australian Journal of Political Science* 32, 2: 169–86.

Hindess, Barry. 2005. "Citizenship and Empire." In *Sovereign Bodies: Citizens, Migrants, and States in the Postcolonial World*, ed. Thomas Blom Hansen and Finn Stepputat, 241–56. Princeton, N.J.: Princeton University Press.

Hirsch Ballin, Ernst. 2014. *Citizens' Rights and the Right to Be a Citizen*. Leiden: Brill Nijhoff.

Hudson, Manley O. 1952. *Report on Nationality, Including Statelessness*. United Nations. A/CN.4/50. http://legal.un.org/ilc/documentation/english/a_cn4_50.pdf.

Human Rights Watch. 2002. "'Illegal People': Haitians and Dominico-Haitians in the Dominican Republic." April 4.

———. 2010. "Stateless Again: Palestinian-Origin Jordanians Deprived of Their Nationality." February 10.

———. 2011. "Prisoners of the Past: Kuwaiti Bidun and the Burden of Statelessness." June 13.

Hussain, Misha. 2011. "Stateless Mothers Fall Through the Cracks in Bangladesh." Association for Women's Rights in Development. https://womennewsnetwork.net/2011/05/08/stateless -refugee-mothers-bangladesh/.

Hynes, Patricia. 2011. *The Dispersal and Social Exclusion of Asylum Seekers: Between Liminality and Belonging*. Bristol: Policy.

Institute on Statelessness and Inclusion (ISI). 2014. "The World's Stateless." http://www.institutesi .org/worldsstateless.pdf.

Inter-American Commission on Human Rights. 2005. Petition 12.271. http://www.cidh.oas.org /annualrep/2005eng/DominicanRep.12271eng.htm.

Inter-American Court of Human Rights (IACtHR). 2005. *Yean and Bosico v. Dominican Republic*. http://www.corteidh.or.cr/docs/casos/articulos/seriec_130_%20ing.pdf.

———. 2014a. *Case of Expelled Dominicans and Haitians v. the Dominican Republic*. http:// corteidh.or.cr/docs/casos/articulos/seriec_282_ing.pdf.

———. 2014b. IACtHR Condemns Judgment of the Constitutional Court of the Dominican Republic. http://www.oas.org/en/iachr/media_center/PReleases/2014/130.asp.

International Conference of American States. 1933. Montevideo Convention on the Rights and Duties of States.

International Court of Justice (ICJ). 1955. *Nottebohm Case (Second Phase), Judgment of April 6*, 4–27. http://www.icj-cij.org/docket/files/18/2674.pdf.

International Foundation for Electoral Systems (IFES). 2016. "ElectionGuide: Bahamas." http://www.electionguide.org/elections/id/2970/.

International Organization for Migration (IOM). 2005. "Haitian Migrants in the Bahamas 2005." http://iom.int/jahia/webdav/site/myjahiasite/shared/shared/mainsite/published_docs/books/Haitian_Migrants_Report.pdf.

———. 2013. "IOM-Haiti Strategic Plan, 2013–2014." Port-au-Prince. http://www.iom.int/files/live/sites/iom/files/pbn/docs/Strategy-IOM-Haiti-Updated-Jan-2013.pdf.

———. 2015. "IOM Monitors Dominican Republic—Haiti Border." http://www.iom.int/news/iom-monitors-dominican-republic-haiti-border.

International Work Group for Indigenous Affairs. 2014. "Self Determination of Indigenous Peoples." http://www.iwgia.org/human-rights/self-determination.

IRIN. 2013. "Sectarian Tension in Myanmar Threatens Aid Workers." http://www.irinnews.org/report/97852/sectarian-tension-myanmar-threatens-aid-workers.

Jackson, Vicki C. 2009. "Citizenships, Federalisms, and Gender." In *Migrations and Mobilities: Citizenship, Borders, and Gender*, ed. Seyla Benhabib and Judith Resnik, 439–86. New York: New York University Press.

Jacobson, David. 1996. *Rights Across Borders: Immigration and the Decline of Citizenship*. Baltimore: Johns Hopkins University Press.

Jirawattanapisal, Thidaporn, Suwit Wibulpolpraset, Sombat Thanprasertsuk, and Thidakorn Noree. 2010. "Human Resources for Health Implications of Scaling Up for Universal Access to HIV/AIDS Prevention, Treatment, and Care: Thailand Rapid Situational Analysis." World Health Organization. http://www.who.int/workforcealliance/knowledge/publications/Thailand_report.pdf.

Johnson, Dexter Reno. 2008. *An Introduction to Critical Problems in Bahamian Constitutional Law*. Nassau: Terenshad.

Joppke, Christian. 1999. *Immigration and the Nation-State: The United States, Germany, and Great Britain*. Oxford: Oxford University Press.

Joseph, Daniel. 2015. "Reconocen nueva cédula de República Dominicana como documento de identidad más seguro y mejor diseñado del mundo en 2014." Junta Central Electoral. http://jce.gob.do/Noticias/reconocen-nueva-cedula-republica-dominicana-documento-identidad-mas-seguro-del-mundo-2014.

Kajouee, Shereen. 2014. "Situation of the Right to Nationality of Dominicans of Haitian Descent Affected by Denaturalization Policies in the Dominican Republic." Human Rights Brief, March 28.

Kanengoni, Alice. 2008. "Editorial." *OpenSpace* 3, 2: 4–6.

Kanics, Jyothi. 2011. "Realizing the Rights of Undocumented Children in Europe." In *Children Without a State: A Global Human Rights Challenge*, ed. Jacqueline Bhabha, 131–49. Cambridge, Mass.: MIT Press.

Kelley, Ninette. 2010. "Ideas, Interests, and Institutions: Conceding Citizenship in Bangladesh." *University of Toronto Law Journal* 60, 2: 349–71.

Kesby, Alison. 2012. *The Right to Have Rights: Citizenship, Humanity, and International Law.* Oxford: Oxford University Press.

Khan, Gerrard. 2001. "Citizenship and Statelessness in South Asia." UN High Commissioner for Refugees. Working Paper 47. http://www.unhcr.org/research/RESEARCH/3bf0ff124.pdf.

Kibreab, Gaim. 1999. "Revisiting the Debate on People, Place, Identity and Displacement." *Journal of Refugee Studies* 12, 4: 384–428.

Kingston, Lindsey N. 2013. "'A Forgotten Human Rights Crisis': Statelessness and Issue (Non) emergence." *Human Rights Review* 14, 2: 73–87.

Kingston, Lindsey N., Elizabeth F. Cohen, and Christopher P. Morley. 2010. "Debate: Limitations on Universality: The 'Right to Health' and the Necessity of Legal Nationality." *BMC International Health and Human Rights* 10: 1–12.

Koopmans, Ruud, Paul Statham, Marco Giugni, and Florence Passy. 2005. *Contested Citizenship: Immigration and Cultural Diversity in Europe.* Minneapolis: University of Minnesota Press.

Korir Sing'oei, Abraham. 2009. "Promoting Citizenship in Kenya: The Nubian Case." In *Statelessness and the Benefits of Citizenship: A Comparative Study*, ed. Brad K. Blitz and Maureen Lynch, 37–49. Geneva: Geneva Academy of International Humanitarian Law and Human Rights and International Observatory on Statelessness.

Kostakopoulou, Theodora. 2008. *The Future Governance of Citizenship.* Cambridge: Cambridge University Press.

Krause, Monika. 2008. "Undocumented Migrants: An Arendtian Perspective." *European Journal of Political Theory* 7, 3: 331–48.

Kristeva, Julia. 1980. *Powers of Horror: An Essay on Abjection.* Trans. Leon S. Roudiez. New York, Columbia University Press.

Kushner, Jacob. 2015. "Birthright Denied." *Moment Magazine.*

Kymlicka, Will. 1995. *Multicultural Citizenship: A Liberal Theory of Minority Rights.* Oxford: Oxford University Press.

League of Nations. 1930. Convention on Certain Questions Relating to the Conflict of Nationality Law. League of Nations, Treaty Series 179, no. 4137.

Leary, Virginia. 1999. "Citizenship, Human Rights and Diversity." In *Citizenship, Diversity and Pluralism*, ed. Alan C. Cairns, John C. Courtney, Peter MacKinnon, Hans J. Michelmann, and David E. Smith, 247–64. Montreal: McGill-Queen's University Press.

Leedy, Paul D., and Jeanne Ellis Ormrod. 2005. *Practical Research.* 8th ed. Upper Saddle River, N.J.: Pearson Education.

Lewa, Chris. 2009. "North Arakan: An Open Prison for the Rohingya in Burma." *Forced Migration Review* 32: 11–13.

Lillich, Richard B. 1984. *The Human Rights of Aliens in Contemporary International Law.* Manchester: Manchester University Press.

Linz, Juan J., and Alfred Stepan. 1996. *Problems of Democratic Transition and Consolidation: Southern Europe, South America, and Post-Communist Europe.* Baltimore: Johns Hopkins University Press.

Liss, Ryan. 2014. "A Right to Belong: Legal Protection of Sociological Membership in the Application of Article 12(4) of the ICCPR." *New York University Journal of International Law and Politics* 46: 1097–1191.

Lubkemann, Stephen C. 2008. "Involuntary Immobility: On a Theoretical Invisibility in Forced Migration Studies." *Journal of Refugee Studies* 21, 4: 454–75.

Lynch, Maureen. 2005. "Lives on Hold: The Human Cost of Statelessness." Washington, D.C.: Refugees International.

———. 2008. "Futures Denied: Stateless Among Infants, Children, and Youth." Washington, D.C.: Refugees International.

———. 2009. "Statelessness: International Blind Spot Linked to Global Concerns." Washington, D.C.: Refugees International.

Lynch, Maureen, and Perveen Ali. 2006. "Buried Alive: Stateless Kurds in Syria." Washington, D.C.: Refugees International.

Lynch, Maureen, and Dawn Calabia. 2007. "Senegal: Voluntary Repatriation Critical for Protecting Stateless Mauritanians." Refugees International. ReliefWeb, February 9.

Lynch, Maureen, and Thatcher Cook. 2004. "Left Behind: Stateless Russians Search for Equality in Estonia." *Refugees International Bulletin*, December 24. http://www.refugeesinternational.org/policy/field-report/left-behind-stateless-russians-search equality-estonia.

———. 2006. "Citizens of Nowhere: The Stateless Biharis of Bangladesh." Refugees International.

Macklin, Audrey. 2007. "Who Is the Citizen's Other? Considering the Heft of Citizenship." *Theoretical Inquiries in Law* 8, 2: 333–66.

Manby, Bronwen. 2009. *Struggles for Citizenship in Africa: A Comparative Study.* London: Zed.

———. 2015. "Nationality, Migration and Statelessness in West Africa: A Study for UNHCR and IOM." http://www.refworld.org/docid/55b886154.html.

Manly, Mark. 2007. "The Spirit of Geneva: Traditional and New Actors in the Field of Statelessness." *Refugee Survey Quarterly* 26, 4: 255–61.

Manly, Mark, and Santhosh Persaud. 2009. "UNHCR and Responses to Statelessness." *Forced Migration Review* 32: 7–10.

Manzano, Sylvia, Matt A. Barreto, Ricardo Ramirez, and Kathy Rim. 2009. "Mobilization, Participation, Solidaridad: Latino Participation in the 2006 Immigration Protest Rallies." *Urban Affairs Review* 44, 5: 736–64.

Marshall, Dawn. 1979. " 'The Haitian Problem': Illegal Migration to the Bahamas." Institute of Social and Economic Research. University of the West Indies, Mona, Kingston, Jamaica.

Martínez, Samuel. 2003. "Not a Cockfight: Rethinking Haitian-Dominican Relations." *Latin American Perspectives* 30, 3: 80–101.

———. 2011. "The Onion of Oppression: Haitians in the Dominican Republic." In *Geographies of the Haitian Diaspora*, ed. Regine O. Jackson, 51–70. New York: Routledge.

Massey, Hugh. 2010. "UNHCR and *De Facto* Statelessness." LPPR/2010/01. Legal and Protection Policy Research Series. Geneva: UN.

McCartney, Juan. 2011. "Hundreds to Get Citizenship." *Nassau Guardian.* July 15.

McDougal, Myres S., Harold D. Lasswell, and Lung-chu Chen. 1974. "Nationality and Human Rights: The Protection of the Individual in External Arenas." *Yale Law Journal* 83: 900–998.

McNevin, Anne. 2011. *Contesting Citizenship: Irregular Migrants and New Frontiers of the Political.* New York: Columbia University Press.

Michelman, Frank I. 1996. "Parsing 'A Right to Have Rights.'" *Constellations* 3, 2: 200–209.

Migration Policy Institute. 2015. Data Hub. http://www.migrationpolicy.org/programs/data-hub/international-migration-statistics.

Miller, David. 1998. "The Ethical Significance of Nationality." *Ethics* 98, 4: 647–62.

Mitchell, Fred. 2014. "Minister Mitchell on Bahamas Immigration Regulatory Changes." *Bahamas Weekly,* October 25.

Modikwa, Onalenna. 2012. "No ARVs for Technically Stateless Woman." Mmegionline. http://www.mmegi.bw/index.php?sid=1&aid=496&dir=2012/August/Tuesday14.

Moellendorf, Darrel. 1996. "Constructing the Law of Peoples." *Pacific Philosophical Quarterly* 77, 2: 132–54.

Monforte, Pierre, and Pascale Dufour. 2011. "Mobilizing in Borderline Citizenship Regimes: A Comparative Analysis of Undocumented Migrants' Collective Actions." *Politics and Society* 39, 2: 203–32.

MOSCTHA (Sociocultural Movement for Haitian Workers). 2012. "Statelessness in the Dominican Republic." http://www.youtube.com/user/moscthamovement.

Movimiento por un Registro Civil Libre de Discriminación (MRCLD). 2013. "Sociedad civil se posiciona de cara al Informe de la Comisión Investigadora de la Cámara de Diputados sobre la situación de la Junta Central Electoral y sus miembros." Santo Domingo.

MSN Arabia. 2012. "Kuwait Police Fire Tear Gas to Break Up Stateless Demo." http://www.aljazeera.com/news/middleeast/2012/01/201211420266902157.html.

Muller, Benjamin. 2004. "(Dis)qualified Bodies: Securitization, Citizenship and 'Identity Management.'" *Citizenship Studies* 8, 3: 279- 94.

Murphy, Michael, and Siobhan Harty. 2003. "Post-Sovereign Citizenship." *Citizenship Studies* 7, 2: 181–97.

Murray, Don. 2015. "World faces major crisis as number of displaced hits record high." June 18. http://www.unhcr.org/5582c2f46.html.

Mutharika, Peter A. 1989. *The Regulation of Statelessness Under International and National Law.* Dobbs Ferry, N.Y.: Oceana.

Nagel, Thomas. 2005. "The Problem of Global Justice." *Philosophy and Public Affairs* 33, 2: 113–47.

Nardin, Terry. 2006. "International Political Theory and the Question of Justice." *International Affairs* 82, 3: 449–65.

Nicolls, Noelle. 2013. "Pindling Faces Unrestrained Post-Modern Examination." *Tribune242,* December 4.

Ní Mhurchú, Aoileann. 2015. "Ambiguous Subjectivity, Irregular Citizenship: From Inside/ Outside to Being-Caught In-Between." *International Political Sociology* 9:158–79.

Nussbaum, Martha C. 2006. *Frontiers of Justice: Disability, Nationality, Species Membership.* Cambridge, Mass.: Harvard University Press.

Nyamnjoh, Francis B. 2007. "From Bounded to Flexible Citizenship: Lessons from Africa." *Citizenship Studies* 11, 1: 73–82.

Nyers, Peter. 2011. "Forms of Irregular Citizenship." In *The Contested Politics of Mobility: Borderzones and Irregularity*, ed. Vicki Squire. New York: Routledge.

Odinkalu, Chidi Anselm. 2008. "Statelessness in Africa: Turning Citizens into Nomads." In *New Challenges to Building Open Societies in Africa*. Open Society.

————. 2009. "Nigeria: The Right to a Passport." *This Day*. http://allafrica.com/stories/200910 200930.html.

Ong, Aihwa. 1999. *Flexible Citizenship: The Cultural Logics of Transnationality*. Durham, N.C.: Duke University Press.

Open Society Justice Initiative (OSJI). 2014. "Dominican Republic's New Naturalization Law Falls Short." https://www.opensocietyfoundations.org/press-releases/dominican-republics -new-naturalization-law-falls-short.

Open Society Justice Initiative and Center for Justice and International Law (OSJI and CEJIL). 2010. "Summary of Initial Petition in the Case of *Emildo Bueno Oguís v. Dominican Republic*." http://www.opensocietyfoundations.org/sites/default/files/Petition%20Summary -20100601.pdf.

————. 2012. "Submission to the United Nations Human Rights Committee: Review of the Dominican Republic." http://www2.ohchr.org/english/bodies/hrc/docs/ngos/OSJI_and_CJIL _DominicanRepublic_HRC104.pdf.

Organization of African Unity. 1969. Convention Governing the Specific Aspects of Refugee Problems in Africa. http://www.achpr.org/files/instruments/refugee-convention/achpr _instr_conv_refug_eng.pdf.

Organization of American States (OAS). 1969. American Convention on Human Rights.

————. 1977. "Third Report on the Situation of Human Rights in Chile. Chapter IX. Right to Nationality." OEA/Ser.L/V/II.40 doc. 10, February 11. http://www.cidh.org/countryrep/chile 77eng/chap.9.htm.

————. 1984. Cartagena Declaration on Refugees. https://www.oas.org/dil/1984_Cartagena _Declaration_on_Refugees.pdf.

————. 2010. "The Prevention and Reduction of Statelessness and Protection of Stateless Persons in the Americas." AG/RES. 2599 (XL-O/10).

————. 2011. "The Prevention and Reduction of Statelessness and Protection of Stateless Persons in the Americas." AG/RES. 2665 (XLI-O/11).

————. 2012. "Fundamental Elements for Identification and Protection of Stateless Persons and Prevention and Reduction of Statelessness in the Americas." http://www.oas.org/dil/state lessness_courses.htm.

————. 2013a. "Preliminary Observations from the IACHR's Visit to the Dominican Republic." http://www.oas.org/en/iachr/media_center/PReleases/2013/097A.asp.

————. 2013b. "Prevention and Reduction of Statelessness and Protection of Stateless Persons in the Americas." AG/RES. 2787 (XLIII-O/13).

————. 2014. "Prevention and Reduction of Statelessness and Protection of Stateless Persons in the Americas." AG/RES.2826 (XLIV-O/14).

Parekh, Serena. 2008. *Hannah Arendt and the Challenge of Modernity: A Phenomenology of Human Rights*. New York: Routledge.

Park, Susin. 2011. "Climate Change and the Risk of Statelessness: The Situation of Low-Lying Island States." UN High Commissioner for Refugees. http://www.unhcr.org/4df9cb0c9.pdf.

Parliament of Australia. 2015. "Australian Citizenship Amendment (Allegiance to Australia) Bill 2015." https://www.legislation.gov.au/Details/C2015A00166.

Parliament of Canada. 2014. "Royal Assent." June 19. http://www.parl.gc.ca/Content/Sen/Chamber /412/Debates/075db_2014-06-19 e.htm?Language=E.

Pérez, Michael Vicente. 2011. "Human Rights and the Rightless: The Case of Gaza Refugees in Jordan." *International Journal of Human Rights* 15, 7: 1031–54.

Perks, Katherine, and Amal de Chickera. 2009. "The Silent Stateless and the Unhearing World. Can Equality Compel Us to Listen?" *Equal Rights Review* 3: 42–55.

Physicians for Human Rights. 2010. "Stateless and Starving: Persecuted Rohingya Flee Burma and Starve in Bangladesh." http://physiciansforhumanrights.org/library/documents/reports /stateless-and-starving.pdf.

———. 2012. "Stateless Children in Western Burma." http://physiciansforhumanrights.org/blog /stateless-children-in-western-burma.html.

Pogge, Thomas. 1994. "An Egalitarian Law of Peoples." *Philosophy and Public Affairs* 23, 3: 195–224.

———. 2002. *World Poverty and Human Rights: Cosmopolitan Responsibilities and Reforms.* Cambridge, Mass.: Blackwell.

Pogge, Thomas, and Darrel Moellendorf. 2008. "Introduction." In *Global Justice: Seminal Essays,* xxv–xxviii. St. Paul, Minn.: Paragon House.

Rawls, John. 1977. "The Basic Structure as Subject." *American Philosophical Quarterly* 14, 2: 159–65.

Redclift, Victoria. 2013. *Statelessness and Citizenship: Camps and the Creation of Political Space.* London: Routledge.

Relph, Edward. 1976. *Place and Placelessness.* London: Pion.

Reynolds, Sarnata. 2012. "South Sudan Nationality: Commitment Now Avoids Conflict Later." Refugees International.

Reynolds, Sarnata, and Kristen Cordell. 2012. "Kuwait: *Bidoon* Nationality Demands Can't Be Silenced." Refugees International.

Riggan, Jennifer. 2011. "In Between Nations: Ethiopian-Born Eritreans, Liminality, and War." *Political and Legal Anthropology Review* 34, 1: 131–54.

Robert F. Kennedy Human Rights Center. 2015. "Dominicanos desnacionalizados y migrantes haitianos en riesgo de expulsiones discriminatorias de República Dominicana." http:// rfkcenter.org/media/filer_public/12/1c/121cc7ab-a02d-411b-85c5-184bad4d033b/espanol .pdf.

Robinson, Nehemiah. (1955) 1997. "Convention Relating to the Status of Stateless Persons: Its History and Interpretation." Institute of Jewish Affairs. http://www.unhcr.org/publ/PUBL /3d4ab67f4.pdf.

Robles, Frances. 2015. "Immigration Rules in Bahamas Sweep Up Haitians." *New York Times,* January 30.

Rojas, Ricardo. 2013. "Dominican Court Ruling Renders Hundreds of Thousands Stateless." http://www.reuters.com/article/us-dominicanrepublic-citizenship-idUSBRE99B01 Z20131012.

Rolle, Krystel. 2012a. "Haitian Embassy Defends President." *Nassau Guardian*, February 10.

———. 2012b. "Ingraham: Haitian Leader 'Mistaken.'" *Nassau Guardian*, February 13.

Rolle, Rashad. 2014. "Homes Destroyed in Shanty Town Fire." *Tribune242*, May 4.

Ross, Patrick, and Alice Galey. 2014. "Stripping UK Citizenship by Stealth." Open Democracy, February 13.

Rumelili, Bahar. 2003. "Liminality and Perpetuation of Conflicts: Turkish-Greek Relations in the Context of Community-Building by the EU." *European Journal of International Relations* 9, 2: 213–48.

———. 2012. "Liminal Identities and Processes of Domestication and Subversion in International Relations." *Review of International Studies* 38, 2: 495–508.

Rürup, Miriam. 2011. "Lives in Limbo: Statelessness After Two World Wars." *Bulletin of the German Historical Institute* 49: 113–34.

Sadiq, Kamal. 2009. *Paper Citizens: How Illegal Immigrants Acquire Citizenship in Developing Countries*. Oxford: Oxford University Press.

Sagás, Ernesto. 1998. "El antihaitianismo en la República Dominicana: Pasado y presente de una ideología dominante." In *Los problemas raciales en la República Dominicana y el Caribe*, 125–51. Santo Domingo: Comisión municipal. Editora Collado.

———. 2000. *Race and Politics in the Dominican Republic*. Gainesville: University Press of Florida.

Sanderson, Mike. 2014. "Statelessness and Mass Expulsion in Sudan: A Reassessment of the International Law." *Northwestern Journal of International Human Rights* 12, 1: 74–114.

Sassen, Saskia. 2006. *Territory, Authority, Rights: From Medieval to Global Assemblages*. Princeton, N.J.: Princeton University Press.

Sawyer, Caroline, and Brad K. Blitz. 2011. "Conclusions." In *Statelessness in the European Union: Displaced, Undocumented, Unwanted*, ed. Sawyer and Blitz, 306–11. Cambridge: Cambridge University Press.

Schaap, Andrew. 2011. "Enacting the Right to Have Rights: Jacques Ranciere's Critique of Hannah Arendt." *European Journal of Political Theory* 10, 1: 22–45.

Schmitt, Carl. (1922) 1985. *Political Theology*. Trans. George Schwab. Cambridge, Mass.: MIT Press.

Sears, Alfred. 1994. "The Haitian Question in the Bahamas." *Journal of the Bahamas Historical Society* 16, 1: 10–20.

Seet, Matthew. 2016. "The Origins of UNHCR's Global Mandate on Statelessness." *International Journal of Refugee Law* 28, 1: 7–24.

Shachar, Ayelet. 2009. *The Birthright Lottery: Citizenship and Global Inequality*. Cambridge, Mass.: Harvard University Press.

Shachar, Ayelet, and Ran Hirschl. 2007. "Citizenship as Inherited Property." *Political Theory* 35, 3: 253–87.

Shacknove, Andrew. 1993. "From Asylum to Containment." *International Journal of Refugee Law* 5, 4: 516–33.

Shiblak, Abbas. 2009. "The Lost Tribes of Arabia." *Forced Migration Review* 32: 37–38.

Singh, Deepak K. 2010. *Stateless in South Asia: The Chakmas Between Bangladesh and India*. Thousand Oaks, Calif.: Sage.

Sironi, Alice. 2004. "Nationality of Individuals in Public International Law: A Functional Approach." In *People Out of Place: Globalization, Human Rights, and the Citizenship Gap*, ed. Alison Brysk and Gershon Shafir, 54–75. New York: Routledge.

Slip, Sai. 2006. "Stateless HIV/AIDS Sufferers Face Earlier Death, Thai Forum Told." Irrawaddy. http://www2.irrawaddy.org/article.php?art_id=6010.

Smith, Gustavius. 2012. "Surviving in The Bahamas: A Haitian Boy Strives for Brighter Future." *Haitian Times*.

Smith, Ianthia. 2012. "FNM Celebrates First Victory." *Bahama Journal*, August 20.

Snyder, Jack. 2000. *From Voting to Violence: Democratization and Nationalist Conflict*. New York: Norton.

Sokoloff, Constantin. 2005. "Denial of Citizenship: A Challenge to Human Security." New York: Advisory Board on Human Security, Office for the Coordination of Humanitarian Affairs.

Somers, Margaret R. 2008. *Genealogies of Citizenship: Markets, Statelessness, and the Right to Have Rights*. Cambridge: Cambridge University Press.

Southwick, Katherine, and Maureen Lynch. 2009. "Nationality Rights for All: A Progress Report and Global Survey on Statelessness." Washington, D.C.: Refugees International.

Soysal, Yasemin Nuhoglu. 1994. *Limits of Citizenship: Migrants and Postnational Membership in Europe*. Chicago: University of Chicago Press.

Spiro, Peter J. 2004. "Mandated Membership, Diluted Identity: Citizenship, Globalization, and International Law." In *People Out of Place: Globalization, Human Rights, and the Citizenship Gap*, ed. Alison Brysk and Gershon Shafir, 87–105. New York: Routledge.

———. 2011. "A New International Law of Citizenship." *American Journal of International Law* 105, 4: 694–746.

Staples, Kelly. 2012. *Retheorising Statelessness: A Background Theory of Membership in World Politics*. Edinburgh: Edinburgh University Press.

Stiks, Igor. 2006. "Nationality and Citizenship in the Former Yugoslavia: From Disintegration to European Integration." *Southeast European and Black Sea Studies* 6, 4: 483–500.

Sturm, Nora. 2014. "Hendricks Commends Efforts to End Statelessness in Côte d'Ivoire." UNHCR. http://www.unhcr.org/53ce16666.html.

Suárez-Navaz, Liliana, Raquel Maciá Pareja, and Ángela Moreno García. 2007. *Las luchas de los sin papeles y la extensión de la ciudadanía. Perspectivas críticas desde Europa y Estados Unidos*. Madrid: Traficantes de Sueños.

Taylor, Lucy. 2004. "Client-Ship and Citizenship in Latin America." *Bulletin of Latin American Research* 23, 2: 213–27.

Teune, Henry. 2009. "Citizenship Deterritorialized: Global Citizenships." In *The Future of Citizenship*, ed. Jose V. Ciprut, 229–52. Cambridge, Mass.: MIT Press.

Thomassen, Bjørn. 2009. "Uses and Meanings of Liminality." *International Political Anthropology* 2, 1: 5–28.

Tiburcio, Carmen. 2001. *The Human Rights of Aliens Under International and Comparative Law*. The Hague: Martinus Nijhoff.

Tilburg University. 2015. "Global Forum on Statelessness: New Directions in Statelessness Research and Policy." http://www.tilburguniversity.edu/research/institutes-and-research -groups/statelessness/forum.htm.

Torpey, John. 2000. *The Invention of the Passport: Surveillance, Citizenship and the State*. Cambridge: Cambridge University Press.

Troeller, Gary. 2003. "Refugees and Human Displacement in Contemporary International Relations: Reconciling State and Individual Sovereignty." In *Refugees and Forced Displacement: International Security, Human Vulnerability, and the State*, ed. Edward Newman and Joanne van Selm, 50–65. Tokyo: UN University Press.

Turner, Victor W. 1984. "Liminality and Performance Genres." In *Rite, Drama, Festival, Spectacle: Rehearsals Toward a Theory of Performance*, ed. John J. MacAloon, 19–41. Philadelphia: Institute for the Study of Human Issues.

——. 1985. *On the Edge of the Bush: Anthropology as Experience*, ed. Edith L. B. Turner. Tucson: University of Arizona Press.

——. [1969] 1995. *The Ritual Process: Structure and Anti-Structure*, 2nd ed. New York: Aldine De Gruyter.

Turnquest, Ava. 2014. "Call for Greater Dialogue After Shanty Town Blaze." *Tribune242*, January 24.

United Nations. 1945. Charter of the United Nations.

——. 1948. Universal Declaration of Human Rights.

——. 1951. Convention relating to the Status of Refugees.

——. 1954. Convention relating to the Status of Stateless Persons.

——. 1957. Convention on the Nationality of Married Women. A/RES/1040.

——. 1960. Declaration on the Granting of Independence to Colonial Countries and Peoples.

——. 1961. Convention on the Reduction of Statelessness.

——. 1965. International Convention on the Elimination of All Forms of Racial Discrimination.

——. 1966a. International Covenant on Civil and Political Rights.

——. 1966b. International Covenant on Economic, Social and Cultural Rights.

——. 1974. Resolution 3274 (XXIX). General Assembly. http://www.unhcr.org/3dc8dca44 .html.

——. 1979. Convention on the Elimination of All Forms of Discrimination against Women.

——. 1989. Convention on the Rights of the Child.

——. 1990. International Convention on the Protection of the Rights of All Migrant Workers and Members of Their Families.

——. 2007a. Convention on the Rights of Persons with Disabilities.

——. 2007b. Declaration on the Rights of Indigenous Peoples.

——. 2011. "Guidance Note of the Secretary-General: The United Nations and Statelessness." http://www.unhcr.org/refworld/pdfid/4e11d5092.pdf.

——. 2016. Treaty Collection. "Chapter V: Refugees and Stateless Persons." https://treaties.un .org/Pages/Treaties.aspx?id=5&subid=A&clang=_en.

United Nations Children's Fund (UNICEF). 2013. "Every Child's Birth Right: Inequities and Trends in Birth Registration." https://www.unicef.org/media/files/Embargoed_11_Dec _Birth_Registration_report_low_res.pdf.

——. 2014a. "Birth Registration." http://www.unicef.org/protection/57929_58010.html.

———. 2014b. "Declárame y me abrirás muchas Puertas." http://www.unicef.org/republic
adominicana/resources_3863.htm.

———. 2014c. "Name and Nationality." http://www.unicef.org/republicadominicana/english
/advocacy_partnerships_12547.htm.

United Nations Committee on the Elimination of Racial Discrimination. 2013. "Concluding
Observations on the Thirteenth and Fourteenth Periodic Reports of the Dominican Repub-
lic, Adopted by the Committee at Its Eighty-Second Session." United Nations. CERD/C/
DOM/CO/13-14.

United Nations Conference on Trade and Development. 2012. *UNCTAD Handbook of Statistics,
2012.* New York: UN. http://unctad.org/en/PublicationsLibrary/tdstat37_en.pdf.

United Nations Department of Economic and Social Affairs (DESA). 2016. "International Migration Report 2015." http://www.un.org/en/development/desa/population/migration/public
ations/migrationreport/docs/MigrationReport2015_Highlights.pdf.

United Nations Development Programme (UNDP). 2013a. "Country Reports." http://hdr.undp
.org/en/countries.

———. 2013b. "Human Development Report 2013: The Rise of the South: Human Progress in a
Diverse World." http://hdr.undp.org/en/media/HDR_2013_EN_complete.pdf.

United Nations High Commissioner for Refugees (UNHCR). 1988. " 'Lawfully Staying'—A Note
on Interpretation." http://www.refworld.org/docid/42ad93304.html.

———. 2003. "Statelessness: Nine Million Ghosts." *Refugees Magazine* 132: 12–15.

———. 2004. "Final Report Concerning the Questionnaire on Statelessness Pursuant to the
Agenda for Protection." http://www.unhcr.org/4047002e4.pdf.

———. 2007. "Q&A: The World's 15 Million Stateless People Need Help." http://www.unhcr.org/en
-us/news/latest/2007/5/464dca3c4/qa-worlds-15-million-stateless-people-need-help.html.

———. 2010a. Brasilia Declaration on the Protection of Refugees and Stateless Persons in the
Americas. http://www.unhcr.org/protection/basic/4cdd3fac6/brasilia-declaration-protec
tion-refugees-stateless-persons-americas-brasilia.html.

———. 2010b. "UNHCR Action to Address Statelessness: A Strategy Note." Division of Internal
Protection. http://www.unhcr.org/4b960ae99.html.

———. 2011a. "Haiti: Universal Periodic Review." http://lib.ohchr.org/HRBodies/UPR/Documents
/session12/HT/UNHCR-eng.pdf.

———. 2011b. "UNHCR Intergovernmental Meeting at Ministerial Level Closing Remarks by
the United Nations High Commissioner for Refugees." http://www.unhcr.org/admin/hcspee
ches/4ef094a89/unhcr-intergovernmental-meeting-ministerial-level-closing-remarks
-united.html.

———. 2012a. "Addressing Statelessness." In *UNHCR Global Report 2011.* http://www.unhcr.org
/4fc8808b0.pdf.

———. 2012b. "Figures at a Glance." http://www.unhcr.org/pages/49c3646c11.html.

———. 2012c. "Guidelines on Statelessness. No. 4: Ensuring Every Child's Right to Acquire a
Nationality." HCR/GS/12/04. http://www.refworld.org/docid/50d460c72.html.

———. 2012d. "Ministerial Intergovernmental Event on Refugees and Stateless Persons-Pledges
2011." http://www.refworld.org/docid/50aca6112.html.

———. 2012e. "UNHCR Global Appeal 2012–2013: Americas." http://www.unhcr.org/public ations/fundraising/4ec230f40/unhcr-global-appeal-2012-2013-americas-regional -summary.html.

———. 2014a. "Ashgabat Meeting Proposes Way Forward on Migration and Statelessness." http://www.unhcr.org/53a96dbd6.html.

———. 2014b. "Asia-Pacific Ministers Agree on Civil Registration for All by 2024." http://www .unhcr.org/en-us/news/latest/2014/11/54787b236/asia-pacific-ministers-agree-civil-regis tration-2024.html.

———. 2014c. Brazil Declaration: A Framework for Cooperation and Regional Solidarity to Strengthen the International Protection of Refugees, Displaced and Stateless Persons in Latin America and the Caribbean. http://www.acnur.org/t3/fileadmin/scripts/doc.php?file =t3/fileadmin/Documentos/BDL/2014/9865

———. 2014d. "General Assembly Resolutions Relating to Statelessness." http://www.unhcr.org /cgi-bin/texis/vtx/search?page=&comid=4a2527ca6&cid=49aea93a20&scid=49aea93a1a &keywords=stateless_res.

———. 2014e. "Global Action Plan to End Statelessness: 2014–2024." http://www.unhcr.org/en-us /protection/statelessness/54621bf49/global-action-plan-end-statelessness-2014-2024.html.

———. 2014f. "Global Forced Displacement Tops 50 Million for First Time Since World War II." http://www.unhcr.org/53999cf46.html.

———. 2014g. Handbook on Protection of Stateless Persons. http://www.unhcr.org/53b698ab9.pdf.

———. 2014h. "Juliana Deguis Pierre Receives Dominican National ID After Long Battle to Regain Citizenship." http://www.unhcrwashington.org/media-news/latest-news/juliana-deguis -pierre-receives-dominican-national-id-after-long-battle-regain.

———. 2014i. "UNHCR Launches 10-Year Global Campaign to End Statelessness." http://www .unhcr.org/545797f06.html.

———. 2014j. "United Colors of Benetton's Fabrica Develops #IBelong Campaign in Support of UNHCR's Aim to End Statelessness by 2024." Nov. 4. http://www.unhcr.org/ibelong/united -colors-of-benettons-fabrica-develops-ibelong-campaign-in-support-of-unhcrs-aim-to -end-statelessness-by-2024/.

———. 2015a. "I Am Here, I Belong: The Urgent Need to End Childhood Statelessness." Division of International Protection. November. http://www.unhcr.org/ibelong/wp-content/uploads /2015-10-StatelessReport_ENG16.pdf.

———. 2015b. "Statistical Online Population Database." http://popstats.unhcr.org/en/overview.

———. 2015c. "2015 UNHCR Regional Operations Profile—Americas." http://www.unhcr.org /pages/4a02da6e6.html.

———. 2015d. "Update on Statelessness." Executive Committee of the High Commissioner's Programme. EC/66/SC/CRP.11.

———. 2015e. "Who Is Stateless and Where?" http://www.unhcr.org/pages/49c3646c15e .html.

———. 2016. "30th Commemorative Anniversary of the Cartagena Declaration on Refugees." http://www.unhcr.org/en-us/30th-commemorative-anniversary-cartagena-declaration -refugees.html.

United Nations High Commissioner for Refugees and the Inter-Parliamentary Union. 2005. *Nationality and Statelessness: A Handbook for Parliamentarians*. Geneva: Interparliamentary Union.

United Nations High Commissioner for Refugees and Plan International. 2012. "Under the Radar and Under Protected: The Urgent Need to Address Stateless Children's Human Rights." http://www.unhcr.org/509a6bb79.pdf.

United Nations Human Rights Council (UN HRC). 2008a. "Human Rights and Arbitrary Deprivation of Nationality." March 27. A/HRC/RES/7/10.

———. 2008b. "Promotion and Protection of All Human Rights, Civil, Political, Economic, Social and Cultural Rights, Including the Right to Development." Human Rights Council. Seventh Session. A/HRC/7/23.

———. 2008c. "Report of the Special Rapporteur on Contemporary Forms of Racism, Racial Discrimination, Xenophobia and Related Intolerance, Doudou Diène, and the independent expert on minority issues, Gay McDougall, Addendum: Mission to Dominican Republic." Human Rights Council. A/HRC/7/19/Add.5 and A/HRC/7/23/Add.3.

———. 2009a. "Arbitrary Deprivation of Nationality: Report of the Secretary-General." January 26. A/HRC/10/34.

———. 2009b. "Human Rights and Arbitrary Deprivation of Nationality: Report of the Secretary-General." December 14. A/HRC/13/34.

———. 2009c. "Resolution 10/13: Human Rights and Arbitrary Deprivation of Nationality." March 26. Resolution 10/13. http://www.refworld.org/docid/4bce9da22.html.

———. 2010. "Human Rights and Arbitrary Deprivation of Nationality: Resolution Adopted by the Human Rights Council." April 14. A/HRC/RES/13/2.

———. 2011. "Human Rights and Arbitrary Deprivation of Nationality: Report of the Secretary-General." December 19. A/HRC/19/43.

———. 2012a. "Human Rights and Arbitrary Deprivation of Nationality." Human Rights Council. Twentieth Session of the General Assembly. A/HRC/20/L.9.

———. 2012b. "Human Rights and Arbitrary Deprivation of Nationality: Resolution Adopted by the Human Rights Council." July 16. A/HRC/RES/20/5.

———. 2013a. "Discrimination Against Women on Nationality-Related Matters, Including the Impact on Children: Report of the Office of the United Nations High Commissioner for Human Rights." March 15. A/HRC/23/23.

———. 2013b. "Human Rights and Arbitrary Deprivation of Nationality: Report of the Secretary-General." December 19. A/HRC/25/28.

———. 2014. "Human Rights and Arbitrary Deprivation of Nationality: Resolution Adopted by the Human Rights Council." July 11. A/HRC/RES/26/14.

———. 2015. "Birth Registration and the Right of Everyone to Recognition Everywhere as a Person Before the Law: Resolution Adopted by the Human Rights Council." April 7. A/HRC/RES/28/13.

United Nations Office of the High Commissioner for Human Rights (OHCHR). 2006. *The Rights of Non-Citizens*. HR/PUB/06/11. New York: United Nations.

———. 2008. "Racial Discrimination against Dominicans of Haitian Descent in Access to Nationality." http://tbinternet.ohchr.org/_layouts/treatybodyexternal/Download.aspx?symbolno=INT%2FCERD%2FNGO%2FDOM%2F72%2F8613&Lang=en.

United Nations Secretary General (UNSG). 2011. "Guidance Note of the Secretary General: The United Nations and Statelessness." http://www.refworld.org/docid/4e11d5092.html.

UNAIDS. 2011. "HIV and Social Protection: Guidance Note." http://www.unaids.org/sites/default /files/media_asset/2014unaidsguidancenote_HIVandsocialprotection_en.pdf.

United States Citizenship and Immigration Service (USCIS). 2015. "Chapter 2: Grounds for Revocation of Naturalization." http://www.uscis.gov/policymanual/HTML/PolicyManual -Volume12-PartL-Chapter2.html.

United States Department of State. 2015. "Dominican Republic 2015 International Religious Freedom Report." https://www.state.gov/documents/organization/256563.pdf.

United States Office of Personnel Management. 2001. "Citizenship Laws of the World." http:// www.multiplecitizenship.com/documents/IS-01.pdf.

United States Supreme Court. 1958. *Perez v. Brownell*. 1958. 356 U.S. 44, 64.

van Panhuys, H. F. 1959. *The Role of Nationality in International Law: An Outline*. Leyden: Sythoff.

van Selm, Joanne. 2009. "Stateless Roma in Macedonia." *Forced Migration Review* 32: 46–47.

van Waas, Laura. 2008. *Nationality Matters: Statelessness Under International Law*. Antwerp: Intersentia.

———. 2010. *The Situation of Stateless Persons in the Middle East and North Africa*. UNHCR.

———. 2013. "2014 Global Forum: A 'Meeting Place' for People Concerned About Statelessness." European Network on Statelessness. http://www.statelessness.eu/blog/2014-global-forum -"meeting-place"-people-concerned-about-statelessness.

Vernon, Richard. 2010. *Cosmopolitan Regard: Political Membership and Global Justice*. New York: Cambridge University Press.

Vishniak, Marc. 1945. *The Legal Status of Stateless Persons*. Jews and the Post-War World Pamphlet Series 6. New York: American Jewish Committee.

Voice of America. 2009. "Refugee Group Highlights Plight of World's Stateless People." http:// www.voanews.com/content/a-13-2005-02-15-voa55-67378492/274567.html.

Walzer, Michael. 1983. *Spheres of Justice: A Defense of Pluralism and Equality*. New York: Basic.

Weatherford, Robin. 2011. *Great Things He Has Done: A Life of Service and Surrender to God*. Abaco, Bahamas: Abaco Print Shop.

Weil, Simone. 1955. *The Need for Roots*. Boston: Beacon Press.

Weis, Paul. 1956. *Nationality and Statelessness in International Law*. London: Stevens & Sons.

Weissbrodt, David S. 2008. *The Human Rights of Non-Citizens*. New York: Oxford University Press.

Weissbrodt, David S., and Clay Collins. 2006. "The Human Rights of Stateless Persons." *Human Rights Quarterly* 28, 1: 245–76.

Welsh, Teresa. 2015. "Dominican Republic Temporarily Halts Deportation of Haitians." *U.S. News and World Report*, July 10.

Wood, William B. 1994. "Forced Migration: Local Conflicts and International Dilemmas." *Annals of the Association of American Geographers* 84, 4: 607–34.

Wooding, Bridget. 2008. "Contesting Dominican Discrimination and Statelessness." *Peace Review* 20, 3: 366–75.

———. 2009. "Contesting Discrimination and Statelessness in the Dominican Republic." *Forced Migration Review* 32: 23–25.

Wooding, Bridget, and Richard Moseley-Williams. 2004a. "Inmigrantes haitianos y dominicanos de ascendencia haitiana en la República Dominica." Cooperación Internacional para el Desarollo y el Servicio Jesuita a Refugiados y Migrantes. http://www.obmica.org/images /Publicaciones/Libros/Wooding%20and%20Mosely%202004%20Inmigrantes_haitianos.pdf.

———. 2004b. *Needed But Unwanted: Haitian Immigrants and Their Descendants in the Dominican Republic.* London: Catholic Institute for International Relations.

World Bank. 2013a. "The Bahamas." http://data.worldbank.org/country/bahamas/.

———. 2013b. "Haiti." http://data.worldbank.org/country/haiti#cp_wdi.

Zilbershats, Yaffa. 2002. *The Human Right to Citizenship.* Ardsley, N.Y.: Transnational.

Zorn, Jelka. 2004. "The Politics of Exclusion: Citizenship, Human Rights and the Erased in Slovenia." *Croatian Sociological Association* 35: 1–2. http://skylined.org/.

INDEX

254 Index

forced displacement in situ, 9; ambiguous belonging and, 122, 172; Bahamian-born of Haitian descent, 122, 151–52; democracies engaging in, 15; Dominican-born of Haitian descent, 122, 151–52; effects of, 23, 136; human rights and, 14; Mozambican civil war (1977–1992) and, 15; reconceptualizing statelessness as, 12–13, 14–15, 176. *See also* rooted displacement.

Forced Migration Online, 208n36

Forced Migration Review's "Crisis" issue (2014), 208n36

foreign nationals, created by denationalization, 33

foreigner's book in DR. *See* "Registry of Births to Foreign Non-Resident Mothers in the Dominican Republic"

former Soviet states. *See* post-Communist states

France: Algeria, French citizens of Arab descent in, 220n2; Haiti as colony of, 86; political action among noncitizens in, 207n32

fraudulent documentation, 76–77, 102, 106

Free National Movement (FNM, The Bahamas), 57, 59–60, 214n7

Freedom House, 16, 213n6

freedom to travel: Bahamian-born persons of Haitian descent traveling to DR, 222n42; Dominican-born of Haitian descent, limitations on, 222n44; fear of deportation limiting, 140–41. *See also* immobilization

Freeman, Michael, 223n1

Fundación Zile, 217n11

Gamboa, Liliana, 88–94, 96–97, 104–6, 109, 144, 175

GDJ. *See* global distributive justice

gender bias in nationality laws, 35–36, 44, 72, 152, 211n23

Generation Y Haitian-Bahamians, 148

Georgetown University Law School's Human Rights Institute (GULSHRI), 134–35, 138

Germany, guest workers in, 158

"ghosts." *See* noncitizen insiders

Giovanni, Andrea, 223n10

Girard, Philippe, 213n1

Global Action Plan to End Statelessness: 2014–2024 (GAP, 2014), 48, 212n60

global citizenship, 8

global distributive justice (GDJ): framework of, 26, 152–55, 177; human capabilities and, 162–63, 223n5; just membership and, 155–59, 167, 169, 172, 174, 224n15; right to a nationality as matter of, 159–65; shared risk society and, 163–65

"Global Forum on Statelessness: New Directions in Statelessness Research and Policy" (Tilburg University, 2015), 14, 208n34

global stateless populations, 30, 31*fig*, 200*t*

globalization lessening importance of citizenship, 7–9

Goldston, James, 83–84, 112–13

Gonçalves Margerin, Marselha, 79

Gonzalez, Roberto G., 222n41

Goris, Indira, 87–90, 95–98, 100, 171, 217n9

guest workers, 10, 158, 225n23

Gulf region. *See* Persian Gulf states

GULSHRI (Georgetown University Law School's Human Rights Institute), 134–35, 138

Guterres, António, 14, 47

Hailbronner, Kay, 161, 162

Haiti: compared to The Bahamas, 56; earthquake (2010), 56; economic situation of, 56, 87; history of, 86, 217n4; human development status of, 87, 213n2, 217n7; lack of culture of documentation in, 107; nationality law, 79; political situation of, 56, 213n1; refusal to accept Dominican-born Haitians, 111; Registrar's office, 73; slavery in, 86. *See also* Haitian migrants

Haitian Constitution, 79; Article 11, 22, 78, 82, 89, 94

Haitian Embassy: The Bahamas, 61, 63, 73, 75–78, 80, 82, 107, 146, 171, 216n54; birth registration for child born to Haitian migrant in DR, 106, 111; Dominican Republic, 90, 106–7, 111, 220n50; interview with diplomat in DR, 19

Haitian Haitians vs. Bahamian Haitians, 128, 145

political action among noncitizens in, 207n32; U.S.-born children of undocumented parents, citizenship of, 34–35
Universal Declaration of Human Rights (UDHR), 132, 212n49; Article 13, 40; Article 15, 6, 31, 33, 165; right to nationality, 6, 162, 164
University of The Bahamas. *See* College of The Bahamas

vaccinations, 39–40
Valdez-Cox, Juanita, 34–35
van Waas, Laura, 40, 211n25
Vargas, Tahira, 128, 221n18
Vernon, Richard, 163–64, 224n13; *Cosmopolitan Regard*, 155
Vishniak, Marc, 28
the voiceless. *See* noncitizen insiders

Walzer, Michael, 158–59, 164, 165, 168, 172; *Spheres of Justice*, 156–57
Weatherford, Robin, 129–30
Weis, Paul, 6, 206n14
women. *See* gender bias in nationality laws; mother's citizenship and passing citizenship rights to children
Wooding, Bridget, 79, 90, 100, 106
World War II-created situations of statelessness, 30–31, 109, 200t, 225n25

Yean and Bosico v. Dominican Republic (IACtHR 2005), 22, 88–89, 96, 100–101, 109, 132

Zaiem, Bianca, 64, 65t, 66–69, 209n56, 215n29
Zilbershats, Yaffa, 165, 169, 224n15, 225n22

ACKNOWLEDGMENTS

Writing a book is far from a solitary activity. I have had the good fortune of strong support and encouragement from family, friends, and colleagues while this book was coming into being. My greatest champion throughout this process has been my best friend and husband, Jevon Knowles. He kept me moving forward on the days when I felt like I was treading water and his patience, flexibility, and understanding allowed me the space and time to do all that was necessary to write this book.

I am forever grateful to Shareen Hertel, who took me under her wing and guided me through the book writing process. Her unfailing support, enthusiasm, and constructive critique have made this book a better manuscript and me a better scholar. I am also fortunate to have within my circle of friends Mark Boyer, Jennifer Sterling-Folker, and Serena Parekh. Mark has been my go-to person for advice of nearly every kind. His confidence is inspiring and his "look-at-the-big-picture" attitude has kept me grounded on more than one occasion. Jennifer's belief in my ability to be a "theorist," and her enthusiasm for my work, has given me the confidence to tread in academic areas I perhaps otherwise would not have. Without Serena's class on Global Justice and the Ethics of Belonging, I may never have thought about statelessness from the perspective of global distributive justice and I thank her tremendously for opening my eyes to this subject matter.

I would also like to express my heartfelt gratitude to the University of Connecticut, the ZEIT-Stiftung Ebelin und Gerd Bucerius Foundation, and the University of Dayton. These institutions provided me with incredibly supportive environments for research and writing over the years. At UConn, I was the recipient of the Outstanding Scholars Program fellowship, a Tinker Field Research Grant from the Center for Latin American and Caribbean Studies, and numerous summer fellowships from the Department of Political Science, among other awards. These sources of funding provided me opportunities to conduct fieldwork overseas and to attend conferences where I presented earlier drafts of this work. As a recipient of a Settling into Motion Scholarship in Migration Studies from the ZEIT-Stiftung Ebelin und Gerd Bucerius Foundation, I joined the ranks of fellow migration enthusiasts and parlayed ideas with my cohort at a workshop in Hamburg. I am grateful for their feedback and for the time that the fellowship provided me to delve into my work.

The University of Dayton (UD) likewise deserves resounding thanks. If it were not for Jason Pierce, Mark Ensalaco, Natalie Hudson, and Kelly Johnson, I would not have had the opportunity to become part of UD's vibrant human rights community. The two years I spent at UD at the Human Rights Center provided me the ability to take part in UNHCR's Cartagena +30 events in Latin America and the Caribbean, which presented me with an entirely new side of statelessness advocacy. A special thanks must also go out to Grant Neeley for always graciously accommodating my work requests as the mother of a newborn.

I have been fortunate to have multiple occasions in which to present my work for feedback. From the International Studies Association and Caribbean Studies Association's annual conferences to Wayne State University's annual Citizenship Studies Conference, Columbia University's Human Rights Seminar and a terrific workshop, hosted by Serena, on the Ethics of Exclusion at Northeastern. Likewise, I have benefited from the feedback received from reviewers on earlier iterations of this work for the *Journal of Global Ethics* and *Citizenship Studies,* and the Wayne State University Press edited volume, *The Meaning of Citizenship.*

I would like to express my gratitude to Zehra Arat and Sam Martínez for their invaluable input on this book project, as well as Shayna Plaut for encouraging me to "position" myself within the research and to write from the first-person perspective. In that light, I would like to gratefully acknowledge Peter Agree and the rest of the University of Pennsylvania Press team for taking my book project under their wing and allowing it to blossom. I would also like to thank the anonymous reviewers of my book manuscript for their thorough reading and thoughtful comments.

To my dad, who was there with me during a large portion of my Dominican Republic fieldwork, and to my mom, who always provided her car whenever I needed it for interviews in Nassau, thank you both for your unfailing support and for instilling a strong sense of justice in me. Thanks, too, to my Uncle Philip and Aunt Nancy for making me feel at home while I conducted fieldwork in Abaco, and to Debbie Sylvester who took such wonderful care of my daughter when I was in the early stages of writing.

To Bridget Wooding, thank you for including me in the local conversation on statelessness in the Dominican Republic and for providing me the incredible opportunity to travel to a batey. To my colleagues who work on statelessness in the advocacy, policy, and academic worlds, your work inspires me and I am humbled to write in your light. My deepest thanks to all the study participants, named and unnamed, who took the time to discuss this highly sensitive topic. This book is rooted in your words.

Finally, I would like to acknowledge Emmi and Owen's role in motivating me to finish this book. Emmi came into our world when I was writing the first draft and Owen came on her heels while I was at UD. Their presence always grounds me and draws me back to the reality of what counts. They remind me that we scholar-advocates do what we do because we want the world to be a better place for them and for the others to come.

Earlier versions of portions of "Exclusion, Island Style: Citizenship Deprivation and Denial in the Caribbean," appeared in *The Meaning of Citizenship*, eds. Richard Marback and Marc W. Kruman, copyright ©2015 Wayne State University Press, with the permission of Wayne State University Press.

Earlier versions of portions of articles appeared in the *Journal of Global Ethics* and *Citizenship Studies*, used by permission of Taylor & Francis Ltd.